NEO-ARAMAIC AND KURDISH FOLKLORE FROM NORTHERN IRAQ

VOLUME I

Neo-Aramaic and Kurdish Folklore from Northern Iraq

A Comparative Anthology with a Sample of Glossed Texts

Volume I

Geoffrey Khan, Masoud Mohammadirad, Dorota Molin and Paul M. Noorlander

in collaboration with
Lourd Habeeb Hanna, Aziz Emmanuel Eliya Al-Zebari and Salim Abraham

https://www.openbookpublishers.com

© 2022 Geoffrey Khan, Masoud Mohammadirad, Dorota Molin and Paul M. Noorlander, in collaboration with Lourd Habeeb Hanna, Aziz Emmanuel Eliya Al-Zebari and Salim Abraham.

This work is licensed under an Attribution-NonCommercial 4.0 International (CC BY-NC 4.0). This license allows you to share, copy, distribute and transmit the text; to adapt the text for non-commercial purposes providing attribution is made to the authors (but not in any way that suggests that they endorse you or your use of the work). Attribution should include the following information:

Geoffrey Khan, Masoud Mohammadirad, Dorota Molin and Paul M. Noorlander, *Neo-Aramaic and Kurdish Folklore from Northern Iraq: A Comparative Anthology with a Sample of Glossed Texts, Volume 1*. Cambridge Semitic Languages and Cultures 12. Cambridge, UK: Open Book Publishers, 2022, https://doi.org/10.11647/OBP.0306

Copyright and permissions for the reuse of many of the images included in this publication differ from the above. Copyright and permissions information for images is provided separately in the List of Illustrations.

In order to access detailed and updated information on the license, please visit, https://doi.org/10.11647/OBP.0306#copyright

Further details about CC BY-NC licenses are available at, https://creativecommons.org/licenses/by-nc/4.0/

All external links were active at the time of publication unless otherwise stated and have been archived via the Internet Archive Wayback Machine at https://archive.org/web

Updated digital material and resources associated with this volume are available at https://doi.org/10.11647/OBP.0306#resources

Every effort has been made to identify and contact copyright holders and any omission or error will be corrected if notification is made to the publisher.

Semitic Languages and Cultures 12.

ISSN (print): 2632-6906
ISSN (digital): 2632-6914

ISBN Paperback: 9781800647664
ISBN Hardback: 9781800647671
ISBN Digital (PDF): 9781800647688
DOI: 10.11647/OBP.0306

Cover images:

Cover design: Anna Gatti

Volume I

Prolegomena and Glossed Texts

CONTENTS

VOLUME I

LIST OF TABLES AND MAPS x

LIST OF ABBREVIATIONS AND SYMBOLS xi

CONTRIBUTORS AND COLLABORATORS xiii

PREFACE xvii

REFERENCES xxi

PROLEGOMENA

Paul M. Noorlander and Dorota Molin

1. Introduction to a Comparative Corpus of Oral Literature 1

Dorota Molin

2. The Folkloristic Heritage of Kurds, Jews and Syriac Christians of Northern Iraq 35

Paul M. Noorlander and Masoud Mohammadirad

3. Narrative Style and Discourse in Kurdish and Neo-Aramaic Oral Literature 85

SAMPLE OF GLOSSED TEXTS

NEO-ARAMAIC

Geoffrey Khan

    ChA. Dure (Text 8) 159

    ChA. Shaqlawa (Text 28) 165

Dorota Molin

    ChA. Duhok (Text 14) 179

    JA. Duhok (Text 16) 196

    ChA. Enishke (Text 6) 205

    JA. Zakho (Text 25) 216

    ChA. Zakho (Text 10) 222

Paul M. Noorlander

    ChA. Harmashe (Text 33) 234

KURDISH

Masoud Mohammadirad

    NK. Duhok (Text 30) 248

    NK. Dure (Text 20) 274

    NK. Khizava (Text 7) 286

    NK. Zakho (Text 11) 302

    CK. Shaqlawa (Text 19) 316

INDEX 331

VOLUME II

THEME I: ZAMBILFROSH 1

THEME II: THE BRIDGE OF DALALE 61

THEME III: ANIMALS AND HUMANS 105

THEME IV: SOCIAL STATUS 221

THEME V: FAMILY RELATIONS 347

THEME VI: MIRZA MUHAMMAD 435

THEME VII: RELIGIOUS LEGENDS 547

LIST OF TABLES AND MAPS

Tables

Table 1. Selection of features of Jewish dialects of NENA

Table 2. Selection of features of Christian dialects of NENA

Table 3. Selection of features of Northern and Central Kurdish

Table 4. General transcription of Kurdish and Neo-Aramaic

Table 5. Basic transcription of Kurdish in this volume

Table 6. Correspondence between Kurdish and NENA transcription

Table 7. The stories categorised according to genre

Table 8. Stories with multiple versions in the corpus

Table 9. Folkloristic motifs occurring in the stories (categorised with Aarne-Thomson-Uther's and Thompson's indexes)

Table 10. Near demonstrative pronouns in NENA and Kurdish

Table 11. Main discourse functions of verbal forms in Kurdish and NENA

Table 12. Overview of some shared narrative hallmarks

Maps

Map 1. The respective locations of the dialects of Aramaic and Kurdish represented in this book

LIST OF ABBREVIATIONS AND SYMBOLS

ADD	additive	M	masculine
AUX	auxiliary	NA	not analysed
CAUS	causative	NEG	negative
CMPR	comparative	O	affixal object
COMPL	complementiser	OBL	oblique
COP	copula	PERF	perfect
DEF	definite	PFV	perfective
DEIC	deictic	PL	plural
DEM	demonstrative	PN	proper noun
DIM	diminutive	POST	postposition
DIR	direct	PRS	present
DIST	distal	PROG	progressive
DRCT	directional	PRON	pronominal
EMPH	emphatic	PROX	proximate
EP	epenthetic	PST	past
EXIST	existential	PTCL	particle
EXCM	exclamative	PTCP	participle
EZ	ezafe	PVB	preverbal derivational particle
F	feminine		
FUT	future	REFL	reflexive
HORT	hortative	REL	relativiser
IMP	imperative	RDP	reduplicant
IND	indicative (realis)	SG	singular
INDF	indefinite	SBJV	subjunctive
IPFV	imperfective	SBR	subordinator
INF	infinitive	TAM	tense-aspect-mood
INTJ	interjection		
LVC	light verb complement	TELIC	telicity

ChA.   Christian Neo-Aramaic
JA.   Jewish Neo-Aramaic
CK.   Central Kurdish
NK.   Northern Kurdish
St. K. Standard Kurmanji

| intonation group boundary
=   clitic boundary
-     separates segmentable morphemes
Ø   non-overt, but reconstructable morpheme
.   separates several metalanguage elements represented by a single object language element
_   separates several object language elements represented by a single metalanguage element or by a unity of several metalanguage elements

CONTRIBUTORS

Dorota Molin (PhD, University of Cambridge, 2021) is a Research Associate in Hebrew and Aramaic Studies at the University of Cambridge and a Lecturer in Biblical Hebrew Language at the University of Oxford. She has published on language contact in Semitic, Biblical Hebrew phonology and on issues in Neo-Aramaic syntax from a typological and diachronic perspective. Her doctoral thesis is a comparative grammar of a critically endangered Jewish Neo-Aramaic variety.

Paul M. Noorlander (PhD, Leiden University, 2018) is a Research Associate in Hebrew and Aramaic Studies at the University of Cambridge. He has published widely on Semitic languages, both ancient and modern. His main research concerns the typology of the endangered Neo-Aramaic dialects from an areal-diachronic perspective. He is the author of *Ergativity and Other Alignment Types in Neo-Aramaic: Investigating Morphosyntactic Microvariation* (Leiden: Brill, 2021).

Masoud Mohammadirad (PhD, New Sorbonne University, 2020) is a Research Associate in Kurdish language and linguistics at the University of Cambridge. His PhD thesis was a synchronic and diachronic study of pronominal clitics in modern West Iranian languages. His current research focuses on language contact between Iranian languages (Kurdish and Gorani) and Neo-Aramaic. He has published papers on Iranian linguistics in linguistic journals such as *STUF*, *Folia Linguistica*, and *Folia Linguistica Historica*.

Geoffrey Khan (PhD, School of Oriental and African Studies, London, 1984) is Regius Professor of Hebrew at the University of Cambridge. His research publications focus on three main fields: Biblical Hebrew language (especially medieval traditions), Neo-Aramaic dialectology and medieval Arabic documents. He is the general editor of *The Encyclopedia of Hebrew Language and Linguistics* and is the senior editor of *Journal of Semitic Studies*. His most recent book is *The Tiberian Pronunciation Tradition of Biblical Hebrew*, 2 vols, Cambridge Semitic Languages and Cultures 1 (University of Cambridge & Open Book Publishers, 2020).

Oz Aloni (PhD, University of Cambridge, 2018) is a Research Fellow at the Martin Buber Society of Fellows at the Hebrew University of Jerusalem. He has recently published the book *The Neo-Aramaic Oral Heritage of the Jews of Zakho*, Cambridge Semitic Languages and Cultures 11 (University of Cambridge & Open Book Publishers, 2022). He is currently working on a corpus of Neo-Aramaic folktales recorded from Mamo Yona Gabbay in 1964.

Collaborators

Lourd Habeeb Hanna Chechman is a native speaker of Neo-Aramaic and fluent in different varieties of Kurdish. She has been working to rebuild trust between the different religious and ethnic communities of the region after the trauma of the invasion of Islamic State. She co-founded and was president of the Middle East Sustainable Peace Organization (2016-17). In 2018 she became the leader of a project on social cohesion for the Catholic

Relief Services and USAID. She has also been a fellow in the United States Institute of Peace. Currently Lourd heads the Civil Society Initiatives Unit at the International Commission on Missing Persons in Iraq.

Aziz Emmanuel Eliya Al-Zebari (PhD, Salahaddin University, Erbil, 2018) is a lecturer in the English Department of the Catholic University of Erbil, Iraq. He was born in the village of Upper Gerbish in the area of Nekhla, North of Aqra. For his PhD thesis he documented the Neo-Aramaic dialect of the Aqra region.

Salim Disho Lazar Abraham is a freelance journalist working currently on a book on the most recent suffering of Assyrians at the hands of the Islamic State organization (ISIS.) He obtained his Master of Science degree in journalism from Columbia University, New York, USA, in 2006. He also holds a bachelor degree and post-graduate degree in English literature and Arabic-English translation from Aleppo and Damascus universities in Syria. He was born in the Assyrian quarter of Qamishli (north-eastern Syria), where almost all Assyrian dialects of Hakkari (south-eastern Turkey) were represented. He himself hails from Birij, Tkhuma, one of the largest tribes of Hakkari Assyrians.

PREFACE

Kurdish and Neo-Aramaic speaking communities have been neighbours in northern Iraq for centuries long before modern ethnic nationalist politics became dominant. The documentation and analysis of Neo-Aramaic and Kurdish folktales has long been a desideratum in the field of Middle Eastern literature. Like most oral literature today, it is highly endangered and likely to disappear within the next few decades. Recent violent conflicts in northern Iraq, fuelled by religious and ethnic ideologies, have had devastating effects on minority communities, resulting in their mass displacement and the endangerment of their language and oral culture. In northern Iraq the diverse ethnic and religious communities share many folktales, which they tell, often with local variations, in their various different languages. How similar are the shared folktales in their motifs and how have the shared tales been adapted to the particular ethno-religious identity of the community in question?

This book is a comparative collection of folklore as narrated by members of three ethno-religious communities from northern Iraq: Kurdish Muslims, Syriac Christians and—to a lesser degree—Aramaic-speaking Jews. Each story is transcribed to reflect as authentically as possible the language and dialect of the speaker. Several varieties of Northern and Central Kurdish, as well as Christian and Jewish Neo-Aramaic are included. All of these communities are understood here as belonging to a shared, though not homogeneous, cultural space, described here as 'northern Iraq', and elsewhere referred to as 'Iraqi Kurdistan' and

© 2022 Chapter Authors CC BY-NC 4.0   https://doi.org/10.11647/OBP.0306.17

'Kurdistan'. The latter terms refer to the ethnically diverse region of northern Iraq, nowadays politically recognised as the 'Kurdistan Regional Government'. Though now Kurdish-speaking and Muslim in its majority, this region has historically hosted a wide range of ethno-religious communities, including Kurdish-speaking Yezidis, Arabic- and Aramaic-speaking Jews and Christians, as well as Gorani-speaking Shia Shabaks and Yarsanis.

The shared political and social history as well as geography of the region's communities has led to a significant degree of cultural convergence, along with the preservation of firm boundaries of religion and—to a lesser degree—language. This reality justifies considering the various communities of Iraqi Kurdistan as part of a larger cultural space. For the lack of a better term, this multi-cultural space is referred to as 'northern Iraq' in this publication.

With its comparative approach, this volume serves as a case-study of the intimate and long-standing relations between the three aforementioned ethno-religious communities: the Kurds, Jews and Syriac Christians. Many Christians of Iraq who speak Neo-Aramaic, i.e. *surəθ* or *surət* 'Syriac', identify themselves as *suraye* 'Syrian Christians'. The vast majority of them belong to the Chaldean Catholic Church and Assyrian Church of the East. Most speakers, therefore, identify themselves as Chaldeans and Assyrians, respectively.

This volume is the outcome of a collaboration between linguists based at the University of Cambridge and members of the Syriac Christian and Kurdish Muslim communities in northern

Iraq. It has been funded by a grant awarded by the Heritage, Dignity and Violence programme (HDV190229) of the British Academy in 2019 and directed by Geoffrey Khan and Paul M. Noorlander. The main aim has been to produce parallel corpora of Kurdish and Neo-Aramaic folktales and to investigate the exchanges between the two neighbouring communities in order to foster an understanding of shared cultural heritage, and so contribute to the resolution and prevention of conflict.

Our main collaborator in Iraq, Lourd Hanna, was responsible for conducting the fieldwork and collecting the majority of the stories in northern Iraq. Lourd has experience in working with peace-building NGOs in northern Iraq. It was she who had the idea of using the shared cultural heritage of folktales as a means of fostering understanding between the different religious communities of the region. The funding of the project by the British Academy has allowed Lourd and the Cambridge team to make this vision a reality. This open-access publication will be used by Lourd as the basis for peace-building workshops between Christians and Muslims in northern Iraq.

We would like to thank Aziz Al-Zebari and Salim Abraham, both native speakers of Neo-Aramaic, for their assistance with transcription and translation. We are also grateful to Oz Aloni for giving us access to the story *The Princess and the Lazy Boy*, which he had collected in his own fieldwork,[1] and for sharing his own transcription, which served as the basis for the text of the tale in the present volume.

---

[1] https://nena.ames.cam.ac.uk/audio/173/.

The audio recordings of the corpus of parallel Neo-Aramaic and Kurdish folktales can be accessed at nena.ames.cam.ac.uk, and kurdic.ames.cam.ac.uk, which are databases maintained by the University of Cambridge.

The fieldwork and documentation work for this volume was made possible, as remarked, by a grant from the British Academy. Financial support for some of the groundwork of the project came from a grant by the University of Cambridge from the university's Global Challenges Research Fund. The research and preparations for this volume were partly funded by the European Research Council. Some of the native speaker assistants were supported by donations from the Assyrian community in the USA. We would like to thank in particular Francis Sarguis and Rebecca Simon for their generous support.

It is our hope that the stories about universal human experiences passed down over generations and communities will help build bridges across cultural divides.

Geoffrey Khan, Masoud Mohammadirad, Dorota Molin,
Paul M. Noorlander
Cambridge, May 2022

REFERENCES

Abeghyan, Manuk. 1899. 'Armenian Folk Beliefs'. PhD Dissertation, Leipzig University. Translated from Armenian by Robert Bedrosian (New Jersey, 2012), <https://archive.org/stream/ArmenianFolkBeliefs/Abeghyan_Armenian_Folk_Beliefs_djvu.txt.> last accessed June 2021

Akin, Cahit, Jastrow, Otto, and Shabo Talay. 2020. 'Zwei Texte im anatolisch-arabischen Dialekt von Nōršēn (Sason-Muş-Gruppe)'. *Zeitschrift für Arabische Linguistik* 17: 84–102.

Allison, Christine. 2001. 'Folklore and Fantasy; the Presentation of Women in Kurdish Oral Tradition'. In *Women of a non-state nation : the Kurds*, edited by Shahrzad Mojab, 181–194. Costa Mesa: Mazda Press.

———. 2010. 'Kurdish Oral Literature'. In *Oral Literature of Iranian Languages: Kurdish, Pashto, Balochi, Ossetic, Persian and Tajik: Companion Volume II*, edited by Ulrich Marzolph and Philip Kreyenbroek, 129-168. London: Bloomsbury.

———. 2016. 'The Shifting Borders of Conflict, Difference, and Oppression: Kurdish Folklore Revisited'. In *The Kurdish Question Revisited*, edited by Gareth R. Stansfield and Shareef Mohammad. London: Hurst.

Aloni, Oz. 2022. *The Neo-Aramaic Oral Heritage of the Jews of Zakho*. Cambridge Semitic Languages and Cultures 11. Cambridge: University of Cambridge and Open Book Publishers.

Amani, Mohammad S. 2021. 'Sammeln und Klassifikation der kurdischen Volksmärchen'. PhD dissertation, University of Göttingen.

Arekalova, Victoria. 2021. 'Yezidism'. In *Handbook of Islamic Sects and Movements,* edited by Muhammad A. Upal and Carole M. Cusack, 743-760. Boston/Leiden: Brill.

Ashliman, Dee L. 2004. *Folk and Fairy Tales: A Handbook*. Westport/London: Greenwood.

Asmussen, Jes Peter. 1968. 'Ein iranisches Wort, ein iranischer Spruch und eine iranische Märchenformel als Grundlage historischer Forschungen'. *Temenos* 3: 7–18.

Bayley, Denise. 2018. 'A Grammar of Gawrajū Gūrānī'. PhD. Dissertation, University of Göttingen.

Beckwith, Marc. 1987. 'Italo Calvino and the Nature of Italian Folktales'. *Italics* 64(2): 244–262.

Bickel, Balthasar. 2003. 'Referential Density in Discourse and Syntactic Typology'. *Language* 79 (4): 708–736.

Borysov, Eduard. 2020. 'The Pattern of Primogeniture Reversal as an Evidence for the Unified Nature of Genesis'. *Theological Reflections: Euro-Asian Journal of Theology* 24: 13-28.

Bošković-Stulli, Maja. 1966. 'Regional Variations in Folktales'. *Journal of the Folklore Institute* 3(3): 299–314.

Brauer, Erich. 1993. *The Jews of Kurdistan*. Detroit: Wayne State University Press.

Chrzanowski, Jaroslaw. 2011. 'Verbal Hendiadys Revisited: Grammaticalization and Auxiliation in Biblical Hebrew Verbs'. PhD Dissertation. The Catholic University of America, Washington, D.C.

Chyet, Michael L. 1991. "'And a Thornbush Sprang up between Them': Studies in 'Mem u Zin', A Kurdish Romance'. PhD dissertation, University of California, Berkeley.

———. 1995. 'Neo-Aramaic and Kurdish: An Interdisciplinary Consideration of Their Influence on Each Other'. *Israel Oriental Studies* 15: 219–252.

———. 2003. *Kurdish-English Dictionary Ferhenga Kurmanci-Inglizi*. New Haven and London: Yale University Press.

Coghill, Eleanor. 2009. 'Four Versions of a Neo-Aramaic Children's Story'. *ARAM Periodical* 21: 251–280.

———. 2020a. 'North-Eastern Neo-Aramaic Narrative Techniques and their Areal Parallels (Kurdish and Arabic)'. Paper presented at Cambridge Endangered Languages and Cultures Group, Cambridge, UK, 19 February 2020.

———. 2020b. 'Neo-Aramaic'. In *Arabic and Contact-Induced Change*, edited by Christopher Lucas and Stefano Manfredi, 371–402. Contact and Multilingualism 1. Berlin: Language Science Press.

Cohen, Eran. 2012. *The Syntax of Neo-Aramaic: The Jewish Dialect of Zakho. Gorgias Neo-Aramaic Studies*. Piscataway: Gorgias Press.

Da Silva, Sara G., Tehrani, Jamshid J. 2016. 'Comparative Phylogenetic Analyses Uncover the Ancient Roots of Indo-European Folktales'. *Royal Society Open Science* 3: 150645.

Dobbs-Allsopp, F. W. 1995. 'Ingressive *qwm* in Biblical Hebrew'. *Zeitschrift für Althebraistik* 8: 31–55.

Du Bois, John. 1987. 'The Discourse Basis of Ergativity'. *Language* 63(4). 805–855.

Dundes, Alan. 1962. 'From Etic to Emic Units in the Structural Study of Folktales'. *The Journal of American Folklore* 75: 95–105.

———. 1988. *Cinderella, A Casebook*, 2nd edition. Madison/London: Universtity of Wisconsin Press.

Ferguson, Charles A. and Frank A. Rice. 1960. 'Iraqi Children's Rhymes'. *Journal of the American Oriental Society* 80: 335–40.

Fischer, Wolfdietrich and Otto Jastrow. 1980. *Handbuch der arabischen Dialekte*. Harrassowitz: Wiesbaden.

Forker, Diana. 2016. 'Toward a Typology for Additive Markers'. *Lingua* 180: 69–100.

Garbell, Irene. 1965. 'The Impact of Kurdish and Turkish on the Jewish Neo-Aramaic Dialect of Persian Azerbaijan and the Adjoining Regions'. *Journal of the American Oriental Society* 85(2): 159–77.

Grigore, George. 2007. *L'arabe parlé à Mardin*. Bucharest: Bucharest University Press.

Guillaume, Antoine. 2011. 'Subordinate Clauses, Switch-reference and Tail-head Linkage in Cavineña Narratives'. In *Subordination in Native American Languages*, edited by Rik van Gijn, Katharina Haude and Pieter Muysken, 109–140. Typological Studies in Language 97. Amsterdam: John Benjamins.

Häberl, Charles G. 2009. *The Neo-Mandaic Dialect of Khorramshahr*. Wiesbaden: Harrassowitz.

Haig, Geoffrey and Baydaa Mustafa. 2019. 'Language Choice and Patterns of Usage Among Kurdish Speakers of Duhok: An Empirical Intergenerational Study'. In *Current Issues in Kurdish Linguistics*, edited by Gündoğdu, Songül, Ergin

Öpengin, Geoffrey Haig and Erik Anonby, 145–67. Bamberg: Bamberg University Press.

Haig, Geoffrey and Ergin Öpengin. 2014. 'Kurdish in Turkey: An Overview of Grammar, Dialectal variation and Status'. In *Minority Languages in Turkey*, edited by C. Bulut. Wiesbaden: Harrassowitz

Haig, Geoffrey and Geoffrey Khan. 2018. *The Languages and Linguistics of Western Asia*. Berlin/Boston: De Gruyter.

Haig, Geoffrey. 2018. 'The Iranian Languages of Northern Iraq'. In *The Languages and Linguistics of Western Asia*, edited by Geoffrey Haig and Geoffrey Khan, 267–304. Berlin/Boston: De Gruyter.

Ingham, Bruce. 2005. 'Persian and Turkish Loans in the Arabic Dialects of North Eastern Arabia'. In *Linguistic Convergence and Areal Diffusion: Case Studies from Iranian, Semitic and Turkic*, edited by Éva Ágnes Csató, Bo Isaksson and Carina Jahan, 173–80. London: Routledge.

Jakobson, Roman and Bogatyrev, Petr. 1982 [1929]. 'Folklore as a Special Form of Creation. Translated by Manfred Jacobson'. In *The Prague School: Selected Writings, 1929–1946*, edited by Peter Steiner, 33–46. Austin: University of Texas Press.

Jastrow, Otto and Talay, Shabo. 2019. *Der neuaramäische Dialekt von Midyat (Miḍyoyo). Band I: Texte* (Semitica Viva, 59). Wiesbaden: Harrassowitz.

Joseph, Brian. 1997. 'How General are our Generalizations? What Speakers Actually Know and What They Actually Do'. In *ESCOL '96. Proceedings of the Thirteenth Eastern States*

Conference on Linguistics, edited by Anthony D. Green and V. Motopanyane, 148–60. Ithaca: Cascadilla Press.

Khan, Geoffrey. 2008. *The Neo-Aramaic Dialect of Barwar*. Volumes 1-3. Leiden/Boston: Brill.

———. 2009. 'The Syntax and Discourse Structure of Neo-Aramaic Narrative Texts'. *ARAM Periodical* 21: 163–78.

———. 2012. 'The Evidential Function of the Perfect in North-Eastern Neo-Aramaic Dialects'. In *Language and Nature. Papers Presented to John Huehnergard on the Occasion of His 60th Birthday*, edited by Rebecca Hasselbach and Na'ama Pat-El, 219–28. Studies in Ancient Oriental Civilization 67. Chicago: University of Chicago.

———. 2016. *The Neo-Aramaic Dialect of the Assyrian Christians of Urmi*. 4 vols. Leiden: Brill.

———. 2020. 'The Perfect in North-Eastern Neo-Aramaic'. In *Perfects in Indo-European Languages and Beyond*, edited by Robert Crellin and Thomas Jügel, 311–50. Amsterdam: John Benjamins.

———. 2021. 'Verbal Forms Expressing Discourse Dependency in North-Eastern Neo-Aramaic'. In *Studies in the Grammar and Lexicon of Neo-Aramaic*, edited by Geoffrey Khan and Paul M. Noorlander, 143–193. Cambridge Semitic Languages and Cultures 5. Cambridge: University of Cambridge and Open Book Publishers.

———. 2022. 'Remarks on the Christian Neo-Aramaic Dialect of Shaqlawa'. *Israel Oriental Studies* 21: 192–231.

Lahdo, Ablahad. 2009. *The Arabic Dialect of Tillo in the Region of Siirt.* Studia Semitica Upsaliensia 26. Uppsala: Upsala University.

Lazard, Gilbert. 1999. 'Mirativity, Evidentiality, Mediativity, or Other? *Linguistic Typology,* 3 (1): 91–110.

MacKenzie, David N. 1962. *Kurdish Dialect Studies.* Vol. 2. London: Oxford University Press.

Marzolph, Ulrich. 2010. 'Persian Popular Literature'. In *Oral Literature of Iranian Languages: Kurdish, Pashto, Balochi, Ossetic, Persian and Tajik: Companion Volume II to a History of Persian Literature,* edited by Ulrich Marzolph and Philip Kreyenbroek, 208–39. London: Bloomsbury.

Mohammadirad, Masoud. 2021. 'Kurdish (Central, Sanandaj)'. In *WOWA — Word Order in Western Asia: A Spoken-Language-Based Corpus for Investigating Areal Effects in Word Order Variation.*, edited by Geoffrey Haig, Donald Stilo, Mahîr C. Doğan, and Nils N. Schiborr. Bamberg: Bamberg University Press. (multicast.aspra.uni-bamberg.de/resources/wowa/) (accessed 19/01/2022).

Molin, Dorota. 2021a. 'The Jewish Neo-Aramaic Dialect of Dohok: Two Folktales and Selected Features of Verbal Semantics'. In *Studies in the Grammar and Lexicon of Neo-Aramaic,* edited by Geoffrey Khan and Paul M. Noorlander, 95–143. Cambridge Semitic Languages and Cultures 5. Cambridge: University of Cambridge and Open Book Publishers.

———. 2021b. 'The Jewish Neo-Aramaic Dialect of Dohok: A Comparative Grammar'. PhD thesis, University of Cambridge.

Mouse, Anon E. 2018. *The Golden Maiden and Other Stories from Armenia.* Yateley: Abela.

Mutzafi, Hezy. 2002. Barzani Jewish Neo-Aramaic and its Dialects. *Mediterranean Language Review* 14: 41–70.

———. 2008a. *The Jewish Neo-Aramaic Dialect of Betanure (Province of Dihok).* Wiesbaden: Harrasowitz.

———. 2008b. 'Trans-Zab Jewish Neo-Aramaic'. *Bulletin of the School of Oriental and African Studies* 71 (3): 409–31.

Noorlander, Paul M. 2014. 'Diversity in Convergence: Kurdish and Aramaic Variation Entangled'. *Kurdish Studies* 2 (2): 201–24.

Noorlander, Paul M. 2021. *Ergativity and Other Alignment Types in Neo-Aramaic: Investigating Morphosyntactic Microvariation.* Studies in Semitic Languages and Linguistics 103. Leiden: Brill.

Noorlander, Paul M. and Molin, Dorota. 2022. 'Word order Typology in North-Eastern Neo-Aramaic: Towards a Corpus-Based Approach'. In *Word Order Variation: Semitic, Turkic and Indo-European Languages in Contact (Supplement of Language Typology and Universals,* vol. 31), edited by Hiwa Asadpour and Thomas Jügel, 232-258. Berlin: De Gruyter

Ogden, David. 2013. *Drakon: Dragon Myth and Serpent Cult in the Greek and Roman Worlds.* Oxford: Oxford University Press.

Öpengin, Ergin and Geoffrey Haig. 2014. 'Regional Variation in Kurmanji: A Preliminary Classification of Dialects'. *Kurdish Studies* 2(2): 143–76.

Orsatti, Paola. 2006. 'K̲osrow o Shirin'. In *Encyclopedia Iranica,* online edition. Available at zarinaia (accessed on 1 November 2021).

Pavelka, Karel. 2009. 'Detailed Documentation and 3d Model Creation of Dalal Bridge Using Terrestrial Photogrammetry In Zakhu, Northern Iraqi Kurdistan'. *22nd CIPA Symposium, October 11–15, 2009,* Kyoto, Japan.

Pike, Kenneth L. 1954. *Language in Relation to a Unified Theory of the Structure of Human Behavior. Part I.* Preliminary Edition. Glendale: Summer Institute of Linguistics.

Pinault, David. 1992. *Story-Telling Techniques in the Arabian Nights.* Studies in Arabic Literature 15. Leiden; New York: Brill.

Ritter, Helmut. 1969. *Ṭūrōyō: Die Volksprache der syrischen Christen des Ṭūr ₴Abdîn. A: Texte.* Vol 2. Beirut: Steiner.

Sabar, Yona. 1982. *The Folk Literature of the Kurdistani Jews: An Anthology.* New Haven/London: Yale University Press.

Sabar, Yona. 1995. 'The Christian Neo-Aramaic Dialects of Zakho and Dihok: Two Text Samples'. *Journal of the American Oriental Society* 11 (1): 33-51.

Sandfeld, Kr. 1930. *Linguistique balkanique: problèmes et résultats.* Paris: Société de Linguistique.

Schäfers, Marlene. 2018. "It Used to be Forbidden': Kurdish Women and the Limits of Gaining Voice'. *Journal of Middle East Women's Studies* 14 (1): 3-24.

Schiffrin, Deborah. 1981. 'Tense Variation in Narrative'. *Language* 57 (1): 45–62.

Shai, Donna. 1976. 'A Kurdish Jewish Variant of the Ballad of 'The Bridge of Arta''. *AJS Review* 1: 303-10.

Shuman, Amy and Hasan-Rokem, Galit. 2012. 'The Poetics of Folklore'. In *A Companion to Folklore,* edited by Regina F. Bendix and Galit Hasan-Rokem, 55–74. Oxford: Wiley-Blackwell.

Stilo, Donald and Paul M. Noorlander. 2015. 'On the Convergence of Verbal Systems of Aramaic and its Neighbors. Part

II: Past Paradigms Derived from Present Equivalents'. In *Neo-Aramaic in its Linguistic Context,* edited by Geoffrey Khan and Lydia Napiorkowska, 453–84. Piscataway, NJ: Gorgias Press.

Surmelian, Leon Z. 1968. *Apples of Immortality : Folktales of Armenia. London: Allen & Unwin, 1968.* UNESCO Collection of Representative Works. Ser. of Translations from the Literature of the Union of Soviet Socialist Republics. London: Allen & Unwin.

Talay, Shabo. 2008. 'The Neo-Aramaic Dialects of the Tiyari Assyrians in Syria: with Special Attention to Their Phonological Characteristics'. In *Neo-Aramaic Dialect Studies,* edited by Geoffrey Khan, 39-64. Piscataway: Gorgias Press.

Talmon, Rafael. 2001. 'Some Syntactic and Stylistic Features of Interest in Galilean Arabic Folk-Tales'. In *Linguistic and Cultural studies in Arabic and Hebrew: Essays Presented to Professor Moshe Piamenta for his 80th Birthday,* edited by J. Rosenhouse and A. Elad-Bouskila, 211–30. Wiesbaden: Harrassowitz.

Thackston, Wheeler M. 1991. all articles (folktale transcriptions) in *The International Journal of Kurdish Studies* 13 (2); specific pages cited from: 'Kurdish folklore' (i-iv) and 'King Ahmad' (91–95).

Thompson, Stith. 1922–1936. *Motif-Index of Folk-Literature; a Classification of Narrative Elements in Folktales, Ballads, Myths, Fables, Mediaeval Romances, Exempla, Fabliaux, Jest-Books, and Local Legends,* 6 volumes. Bloomington: Indiana University Press.

Thurman, Robert C. 1975. 'Chuave medial verbs'. *Anthropological Linguistics* 17 (7): 342–52.

Uther, Hans-Jörg. 2004. *The Types of International Folktales: A Classification and Bibliography, Based on The System of Antti Aarne and Stith Thompson*. Helsinki: Suomalainen Tiedeakatemia, Academia Scientiarum Fennica.

Vries, Lourens de. 2005. 'Towards a Typology of Tail-Head Linkage in Papuan Languages'. *Studies in Language* 29 (2): 363–84.

Woods, John E. 1990. *The Timurid Dynasty*. Bloomington: Indiana University, Research Institute for Inner Asian Studies.

Zeyrek, Deniz. 1993. 'Runs in Folktales and the Dynamics of Turkish Runs: A Case Study'. *Asian Folklore Studies* 52: 161–75.

PROLEGOMENA

1. INTRODUCTION TO A COMPARATIVE CORPUS OF ORAL LITERATURE[1]

Paul M. Noorlander and Dorota Molin

1.0. The Aramaic and Kurdish Dialects of Northern Iraq

1.1. The Dialects of NENA

The Neo-Aramaic dialects represented in this collection are all subsumed under 'North-Eastern Neo-Aramaic' and its acronym NENA, which are most closely related to the Neo-Aramaic dialects of Ṭur ʿAbdin (Ṭuroyo) and Mlaḥsó in south-eastern Turkey, also known as Central Neo-Aramaic, and Neo-Mandaic spoken further south-east in Iranian Khuzestan. The NENA dialects are generally referred to by their geographic location, i.e. the name of the town, as well as the religious affiliation of the community, i.e. Christian (represented in this anthology by the abbreviation ChA., i.e. Christian Aramaic) or Jewish (represented by the abbreviation JA.). The Christian and Jewish stories are thus nar-

[1] We gratefully acknowledge Masoud Mohammadirad's helpful comments on Section 1.2. in an earlier draft of this chapter.

© 2022 Chapter Authors, CC BY-NC 4.0   https://doi.org/10.11647/OBP.0306.01

rated in the respective Neo-Aramaic dialect of these communities. The Jewish dialects belong to the subgroup *lishana deni* 'our language' distinct from the eastern Jewish dialects subsumed under Trans-Zab Jewish NENA (Muftazi 2008). A sample of ChA. Duhok and ChA. Zakho texts with a linguistic commentary may be found in Sabar (1995). For the JA. Duhok dialect, see Molin (2021b), and for the syntax of JA. Zakho, Cohen (2012).

The following varieties of Neo-Aramaic are represented in the corpus and referred to as:

North-Western Iraq		**North-Eastern Iraq**
Jewish	**Christian**	
JA. Duhok	ChA. Duhok	ChA. Shaqlawa
JA. Zakho	ChA. Zakho	
	ChA. Dure	
	ChA. Enishke	
	ChA. Harmashe	

The locations of these towns are displayed on Map 1. Some features of these dialects are listed in Table 1. and 2. at the end of this section.

The Christian dialect of Shaqlawa, spoken in north-eastern rather than north-western Iraq, differs from the other NENA dialects in a number of ways. The NENA varieties in this region are known for the alveolar articulation of the affricates that correspond to postalveolar affricates in other dialects, e.g.

ChA. Shaqlawa	**Elsewhere**	
tsə	ču, čə	'not any'
ʾaxtsa	ʾaxča	'only'
xantsa	xanča	'a little'
tsōl	čōl	'wasteland'

ChA. Shaqlawa	Elsewhere	
dzwān	*jwān*	'beautiful'
dzwanqa	*jwanqa*	'handsome'

The ChA. Shaqlawa dialect furthermore does not preserve the historical Aramaic interdentals *θ and *ð, which shifted to alveolar plosives *t* and *d* respectively. This shift incidentally also took place in ChA. Zakho, with the exception of the existential particle, e.g. *liθən* 'there is not'.

The ChA. Enishke dialect furthermore shares an affinity with the varieties from the nearby Barwar region (Christian dialects), represented in this corpus by material from the village Dure,[2] which in some cases also makes it diverge from the nearby ChA. Duhok and/or ChA. Zakho and/or ChA. Harmashe. Both ChA. Enishke and ChA. Barwar lie in the mountains east of Duhok and Zakho. An example of this parallel between ChA. Enishke and ChA. Barwar in contrast to ChA. Duhok and ChA. Zakho is the double marking of pronominal recipients of ditransitive verbs, attested in both dialects, and illustrated here by ChA. Enishke (the double object marking is indicated here in bold):

(1) *yawax xa brata* **ṭale diye**

If we [do not] give a girl **to him**. (ChA. Enishke, Text 36: *Mar Giwargis*, §2)

The Jewish and Christian dialects of Duhok are at face value rather similar. Both communities have preserved the interdentals /θ/ and /ð/ and have the preverb *k-* / *g-* throughout. The historically low vowel /a/ is raised in the indicative stem of the

---

[2] For ChA. Barwar, see Khan (2008), vols. 1-3.

historically initial-aleph verbs, e.g. *kaxəl > JA. Duhok kexəl, ChA. Duhok kixəl. Compare:

JA. Duhok	ChA. Duhok	
gəbe	gəbe	'he wants'
muxðaðe	ʾuxðaðe	'(with) each other'
θele	θele	'he came'
ʾaθe	ʾaθe	'that he come' (subj.)
keθe	kiθe	'he comes' (ind.)
kiʾe	kiðe	'he knows' (ind.)

In other respects, the dialects of this town diverge more strongly, for example the possessive suffixes of the third person and the third plural L-suffix, as shown below. It is not unlikely, however, that the Jewish and Christian varieties of Duhok would have been largely mutually intelligible.

JA. Duhok	ChA. Duhok	
šəmmu	šəmmay(hən)	'their name'
šəmme	šəmmeḥ	'his name'
šəmma	šəmmaḥ	'their name'
wədlu	wəðlay	'they did'

The distinct confessional communities betray starker differences further west in the town of Zakho. In JA. Zakho, the interdental fricatives *θ and *ð have shifted mainly from flat to grooved fricatives, i.e. /s/ and /z/ respectively, whereas they shifted to equivalent stops /t/ and /d/ in the corresponding Christian variety. Contrary to other dialects where the preverb k-/g- prevails, the Christian dialect mainly uses the indicative preverb y-, and only sporadically k-:

JA. Zakho	ChA. Zakho	
gəbe	kəbe	'he wants'
ʾəzġas	ʾəxdade	'each other'
sele	tele	'he came'
ʾase	ʾate	'that he come' (subj.)
kese	yate	'he comes' (ind.)
kiʾe	yede	'he knows'

Here, too, the differences are even more drastic in the third person possessive suffixes, but in this case not the 3pl. L-suffix:

JA. Zakho	ChA. Zakho	
didu	diyehən	'theirs'
dide	diyu	'his'
dida	diyaw	'hers'
ʾuzlu	wədlu	'they did'

Table 1. and 2. at the end of this section offer lists of a few features of the Jewish and Christian dialects of NENA in this book.

1.2. The Dialects of Kurdish

Kurdish dialects are generally divided into Northern, Central and Southern Kurdish (Haig and Öpengin 2014, 110–11). The Northern Kurdish varieties represented in this book have been recorded in the Duhok province of Iraq and, together with the Hakkari province of Turkey, comprise a dialect region that is generally referred to as Badini, Bahdinī, or Southeastern Kurmanji

(Öpengin and Haig 2014).³ This book includes the following varieties of Northern Kurdish: Zakho, Duhok, Dure (in the Barwari Bala region) and Khizava (district of Zakho); see Map 1 for their respective location. These varieties share a number of features that set them apart from the rest of Northern Kurdish or the rest of Kurmanji respectively. Central Kurdish, also more generally known as Sorani, is represented by the dialect of Shaqlawa, which is situated between the regional dialects of Mukri (northwestern Iran) and Hewlêr (Erbil).

The aforementioned Kurdish dialects will be referred to as follows:

Northern Kurdish	**Central Kurdish**
NK. Zakho	CK. Shaqlawa
NK. Duhok	
NK. Dure	
NK. Khizava	

Table 3. offers a list of a few common features of the Northern Kurdish varieties and Shaqlawa represented here. A selection of features will be discussed further below.

Generally speaking, Northern Kurdish is distinct from Central Kurdish by features such as its preservation of nominal gender in the singular, its predominant use of independent pronouns rather than enclitic pronominals, and the lack of a definite article (Haig and Öpengin 2014), e.g.

---

[3] A grammatical synopsis of Bahdinī can be found in Haig (2018, 287–295).

Introduction to a Comparative Corpus of Oral Literature

Northern K.	Central K. (Shaqlawa)	
wī got	*got꞊ī*	'he said'
wē got	*got꞊ī*	'she said'
nāvē mən	*nāw꞊əm*	'my name'
gundak	*gundak*	'a village'
gund	*gundaka*	'the village'

The Northern Kurdish dialects of north-western Iraq differ from the dialects further north in Turkey in a number of respects. For instance, the Iraqi varieties exhibit the pharyngealisation of the consonants /ṭ/, /ṣ/ and /ẓ/, as has been observed *inter alia* by other scholars (MacKenzie 1961, 35–36; Haig 2018, 288). Such pharyngealisation is absent in the rest of Kurdish, as the contrast below demonstrates. The dialect of Shaqlawa, however, may also retain this backing in Arabic loanwords, e.g. *maṭrān* 'bishop', and words of Iranian origin, e.g. *ṣa* 'dog'.

Dure (NK)	Shaqlawa (CK)	
ṭərs	*tərs*	'fear'
ẓānī	*zānī*	'know' (pres. 2sg.)

The loss of the labial articulation in the sequence /xw/, which is typical of Bahdinī (Haig and Öpengin 2018; Haig 2018, 288), is generally but not always also found in the Northern Kurdish material, and sporadically also in Shaqlawa:

Duhok (NK)	Khizava (NK)	Shaqlawa (CK)	
xārən	*xwārən*	*xwārdən*	'food; to eat'
xodē	*xodē*	*xodā*	'god'

The Central Kurdish dialect of Shaqlawa also deviates from the Northern Kurdish varieties in its alveolar articulation of the affricates that correspond to postalveolar affricates in other dialects, similarly to the Christian Neo-Aramaic dialect of the same town (see above):

Shaqlawa (CK)	**Northern**	
tsə	čə	'what'
dzəwān	jəwān	'beautiful'
tsīrok	čīrok	'tale'

The velar stops /k/ and /g/ have the palatalised allophones [t͡ɕ] and [d͡ʑ] before front vowels in the dialect of Shaqlawa.[4]

In nominal inflection, the north-western Iraqi varieties exhibit the distinctive plural suffixes -ē and -ēt characteristic of Bahdinī, e.g.

Duhok (NK)	**Standard (NK)**	
kuř-ēt mīrī	kur-ēn mīr	'the sons of the prince'
kuř-ēt wī	kur-ēn wī	'his sons'

The dialect of Shaqlawa, by contrast, generally follows the pattern typical of Central Kurdish with the generalised linker/*ezafe* =ī, but sporadically still shows instances of feminine =ē.

As for the personal pronouns, the dialect of Duhok shows the following distinctive second person plural forms:

Duhok (NK)	**Standard (NK)**	
hīn, hawa	hūn, wa	'you' (2pl.)

A feature unique to the Bahdinī dialects is the use of a construction dedicated to the future, which is otherwise identical to

---

[4] Mohammadirad (p.c.).

the indicative present. The future particle *dē* and its alternative =*ē* in the dialects of Duhok and Khizava is followed by the subjunctive to form the future:

Duhok (NK)	Khizava (NK)	Shaqlawa (CK)	
az dē čəm	az=ē čəm	a-čəm	'I will go'

The subjunctive form of the verb is also combined with the verbal particle *dā* to express the past habitual in Northern Kurdish (cf. Chyet 1985, 246-47), e.g.

(2) **har řo dā bēžē**

Every day he would say. (NK. Khizava, Text 7: *Zanbil-firosh—The Basket-Seller*, §9)

These dialects also generally use the enclitic =*ē*, a reduced form of the oblique third person pronouns, to denote a recipient or addressee. It is attached directly to the inflected verbal form. In other dialects of Kurdish the recipient or addressee is generally expressed by an adpositional phrase:

Duhok (NK)	Standard (NK)	
(awē) got=ē	wē ž-ē ra got	'she said to him'
(aw) ət-bēžt=ē	aw ž-ē ra də-bēža	'she says to him'

The Northern Kurdish storytellers use this enclitic more frequently than not with the past base of the verb *gotin* ~ *gūtin* 'say' without an explicit reference to an agent, e.g.

∅ got=ē ~ gūt=ē 'he/she/they said to him/her/them'

By contrast, the addressee is generally not expressed with the verb *gotin* in the Shaqlawa narratives. This verb also has the present stem *bēž* in Northern Kurdish in contradistinction to Shaqlawa *rē*, e.g. *pē=y a-rē* 'she says to him'.

Features shared between the Northern Kurdish dialects and the Central Kurdish dialect of Shaqlawa are the distinctive 1pl. ending *-īn/-yn*, (Öpengin and Haig 2014, 162), which in other dialects merges with the 3pl. and 2pl. suffix *-ən*, and the aspectual and directional particles *-ava / -awa* and *=a* respectively.

Table 1. Selection of features of Jewish dialects of NENA

	Duhok	Zakho
*θ (*ṯ*)	/θ/	/s/
*ð (*ḏ*)	/ð/	/z/
3sg.m. pronoun	ʾawa	ʾawa
pronoun 'what'	ma	ma
indicative preverb	k- / g-	k- / g-
indicative stem of *yðy 'know'	kiʾ-	kiʾ-
past perfective preverb	qam-	qam-
recipient marker	ta / ṭal-	ta / ṭal-
3pl. L-suffix	-lu	-lu
3pl. possessive	-u	-u
3sg.m. L-suffix	-le	-le
3sg.m. possessive	-e	-e

Table 2. Selection of features of Christian dialects of NENA

	Duhok	Harm.	Enish.	Zakho	Shaql.
*θ (*ṯ*)	/θ/	/θ/	/θ/	/t/	/t/
*ð (*ḏ*)	/ð/	/ð/	/ð/	/d/	/d/
3sg.m. pronoun	ʾaw ʾahu	ʾaw	ʾaw ʾawu	ʾaw	ʾaw
pronoun 'what'	mi, ma	ma	ma	ma	ma
indicative preverb	k- / g-	k-	y- / k-*	y- / k-	k- / č-
indicative stem of *yðy 'know'	kið-	kið-	yăð-	yed-	čăd-
past perfective preverb	gəm- ʾəm-qam-	ḵum-	qam-	kəm-	qam-

* k- with the verb 'to want', e.g. *k-əbe* 'he wants'.

Table 2. Selection of features of Christian dialects of NENA (cont.)

	Duhok	Harm.	Enish.	Zakho	Shaql.
recipient marker	ta / ṭal-	ta / ṭal-	ta / ṭal-	ta / ṭal-	qa / qat-
3pl. L-suffix	-lay -le(y)	-lay -lɛy -na	-lu	-lu	-lu
3pl. possessive	-ay(hən)	-ay	-ey	-ehən	-u
3sg.m. L-suffix	-le	-le	-le	-le	-le
3sg.m. possessive	-eḥ / -e	-eu	-e	-u	-u

Table 3. Selection of features of Northern and Central Kurdish

	Northern (Duhok, Khizava)	Central (Shaqlawa)
3sg. oblique	m. (a)wī f. (a)wē	(a)wī* (a)wī*
ezafe inflection	sg.m. -ē sg.f. -ā pl. -ē(t)	sg.m. -ī** sg.f. -ē, -ī** pl. -ī**
'who'	kē, kī	kē
'my name'	nāv-ē mə(n)	nāw=əm
indicative preverb	(ə)t-	a-
'I will go' (future)	az=ē/dē čəm	a-čəm
'we are doing' (1pl. ending)	tə-kayn	a-kayn
'he wants'	wī t-vētən	da=y-hawē
aspectual particle	-(a)va	-awa, -o
directional particle	=a	=a
prefect particle	--	=a
past habitual particle	dā	--

* This is generally expressed by a series of enclitic pronouns in Central Kurdish.
** In Central Kurdish, the plural morpheme -ān as well as the definite article -ak(a) are generally added before the linker -ī, e.g. gund-ak-ān-ī dawrī Xošnawatī 'the villages around Khosnaw', or added to the following adjective, e.g. haqāyat kurdī-ak-ān 'the Kurdish stories'.

Map 1. The respective locations of the dialects of Aramaic and Kurdish represented in this book

2.0. Transcription

2.1. Common Transcription

The general transcription practices that are common to both the Kurdish and Neo-Aramaic texts in this collection are summarised in Table 4. The more language-specific transcription practices are discussed in the next subsections. Throughout the corpus, unaspirated stops are indicated by a circumflex accent below or above the relevant consonant, e.g. *ǩ* [k] as opposed to *k* [kʰ]. Palatalisation is indicated by a superscript *y*, e.g. *gʸ* [gʲ] as opposed to *g* [g]. Additional backing, manifested in pharyngealisation or velarisation respectively, is marked by a dot below the respective consonant, concurring with the so-called 'emphatics' in Semitic languages, e.g. *ṭ* [t~tˠ~tˤ]. When a speaker prolongs a consonant or vowel for considerable time, this may be reflected in the transcription by a series of three or more letters, e.g. *aaa*.

Furthermore, enclitic constituents are separated from the preceding host by the short equals sign (=). This applies to the enclitic copula and other enclitic argument markers, the cliticised codordinator 'and', and the directional particle =*a*.

(1) Neo-Aramaic
    ma=yle　　　'what is it?'
    bréle=llan　　'it happened to us'
    kayf=u ṣafay　'pleasure and jollity'
    ʾərwe=w tawre　'sheep and cows'

(2) Kurdish
　　čī=ya　　　　'what is it?'
　　got=ī　　　　'he / she said'
　　jəl=ū barg　　'clothes and covering'
　　čēlā=w gāyā　'of cows and bulls'
　　hāt=a māḷē　　'he / she came back home'

These elements are written separately when they do not cliticise to the preceding word, e.g.

(3) Neo-Aramaic
　　ʾ*u brele* ʾ*əllan*　'and it happened to us'
　　ʾ*u* ʾ*ana* ʾ*iwən*　'and I am'

(4) Kurdish
　　ū awī gōt　'and he said'
　　ū az　　　'and I'

The hyphen (-) used in transcription does not serve the same purpose as in glossing (see §4). Hyphens have been added to aid the reader in the identification of bound elements often consisting of merely one consonant or vowel. It is convenient to distinguish these from the core lexeme, for instance, to match this with the translation or to search for a particular verbal form. These elements are mainly prefixal prepositions and preverbal Tense-Aspect-Mood modifiers, e.g.

(5) Neo-Aramaic
    b-aw waqət   'at that time' (preposition b-)
    l-qaṣra   'to the palace' (preposition l-)
    b-qaṭəllan   'he will kill us' (future preverb b-)
    qam-šaqəllan   'he took us' (past perfective preverb qam-)
    d-ənna   'of such-and-such' (attributive d-)
    d-zale   'that goes' (subordinator d-)
    ṱ-ile   'that is' (subordinator d-)

(6) Kurdish
    l-gundak̯ə   'in a village' (preposition l-)
    a-čəm   'I go' (indicative preverb a-)
    na-t-k̯am   'I don't do' (negative na- and indicative t-)
    bə-xom   'I eat' (subjunctive preverb bə-)

Neo-Aramaic prepositions and linking particles that serve as a basis for a respective independent series of pronouns are not separated by a hyphen in transcription, e.g.

(7) Neo-Aramaic
    ʾəbbe   '(with) me'
    ʾəlli   '(to / for / on) me'
    dide   'his'
    diyi   'mine'
    daw   'of him; of that (one)'
    dað   'of him; of this (one)'

Finally, a speaker's hesitation is indicated by ellipsis (…). A reconstruction of barely audible segments or instances of unclear speech are placed between square brackets []. Inserted words and phrases from another contemporary language such as (Iraqi) Arabic are added with the initial in supercript, e.g.

(8) Neo-Aramaic

ᴬʿ*al ʾasās*ᴬ from Arabic على أساس

ᴱ*okey*ᴱ from English *okay*

2.2. Kurdish Transcription

The Kurdish transcription in this collection largely follows that of MacKenzie (1961). An overview is provided in Table 5. at the end of this section with the corresponding romanisation in a widely accepted form of Kurdish orthography. The main differences are the absence of the macron in <o>, and the use of <ə> to represent the centralised front unrounded vowel to make the transcription more uniform across the two languages.

2.3. NENA Transcription

The transcription of NENA is based on earlier approaches, relying mainly on more recent grammars of Khan such as ChA. Barwar (Khan 2008). The correspondences between Kurdish and NENA vowels as well as the alveolar trill [r] and velarised lateral approximant [ɫ] are given in Table 6. The main difference is reflected in the indication of length by means of the macron, e.g. *ā* [a:] as opposed to *a* [æ]. The quality and length of NENA tense and lax vowels are more or less predictable in inherited Aramaic words, and, depending on the dialect, the difference between tense and lax vowels is largely neutralised in post-tonic open syllables. The tense vowels [a~ɑ], [i], [e], [o] and [u] typically occur in open syllables and are pronounced longer in stressed syllables,⁵ e.g.

 naše [ˈnaː.ʃe]
 broni [ˈbroː.ni]
 nura [ˈnuː.ɾæ]

The lax counterparts [æ], [ɪ] and [ʊ] typically occur in closed syllables and are always short, e.g.

 ʾaxni [ˈʔæx.ni]
 ʾupra [ˈʔʊpʰ.ɾæ]
 pəšle [ˈpʰɪʃ.le]

In NENA transcriptions, the macron, e.g. *ā*, is only used when the respective tense and long vowel occurs in contexts contrary to the aforementioned tendency, namely in a closed syllable. The breve, e.g. *ă*, by contrast, is used when the lax and typically short vowel occurs in a stressed or pretonic open syllable, e.g.

 ḥălál [ħæˈlaːl]
 Dŭhok [ˈdɔ.hokʰ] ~ [ˈdʊ.hokʰ]
 čōl [ˈtʃʰoːl]

Many of the instances where the lax vowels occur in an open syllable in inherited Aramaic words are historically closed syllables, for example, in ChA. Shaqlawa:

 ʾăra < **ʾarʿa*

---

⁵ For the morpho-phonological rules that govern the distribution of vowel quantity, see Khan (2008, 66–76) and Molin (2021b, 79–88).

kŭla < *kulla

Hence, the NENA transcription of the words below would correspond to the Kurdish ones as follows:

NENA	Kurdish	
xandaq	xandaq	'ditch'
naxwa	naxwa	'otherwise; indeed'
gălak	galak	'very; much'
wărăqa	waraqa	'paper'
dargăvana	dargavān	'gatekeeper'
săwā́l	sawāl	'livestock'
jwān	juwān	'beautiful'
gəra	gər	'hill'
xēr	xēr	'good'
hedi	hēdī	'slow'
ži	žī	'also'
Dŭhok	Duhok	'Duhok'
čōl	čol	'wilderness, wasteland'
ʾu	ʾū	'and' (non-enclitic)

An exception to these rules are short monosyllabic words—typically particles and prepositions—that have an open syllable, for instance:

la	[læ]	'no, not' (verbal negator)
ču	[tʃʊ]	'not any' (nominal negator)
ta	[ta]	'to, for' (prep.)
gu	[gʊ]	'in' (prep.)
xa	[xa]	'one, a certain' (indef. article)

The vowel in these words tends to be short. Since this shortness in monosyllabic words is predicable, however, it is not indicated with the breve sign. Similarly, word-final open syllables generally have a short vowel, which is left here without a breve sign. Thus, it is

dargăvana [dær.gæ.ˈvaː.næ] 'gatekeeper'

2.4. Prosody

Intonation unit boundaries of utterances are indicated by a vertical line in superscript (ˈ). The nuclear accent of the prosodic unit is marked with a grave accent (à) on the stressed syllable of the respective word. Such intonational phrases need not correspond to syntactic units. To illustrate, in example (9) below taken from the Kurdish dialect of Duhok, the phrases *az Bīžān Xošavī ʾÀhmat* 'I am Bizhan Khoshavi Ahmad' and *kuř̄ē Šukrīyāyè* 'son of Shukirya' each constitute their own intonation unit separated by means of a vertical line (ˈ). The same holds for the independent pronoun *ʾana* 'I, me' in (10) below, taken from the Christian Neo-Aramaic dialect of Duhok, which occurs with its own prosodic contour, coinciding with the function of topicalisation.

(9) *az Bīžān Xošavī ʾÀhmat,ˈ kuř̄ē Šukrīyāyè.ˈ*
 'I am Bizhan Khoshavi Ahmad, son of Shukriya.' (NK Duhok, Text 17: *A Woman and a Leopard*, §1)

(10) *ʾànaˈ šəmmi Yawsəp brōnd ʾEliša ʾIshaq Mìxo.ˈ*
 'My name is Yawsep, son of Elisha Isḥaq Mikho.' (ChA. Duhok, Text 32: *Mirza Muhammad and the Forty Monsters*, §1)

Sporadically, one prosodic unit may be characterised as having two instances of a nuclear accent, often because two concepts are represented as two alternatives such as *āxāftənaḵā kərḕt* 'an offensive word' and *āxāftənaḵā saqàt* 'an inappropriate word' in (11) below.

(11) *ū bēyī kū āxāftənaḵā kərḕt ān āxāftənaḵā saqàt bēžīt=a mən.*[|]
 without telling me an offensive word or an inappropriate word (NK. Duhok, Text 17: *A Woman and a Leopard*, §22)

Lexical stress is generally penultimate in NENA dialects. A deviation from this general rule of stress placement is indicated using the acute accent (*á*). In (12) below, for example, there are two intonation unit boundaries; the nuclear accent falls on *ḥàkəm* in the first, and on *yàle* in the second. Since the words *ʾəθwale* 'he had' and *ṭlaθá* do not follow the penultimate stress rule, their deviating lexical stress is indicated by means of the acute accent.

(12) *ʾəθwa xa ḥàkəm*[|] *ʾəθwale ṭlaθá yàle.*[|]
 There once was a ruler who had three children. (ChA. Duhok, Text 32: *Mirza Muhammad and the Forty Monsters*, §3)

2.5. Transcription Tables

Table 4. General transcription of Kurdish and Neo-Aramaic

Transcription	IPA	Transcription	IPA
k	[kʰ]	ḥ	[ħ]
k̭	[k]	ṣ	[sˠ]~[sˤ]
kʸ	[kʲ]~[c]~[t͡ɕ]	ẓ	[zˠ]~[zˤ]
gʸ	[gʲ]~[ɟ]~[d͡ʑ]	ž	[ʒ]
ġ	[ɣ]~[ʁ]	š	[ʃ]
x	[x]~[χ]	č	[t͡ʃʰ]
p	[pʰ]	j	[d͡ʒ]
p̭	[p]	ʿ	[ʕ]
t	[tʰ]	ʾ	[ʔ]
ṭ	[tˠ]~[tˤ]	ə	[ɪ~ɨ~ə]
ṱ	[t]	o	[oː]

Table 5. Basic transcription of Kurdish in this collection

Standard Orthography	MacKenzie (1961)	This book	IPA
a	ā	ā	[aː~ɑ~ɔ]
ê	ē	ē	[eː]
o	ô, ō	o	[oː]
û	ū	ū	[uː]
î	ī	ī	[iː]
o	ø	ö	[œ~ø]
--	û	ü	[yː]
e	a	a	[ɛ~æ~a]
i	i	ə	[ɨ ~ ɪ]
u	u	u	[ʊ]
ş	š	š	[ʃ]
j	ž	ž	[ʒ]
ç	č	č	[t͡ʃʰ]
c	ǰ	j	[d͡ʒ]
r (rr)	r̄	ř	[r]
l (ll)	ḷ	ḷ	[ɫ]

Table 6. Correspondence between Kurdish and NENA transcription

Kurdish	NENA	IPA
ā	a	[a(:)~ɑ(:)]
ē	e	[e(:)]
o	o	[o(:)]
ū	u	[u(:)]
ī	i	[i(:)]
a	a (ă), ɛ	[æ~a~ɑ], [ɛ]
u	u (ŭ)	[ʊ~ɔ]
ə	ə	[ɨ ~ ɪ]
ř	rr	[r]
ł	ḷ	[ɫ]

3.0. Texts

3.1. Organisation

The thirty five texts in Volume II are organised thematically. The seven themes are as follows:

    I: Zambilfrosh (The Basket Seller)
    II: The Bridge of Dalale
    III: Animals and Humans
    IV: Social Status
    V: Family Relations
    VI: Mirza Muhammad
    VII: Religious Legends

The texts are numbered 4–38 and each assigned to one of the themes above. They are arranged by author and subsequently by language and dialect. The title of the story has been added by the respective author, not the storyteller. The Christian and Jewish dialects of Neo-Aramaic are abbreviated to ChA. and JA. respectively before the name of the respective dialect, e.g. ChA. Duhok and JA. Duhok. The abbreviations of Northern and Central Kurdish are placed before the relevant toponym, e.g. NK. Duhok and CK. Shaqlawa.

Texts are divided into numbered paragraphs at the discretion of the author. Reference to the paragraphs of the folktales is given using abbreviations, accompanied by the story title and a number indicating the specific paragraph being referenced. For instance, (ChA. Duhok, Text 14: *A Man and a Lion*, §7) refers to the 7th paragraph of the story *A Man and a Lion*, narrated in the Aramaic dialect of the Christians of Duhok.

3.2. Genre of the Texts

The corpus represents a wide array of genres, and sometimes multiple categorisations are possible. Table 7. below lists the stories according to genre. Nevertheless, the genre of some stories is not altogether clear, as is further discussed in Molin, Chapter 2 this volume. A list of the international folkloristic motifs which are attested in the Aramaic and Kurdish stories is given in Table 9 (Molin, Chapter 2, this volume).

Table 7. The stories categorised according to genre

Genre	Story
Legends (including **saint stories**)	4–7: *Zambilfrosh (The Basket-Seller)*
	35: *Mar Yohanan (St. John)*
	36: *Mar Giwargis (St. George)*
	8–11: *The Bridge of Dalale*
	37: *The Prophet's Horse*
Folktales	17: *A Woman and a Leopard*
	14: *A Man and a Lion*
	16: *A Man and a Wolf*
	15: *A Man and a Snake*
	20: *A Family Horse*
	30: *The Girl, Her Evil Stepmother and the Old Witch*
	23: *The Poor Girl and Her Horse*
	24: *A Woman Builds her Home*
	31: *Firyat and Khajija*
	25: *As Precious as Salt*
	16: *The Girl Pomegranate Grain*
Monster Narratives	32: *Mirza Muhammad and the Forty Monsters*
	30: *The Girl, her Evil Stepmother and the Old Witch*
	36: *Mar Giwargis (St George)*
Sung Stories and Ballads	9: *The Bridge of Dalale* (ChA. Duhok)
	4: *Zambilfrosh* (ChA. Shaqlawa, by A. Sher)
Epic	32–34: *Mirza Muhammad*
Proverbs	At the end of:
	17: *A Woman and a Leopard*
	14: *A Man and a Lion*
	16: *A Man and a Wolf*

Table 7. The stories categorised according to genre (cont.)

Genre	Stories
Fables	22: *A Talking Goat*
	12 & 13: *A 'Pious' Fox*
	18: *A Wolf, a Dog and a Ewe*
	19: *A Ewe and a Wolf*
Aetiology	8–11: *The Bridge of Dalale*
	31: *Firyat and Khajija* ('The Spring of Sorrow')
Anecdotes	38: *The Foul-mouthed Priest*
	28 & 29: *Two Mullahs*
	27: *The Indecent Neighbour*
	21: *A Man and his Dog*

3.3. Neo-Aramaic and Kurdish Versions

Several stories have different versions[6] and are presented in multiple dialects of Neo-Aramaic as well as (corresponding) Kurdish

Table 8. Stories with multiple versions in the corpus

Story	Language	Dialects	No.
Zambilfrosh	NENA	ChA. Shaqlawa (by A. Sher)	4
		ChA. Shaqlawa (by W. Toma)	5
		ChA. Enishke	6
	Kurdish	NK. Khizava	7
The Bridge of Dalale	NENA	ChA. Dure	8
		ChA. Duhok	9
		ChA. Zakho	10
	Kurdish	NK. Zakho	11

[6] There are also stories that overlap with other narratives in a less overarching way, but still in a fashion that suggests a shared origin. For further details, see Molin (Chapter 2, this volume).

Table 8. Stories with multiple versions in the corpus (cont.)

Story	Language	Dialects	No.
A 'Pious' Fox	NENA	ChA. Shaqlawa	12
	Kurdish	CK. Shaqlawa	13
A Human and a Beast	NENA	ChA. Duhok (*A Man and a Lion*)	14
		JA. Duhok (*A Man and a Wolf*)	16
	Kurdish	NK. Dure (*A Woman and a Leopard*)	17
A Wolf and a Ewe	NENA	ChA. Duhok	18
	Kurdish	CK. Shaqlawa	19
Two Mullahs	NENA	ChA. Shaqlawa	28
	Kurdish	CK. Shaqlawa	29
Mirza Muhammad	NENA	ChA. Duhok	32
		ChA. Harmashe	33
	Kurdish	NK. Duhok	34

3.4. List of Speakers with Notes on Idiolect and Style

3.4.1. Neo-Aramaic

ChA. Duhok

Madlen Patu Nagara (Texts 9, 24) uses *qam-* as a transitive past perfective preverb against *gəm-* in the speech of the other informant of ChA. Duhok, and *mi* as opposed to *ma* for 'what'. She has an elaborate story-telling style, though tends to leave some sentences unfinished, which sometimes impedes comprehension.

Yawsep Elisha Yishaq (Texts 14, 15, 18 and 32) has a slightly different dialect from M.P. Nagara (see above). Unlike M.P. Nagara, he uses the transitive perfective preverb *gəm-* alternating with *ʾəm-*. The interdental fricatives θ and ð sporadically shift to their respective stops *t* and *d* before L-suffixes, e.g. *məθle* 'he died' alternates with *mətle*. He often uses the filler *hənna* or *ʾənna* 'thingy, what's-it-called', and feels the need to clarify Kurdish words with an Arabic equivalent, e.g. K. *dargăvana* alongside Arab. *ḥarəs* 'gatekeeper; guard'. His speech is clear overall and at a variable pace. Occasionally, he speaks slowly but dynamically, accenting every word in a sentence, and at other times he can speak rather fast.

JA. Duhok

Sabi Abraham (Text 16) was interviewed in Jerusalem in 2018 by Dorota Molin. Despite having lived in a predominantly Hebrew-speaking environment for 70 years, he remembers in great detail many Neo-Aramaic folktales.[7] He learnt these from his father—a story teller—and he, in turn, had learnt some stories from his Kurdish neighbours.

ChA. Dure

Dawid Adam (Text 8) was interviewed in Turku, Finland, in 2005 by Geoffrey Khan. He was a storyteller in his native village of Dure in Barwar-i Bala. He tells stories with a fluent style and often includes sung ballads in his narratives. The dialect of

---

[7] For another folktale by Sabi Abraham, see Molin (2021a).

Dure belongs to the ChA. Barwar cluster, whose distinctive features include the following (see Khan 2008). The diphthong *ay shifts to /ɛ/, e.g. bɛθa < *bayθa 'house'. When a historically long *ī occurs in a closed syllable and is shortened, it retains its tense quality /i/, e.g. ʾiθwa 'there was'. The past perfective preverb has the form qəm-, which is formally distinct from the preposition qam 'before'.

ChA. Enishke

Zarifa Toma (Texts 6 and 36) has a very elliptical narrative style, so that her stories are for the most part simply summaries of the original creations. Her speech is interspersed with narrator questions (e.g. 'What did he do?').

ChA. Harmashe

Salim Daniel Yomaran (Text 33) was interviewed on site by Khan, Molin and Noorlander on a field trip in Iraq in 2019. He is a fluent speaker of the dialect and an animated storyteller. The interdental /θ/ is preserved before L-suffixes, e.g. məθle 'he died'. The diphthong /ay/ can be raised to [ɛy], and the vowels [o] and [u] are not always clearly distinguished in his speech, e.g. zura 'little', hule 'there is', but smoqa 'red', gora 'big', xona 'brother'. The transitive past perfective preverb qam- (or qām-) alternates with k̭um- and k̭əm- and may also be omitted. He tends to construct a negative imperative with lakun followed by a subjunctive starting with the morpheme ʾət, e.g. lakun ʾət ʾamrutu ta ču naša 'Do not tell anyone!'.

ChA. Shaqlawa

Ayshok Yalda (Text 35) was recorded by Geoffrey Khan and Nineb Lamassu in Shaqlawa 2017.

Warina Toma (Text 5)**, Sare Sawrish** (Text 23)**, Angel Sher** (Text 4) **and Sayran Sher** (Text 12 and 28) were all recorded by Lourd Hanna in Shaqlawa between 2019 and 2020.

They are all lively storytellers and typically speak very fast when they become animated. Some distinctive features of the ChA. Shaqlawa dialect include the following (Khan 2022). The 3sg.m. and 3pl. possessive suffixes both have the form *-u*. There are some asymmetries in the inflection of the various types of copula, e.g. in the 3pl. enclitic positive copula =*ina*, negative copula *lewu*, past enclitic *wənwa*. The particle *na* is used by speakers to express epistemic contrastive focus. It is used to correct what the speaker assumes the hearer believes or presupposes to be the case. Most of the storytellers introduce numerous Arabic and Kurdish words into their speech. A notable loan from Turkic is the particle *gorin*, which is placed after a noun and functions as a definite article, e.g. *yala gorin* 'the boy'. Embedded within the story of Zambilfrosh told by Angel Sher there is a sung ballad that is in the ChA. Alqosh dialect rather than the ChA. Shaqlawa dialect.

ChA. Zakho

Ameen Essa Shimoun's (Text 10) speech contains a significant amount of Arabic material, not only loanwords, but also entire phrases with Aramaic-Arabic code-switching. This includes many Modern Standard (as opposed to dialectal) Arabic phrases and expressions (e.g. *wa-laysa* 'and not' or *ʿəlmiyan* 'scientifically (speaking)', which probably serve to elevate the register.

JA. Zakho

Samra Zaken (Text 25) was recorded by Oz Aloni in July 2011 in Jerusalem, in conversation with **Batya Aloni**. As is the case with most Jewish speakers, her speech includes Aramaic—Modern Hebrew code-switching and loanwords. Samra Zaqen was born in Zakho around 1930. She moved to Jerusalem in 1951.

3.4.2. Kurdish

NK. Dure

Herish Rashid Tawfiq Beg's (Texts 20, 37) speech contains significant pharyngealisation of native words, e.g. *ḥasp* 'horse'. His speech features only a few Arabic loanwords. He consistently uses the 3pl. impersonal form of the verb 'to say' *ət-bēžən* 'lit is said' to signal episode transition in both of his stories.

NK. Duhok

Bizhan Khoshavi Ahmad's (Texts 17, 26, 30) speech is characterised by only limited influence from Arabic, which could be an indication of his education in Kurdish. Occasionally Central Kurdish elements are found in his speech, (e.g. *lā* 'at the place of'), reflecting the sociolinguist situation of Kurdish varieties in Iraqi Kurdistan, namely CK being the official language and the one associated with more prestige. His speech is also characterised by free variation between /ū/, and /o/ in some lexical items, e.g. *bo* vs. *bū* 'was'. Bizhan's dialect contains the largest number of what appears to be unaspirated stops among NK speakers.

Viyan Ramazan's (Texts 34) speech exhibits considerable variation from that of Bizhan. Her speech contains little influence from Standard Bahdini Kurmanji taught in schools and features more Arabic loanwords than Bizhan's. She has an elaborate storytelling style. She uses frequently the verb *īnā* 'S/he brought' to mark transitions in the episodes of the tale. She uses a variant of 3pl. oblique pronoun *wāna*, not attested in the speech of other NK story tellers.

NK. Zakho

Saeid Razvan's (Texts 11) speech exhibits distinctive features of NK. Zakho, e.g. lack of heavy verb stems. He uses Arabic words such as *ʿarrāf* 'fortune-teller' rather than the Kurdish equivalent *xēvzānk* to reflect his literacy in Arabic and the high prestige associated with it among older speakers of Kurdish.

NK. Khizava

Ahmad Abubakir Sleman's (Texts 7, 31) speech contains a considerable number of Arabic loanwords, which also include discourse markers such as *muhəm* 'anyway', *tabʿan* 'indeed'. His dialect shows similarities with the dialect of Zakho, e.g. the (occasional) lack of heavy verb stems, lack of directional particle after verbs of speech. He is from Gulli's tribe, for which a scant grammatical sketch and a text are provided in MacKenzie (1961; 1962).

CK. Shaqlawa

Hawsar Najat Bapir's (Texts 13, 19, 22, 29) speech exhibits some influence from Standard Central Kurdish, e.g., the occasional use of the near singular demonstrative *ama* instead of the distance-neutral *awa* form. He tends to elaborate on the Kurdish culture and folktales associated with Shaqlawa in his tales.

Jalal Sher (Texts 21, 27, 38) is a Neo-Aramaic speaker who is bilingual in Kurdish. His speech is characterised by the use of the impersonal verb 'to say' to mark transition between episodes of the tale. His speech is less influenced by Standard Central Kurdish than that of Hawasar.

4.0. Glossing

A sample of partly glossed texts is given at the end of Volume I, one for each dialect represented here. The glossing is consistent with the Leipzig Glossing Rules, except in the following cases. A few terms have been taken over from Iranian linguistics in the glossing of Kurdish, notably:

EZ for the so-called *ezafe*, i.e. nominal annexation morphemes, and DIR and OBL for the so-called *direct* and *oblique* case, i.e. the unmarked form in contrast to the case that is used in a broad range of other contexts otherwise subsumed under accusative, dative, genitive, and ergative cases. The abbreviation DRCT stands for the 'directional' particle used typically when verbs of movement are followed by goal arguments. The abbreviation TELIC stands for the 'telicity' distinctions, most crucially the endpoint of an action, expressed by the particle *(a)va-/-(a)va* in Northern Kurdish and the cognate *-(a)wa* in Central Kurdish. The particle can be used in alternations marking a change in verbal deixis such as counterdirectionality, e.g. *čūn* 'to go' vs. *čūn-ava* 'to go back', or a shift in lexical semantics, e.g. *xwārdən* 'to eat' : *xwārdən-ava* 'to drink', *kərən* 'to make' : *va-kərən* 'to open'. The abbreviation NA is used to indicate that a morpheme has not been analysed, i.e. the author refrains from judgement on the analysis of the corresponding morpheme.

In the glossing of NENA texts demonstratives, independent personal pronouns, and pronominal affixes on prepositions and nominals are glossed lexically. OBL is used to refer to a dedicated set of genitive third person pronouns corresponding with so-called oblique pronouns in Iranian used in the *ezafe*. Object suffixes on verbs are tagged with 'O', while other grammatical relations, such as subjects, are left unmarked. The participle (PTCP) specifically means the resultative participle, also used in perfect/anterior constructions. The tag INV for 'invariable' is used for non-inflectable adjectives.

5.0. English Translation

The English translation of texts aims to reflect faithfully the original text narrated in the source language with a combination of more formal and dynamic approaches. The outcome of this blending may vary from one translator to the next.

Where the translator has opted for periphrasis, the more literal equivalent rendering is given in footnotes or round brackets (). The frequent use of the verbs literally equivalent to English *rise* and *stand/get up* to express the transition to a new sequence of events is often rendered with the conjunction 'then' or left untranslated. The translation may deviate from the literal equivalent to show stylistic variation. The particles *yăni* or *yaʿni*, for instance, may be translated 'I mean', 'you know', 'indeed', 'that is' and so forth. Similarly, the Neo-Aramaic phrase *mhaymən* or *hemən* may be rendered as 'believe me', 'truly', 'really' and so forth. Frequently used discourse markers such as *ži* or =(*i*)*š* are left untranslated, unless an English equivalent readily presents itself. Repetition in the original language is not always reflected in the English translation.

Finally, words that are missing or implicit in the original text but required for proper use of English and/or for understanding the text have been added between square brackets []. To aid the reader in following the discourse, the referents of pronouns are added in parentheses or directly in the text with a footnote expressing the literal equivalent.

2. THE FOLKLORISTIC HERITAGE OF KURDS, JEWS AND SYRIAC CHRISTIANS OF NORTHERN IRAQ: SHARED MOTIFS, INDEPENDENT DEVELOPMENTS[1]

Dorota Molin

The folklore presented in Volume II is a testament to the intimate and long-standing relations between three ethno–religious communities from northern Iraq: the Kurds, Jews and Syriac Christians.[2] The folklore of these three communities is closely intertwined—not just through folkloristic motifs, which are often uni-

---

[1] I thank Dr Michael Chyet for his valuable comments on this chapter, and especially on cross-cultural parallels of folkloristic motifs. My sincere thanks also to Lourd Hanna, our Iraqi fieldworker, for insights and information about the communities and their folklore.

[2] Unfortunately, Yezidi folklore is not included in this publication. This seems a great shame, since a comparative study with Yezidi folklore would doubtless illuminate the larger extent of northern Iraq's shared cultural history. See, for instance, the discussion on 'Zanbilfirosh'. The overlap of this story's values with those praised in the Yezidi community is striking, and could suggest a Yezidi origin of this tale.

© 2022 Dorota Molin, CC BY-NC 4.0   https://doi.org/10.11647/OBP.0306.02

versal, but also with regard to specific narrative units ('motifemes') and even entire shared stories. In several cases, very similar stories are told by several different communities, with a greater or smaller degree of overlap in details. This chapter traces both folkloristic parallels as well as independent strands in the present corpus, focusing especially on themes, character types and cultural–religious frameworks in which the stories are set.

In general, the oral literature of northern Iraq demonstrates that social and geographic proximity can produce a degree of cultural convergence perhaps as strong as a shared national or ethnic identity and/or religious affiliation.[3] For instance, the *Bridge of Dalale* legend (Theme II) is highly popular throughout the whole region. There are also several animal stories (Theme III; §3.1) told by Muslims, Christians and Jews whose striking similarities suggest a common source. The folktale *As Precious as Salt* (§4) has an even wider trans–communal connection, as this theme occurs also in European folklore.

At the same time, some stories are apparently unique to particular ethno–religious communities.[4] Naturally, therefore, the religious stories in Theme VII introduce figures and/or sets of values that are specific to particular sacred traditions. Moreover,

---

[3] A similar conclusion is reached by Chyet (1995, 233) who—as in the present chapter—uses the term 'Kurdistani folklore' to refer to this trans-communal tradition of oral literature of the region of northern Iraq in which there is a Kurdish majority

[4] That is, our Iraqi fieldworker Lourd Hanna and myself are not aware of another version. In this corpus, see, for instance, the Christian *Mar Yohanan* and the Kurdish–Muslim *The Prophet Muhammad and his horse Dildil* (both §5).

stories such as *Zanbilfirosh* (Theme I) are shared, but nevertheless differ in ways that hint at distinct cultural values. For instance, the Chaldean-Catholic variants praise ascetic piety (a celibate, hermit lifestyle), while the Kurdish-Muslim version has the protagonist married and with a family, focusing instead on the restoration of justice. These points of divergence highlight the limits of cultural convergence among the Christians, Muslims and Jews of northern Iraq, and reflect the persistence of some degree of cultural-religious independence.

Sometimes, however, a story is 'borrowed' along with its culture-specific realia; see for instance, the anecdote *Two Mullahs* told by the Christians of Shaqlawa and, conversely, *The Foul-Mouthed Priest* told by the Muslims of the same town (Theme VII). On other occasions, communities adopt not only each other's folklore, but also religious traditions. In the case of *Zanbilfirosh* (Theme I), both Jews and Christians apparently draw from the story of Joseph and Zulaykha in the Quran (e.g *Joseph or Zambilfrosh*, ChA. Enishke), despite having their own Biblical variant of this narrative (Joseph and Potiphar's wife). Nevertheless, the moral virtues and behaviour patterns extolled in these stories are not in conflict with the norms of the community telling the story (save the reference to religion-specific devotional practices etc.). The existence of such conflicts in a narrative would be likely to discourage a community from borrowing it, at least without adaptions.

The existence of such distinct cultural tendencies, however, should not be equated with complete cultural homogeneity, even in the oral literature of a single community. Thus, for instance, several stories concerning social status (Theme IV) praise resilient, independent women who challenge official, male authority. At other times, the same character in a parallel story (e.g. the builder in *The Bridge of Dalale,* Theme II) receives a drastically different portrayal that makes the character once a villain, then a victim. This variety of behaviour patterns doubtless reflects the unique aesthetics or personalities of the narrators, as well as the fact that folklore is performed with a whole series of different functions and for diverse audiences (see below).

Given the broad approach of this chapter, a brief excursus on folklore theory will suffice. The basic structural units invoked here are themes and motifs, as well as the more specific motifemes. 'Motifeme' is understood here as a motif with a specific function. It is thus used to refer to scenes, narrative units, scene or character types that are shared across a group of closely-related folktales (often of shared origin, at least in part). For instance, while a talking, human-like animal is a universal folkloristic motif, the present corpus includes a specific application of this motif: a wise animal who meets a human on its territory and teaches the human a moral lesson (see Theme III).[5] A list of international folkloristic motifs which are attested in the stories is given in Table 9 below.

---

[5] For the theory of folklore structure and function, and for the distinction between a culture-internal ('emic') and scientific ('etic') analysis, see especially Dundes (1962). See also the useful overview of Elstein & Lipsker's analytical model in Aloni (2022, 187–97). When possible, the motifs discussed here are given indexes according to Stith Thompson's

Table 9. Folkloristic motifs occurring in the stories (categorised with Aarne-Thomson-Uther's and Thompson's indexes)

Motif group	Motif name (number)	Story
Aarne-Thompson-Uther Classification of Folk Tales		
ATU 1–299: **Animal tales**	1–69: The clever fox (other animals)	12–13: *A 'Pious' Fox*
	154: The Jackal and the Farmer	18: *A Wolf, a Dog and a Ewe*
		19: *A Ewe and a Wolf*
	160: Grateful animals; ungrateful man	17: *A Woman and a Leopard*
		14: *A Man and a Lion*
		16: *A Man and a Wolf*
		15: *A Man and a Snake*
		21: *A Man and His Dog*
ATU 300–749: **Tales of magic**	301: The three kidnapped princesses	32: *Mirza Muhammad and the Forty Monsters*
		33: *Mirza Muhammad and the Three Princesses*

Motif Index (1922–1936) and/or Aarne-Thompson-Uther's *Tale Type Index* (2004). Thompson's motifs are referred to with a letter and a number (e.g. S200). A *Tale Type Index* reference has a number preceded by the abbreviation 'ATU'.

Table 9. Folkloristic motifs occurring in the stories (categorised with Aarne-Thomson-Uther's and Thompson's indexes; cont.)

		300: Slaying the dragon	24: *A Woman Builds her Home* 32: *Mirza Muhammad and the Forty Monsters* 36: *Mar Giwargis (St George)*
		510: Cinderella and Cap o' Rushes	16: *The Girl Pomegranate Grain*
		514: The shift of sex	23: *The Poor Girl and Her Horse*
		532: The speaking horsehead	23: *The Poor Girl and Her Horse*
		301: The three stolen princesses	32: *Mirza Muhammad and the Forty Monsters* 33: *Mirza Muhammad and the Three Princesses*
		400: The man on a quest for his lost wife	34: *Mirza Muhammad's Adventures*
ATU 750–849: **Religious tales**		831: The dishonest priest	38: *The Foul-Mouthed Priest*
ATU 850–999: **Realistic tales**		923: Loving the salt	25: *As Precious as Salt*
		850–869: The man marries the princess	25: *As Precious as Salt* 24: *A Woman Builds her Home*
ATU 1200–1999: **Anecdotes and jokes**		1725-1849: Jokes about clergymen and religious figures	38: *The Foul-Mouthed Priest*

Table 9. Folkloristic motifs occurring in the stories (categorised with Aarne-Thomson-Uther's and Thompson's indexes; cont.)

Thompson's index		
B. Animals	B 530: Animals nourish men	17: *A Woman and a Leopard* 14: *A Man and a Lion* 16: *A Man and a Wolf* 15: *A Man and a Snake*
D. Magic	D 150: Transformation: man to bird	30: *The Girl, Her Evil Stepmother and the Old Witch*
	D 1540: Magic object controls the elements	32: *Mirza Muhammad and the Forty Monsters*
F. Marvels	F 628: Strong man slays monster	32: *Mirza Muhammad and the Forty Monsters* 36: *Mar Giwargis (St George)*
G. Ogres	G 100: Giant ogre G 610: Theft from ogre	32: *Mirza Muhammad and the Forty Monsters*
K. Deceptions	K 1300–K1399: Seduction or deceptive marriage	4–7: *Zambilfrosh (The Basket-Seller)*
L. Reversal of Fortune	L 10: Victorious youngest son	32: *Mirza Muhammad and the Forty Monsters* 33: *Mirza Muhammad and the Three Princesses*
	L 50: Victorious youngest daughter & L61: Clever youngest daughter	25: *As Precious as Salt* 24: *A Woman Builds her Home*

Table 9. Folkloristic motifs occurring in the stories (categorised with Aarne-Thomson-Uther's and Thompson's indexes; cont.)

N. Chance and Fate	N343: Lover kills self believing his mistress dead	31: *Firyat and Khajija*
R. Captives and Fugitives	R 10: Abduction	34: *Mirza Muhammad's Adventures*
S. Unnatural Cruelty	S 31: Cruel stepmother	16: *The Girl Pomegranate Grain* 30: *The Girl, her Evil Stepmother and the Old Witch*
	S 261: Foundations sacrifice	8–11: *The Bridge of Dalale*
T. Sex	T 80: Tragic love T 338: Virtuous man seduced by woman	31: *Firyat and Khajija* 4–7: *Zambilfrosh*
	T 481: Wife seduces husband's servant	6: *Joseph or Zambilfrosh*
V. Religion	V462. Kingship renounced to become an ascetic	35: *Mar Yohanan (St John)* 4–7: *Zambilfrosh*

Several folkloristic genres feature in this corpus, including folktales, legends and anecdotes. Legends—narratives presented as history—are represented by stories of saints and religious figures (Theme VII), the *Bridge of Dalale* (Theme II) and *Zanbilfirosh* (the basket seller; Theme I), at least in its Kurdish variant. Stories of humans and animals (Theme III) are for the most part folktales (creations presented as fiction), including the sub-genre of fables (Theme III.C)—stories with a moral, in which human characteristics are taken on by animal protagonists. However, some animal stories (e.g. *A Talking Goat* and *A Family Horse,* Theme III.B) are most likely anecdotes—short (amusing) stories often considered true by the narrator. The boundary between these folkloristic genres is highly fluid, as has long been recognised by folklorists (Shuman & Hasan-Rokem 2012).[6] Statements about genre categorisation, therefore, are simply shortcuts for referring to the characteristic features of the story in question (e.g. presentation as history for legends, sung/poetic elements for ballads, shortness for anecdotes etc.).

The question of genre interacts closely also with the issue of *audience* (cf. Allison 2010, 132; Shuman & Hasan-Rokem 2012). In the culture of northern Iraq, folklore was performed in a variety of contexts for a wide range of audiences. Stories and poetry entertained people during manual labour, which would typically be gender-segregated. This meant that work folklore would be produced, for instance, by and for women. Social and religious occasions such as weddings, too, had their specific genres, such as epithalamia (songs in praise of marriage). In village guest houses (*dīwānxāna*), folklore was performed for and by men. The stories that filled the long winter evenings spent with family and neighbours were intended for a mixed audience, though generally performed by men.[7] Folk poetry and prose were also performed in urban tea houses and even at the courts of

---

[6] For instance, a single creation can have features characteristic of several different genres, and can pass from one genre to another in the course of its transmission.

[7] My Jewish informants from Duhok who left Iraq in the 1950s report that they knew no female storytellers performing for a mixed audience.

emirs—typically by professionally-trained men for other men (Allison 2010). Sung performance especially was the domain of men. Folk singing required specialist training, which was less easily accessible to women. Additionally, female sung performance was considered immodest in many communities (cf. Allison 2010, 143 and the references there).[8]

It is useful to bear in mind the specifics of audience and performance in our discussion, though needless to say, it is not always possible to determine unequivocally the original audience of a given folk creation.

When a story or a part of it exists in both a Kurdish and a Christian Aramaic version, it is most likely to have been taken over by one community from the other, and then re-told. Such sharing and re-telling of stories, in turn, would have been most likely in a context in which the two communities lived near each other. Members of at least one of the communities must have understood or spoken the other's language. Furthermore, the two communities would typically have spent extensive amounts of time together in amicable interaction.[9] Such relations doubtless continued for centuries, surviving even in the living memory of the folktale narrators themselves. The elderly among them de-

---

[8] For women and folklore performance among the Kurds, see Marlene Schäfers, e.g. 2018.

[9] As shown above, folklore was performed in a variety of rural and urban contexts. The region's different ethno-religious communities would interact with each other in a variety of these situations, perhaps especially during manual labour and winter evenings spent with the neighbours.

scribed, for instance, how during the long winter evenings without modern media and electricity, the Muslims, Jews and Christians of a given town or village would visit each other and listen to stories. My Jewish informants report that they were especially close to their Muslim Kurdish neighbours.

Today, folklore performance among communities of northern Iraq—as in many places around the world—is endangered, and indeed on the brink of extinction. For instance, the vast majority of the Jews of northern Iraq now live in Israel, where their traditions and language are no longer transmitted.

There has been some previous scholarly work on the folklore of the region, which includes documentation and analytic research. A collection and classification of Kurdish folktales may be found in the doctoral dissertation of Amani (2021).[10] Several volumes of Kurdish folklore have also been published by Celîl and Celîl (2014–2018). An anthology of Jewish Neo-Aramaic folklore has been published by Sabar (1982), and many grammars of (Jewish and Christian) Neo-Aramaic include text corpora with folkloristic material.[11] A folkloristic analysis focusing on the Jewish community of Zakho has been published by Aloni (2022).

---

[10] See, however, the research by Robins (née Allison), e.g. 2001, 2010 and 2016. See also Chyet (1991) for the romance of Mem and Zin, which he collected in a series of Kurdish and Neo-Aramaic varieties. Existing collections of Kurdish folklore include *The International Journal of Kurdish Studies,* vol. 13 (Thackston 1999).

[11] The largest corpora are found in Khan's work on ChA. Urmi (northwestern Iran; 2016, vol. 4) and ChA. Barwar (north-western Iraq, 2008, vol. 3). See also Mutzafi (2008a) for a corpus of JA. Betanure (north-western Iraq).

More work, however, is urgently needed, especially documentation, given the endangered state of these folklore traditions.

1.0. Zanbilfirosh (Zambilfrosh) and Joseph the Egyptian

Text 4: *Zambilfrosh*, narrated by A. Sher (ChA. Shaqlawa)
Text 5: *Zambilfrosh*, narrated by W. Toma (ChA. Shaqlawa)
Text 7: *Zanbilfirosh* (NK. Khizava)
Text 6: *Joseph or Zambilfrosh* (ChA. Enishke)

Zanbilfirosh tells the story of a pious basket-seller who gives up his royal status (V462)[12] after he has witnessed death and his values are shaken to the core. The story climaxes when the basket-seller successfully resists the seduction of a wealthy married woman.[13] This tale is also the example *par excellence* in our anthology of the fluid boundary between oral and written literature in northern Iraq, as is shown below. The variants included here further subdivide into 'Zanbilfirosh proper'—which includes the

---

[12] 'Kingship renounced to become an ascetic'.

[13] *zanbilfərosh* in Kurdish means simply 'basket-seller'. This Kurdish title of the protagonist, adapted to 'Zambilfrosh', also occurs in the Neo-Aramaic versions of the tale (i.e. is left untranslated). In other words, it is apparently functioning as the protagonist's name. In this chapter, 'Zanbilifrosh' is used when speaking of the character in folklore in general, or of the Kurdish variants of the story, while 'Zambilfrosh' is used for the Neo-Aramaic stories. For further examples of the interaction of oral and literary written traditions in Kurdish culture, see Allison (2010, 131).

two *Zambilfrosh* stories in ChA. Shaqlawa Aramaic[14] and *Zanbilfirosh* (NK. Khizava)—and the tale of *Joseph or Zambilfrosh*. The latter stands apart because it draws chiefly from the Qurʾanic story of Joseph the Righteous, yet its protagonist also self-identifies as *zambilfrosh* (i.e. 'basket-seller').[15] Moreover, in contrast to his Qurʾanic counterpart and in parallel with the folkloristic Zanbilfirosh, the protagonist is of royal descent (ChA. Enishke, *Zambilfrosh*, §1). Presumably, therefore, *Joseph or Zambilfrosh* in ChA. Enishke is informed by both stories. It is a new oral tale formed by the fusion of a sacred (written) tradition, on the one hand, and a popular oral tradition, on the other.

The story of Zanbilfirosh has long inhabited the imagination and formed the collective identity of the various ethno-religious communities of northern Iraq, with many communities considering it a legend. In the present corpus, this certainly applies to the Kurdish version. It is set in Mosul and names the place where the basket-seller was buried; on the road between Zakho

---

[14] The ChA. Shaqlawa tale by A. Sher also contains a sung version (§44–63). It bears a strong resemblance to the spoken one, while also being more concise and open-ended (it is unclear whether the protagonist manages to escape unharmed). For comparative purposes, it is the spoken version which is referred to in this section.

[15] For instance, when offered the king's crown by the woman who tries to seduce him, he responds that he is 'a mere basket-seller' (ChA. Enishke, *Zambilfrosh*, §7), implying that he does not desire any greater honour.

and Batifa in north-western Iraq (NK. Khizava, *Zanbilfirosh*, §3).¹⁶ On the other hand, none of the Christian Aramaic versions give proper names of places or even people, making it unclear whether the story is treated as a legend. In the case of ChA. Enishke, the categorisation as a legend is further problematised by the clear Qurʾanic inspirations.

Several written versions of the story also exist, perhaps most famously by the 16th century Kurdish Faqīyē Tayrān.¹⁷ The Yezidis have also claimed the story as their own. This project's Iraqi fieldworker Lourd Hanna has informed me that the five domes of the famed Yezidi Lalish temple are named after the five sons of Zanbilfirosh—that is, the names that they carry in the Yezidi version(s) of this tale. The Yezidi origin of 'Zanbilfirosh' is in fact not unlikely, considering also the obvious overlap in values praised in the two. The life of the pious, ascetic (though not necessarily celibate) folkloristic basket seller resembles the Sufi-influenced lifestyle of the celebrated Yezidi *faqirs*.¹⁸

Moreover, the story overlaps with the Qurʾanic Joseph story in a way so striking as to suggest a shared history (see below). And indeed, the story of Joseph and Zulaykha in the Qurʾan is itself based on an even older story of Joseph in the Hebrew Bible, doubtless familiar to the Jews and Christians of northern Iraq. Among the Kurds and their Jewish (and other?) neighbours,

---

¹⁶ The communities of Turkey have their own place that is claimed to be the tomb of Zanbilfirosh, near Farqin in Diyarbakir (NK. Khizava, *Zanbilfirosh*, §2).

¹⁷ https://en.wikipedia.org/wiki/Zemb%C3%AElfiro%C5%9F.

¹⁸ See Arekalova (2021) and the references therein.

the story of Joseph and Zulaykha (see below) enjoys a great popularity (Chyet 1995, 233–34), transmitted in prose and poetry in both written and oral media. The poem 'Yusuf and Zulaykha' by the Persian poet Jami (d. 1414) is perhaps the most famous variant.

Considering the origin of Zanbilfirosh, therefore, it seems likely that at some point, one of the creative re-tellings of the Joseph and Zulaykha narrative merged with or morphed into the story of the Kurdish basket-seller, Zanbilfirosh. The Jews of northern Iraq too had their own, rhymed (para-)religious stories about Joseph (Sabar 1976, 171, footnote 61). Interestingly, these were based on the 'Moslem Kurdish traditions' of Joseph (ibid.), rather than on their Biblical counterpart.

Zanbilfirosh: basket-seller, prince, monk, father and Joseph the Egyptian?

The Kurdish version in the present corpus diverges somewhat from the two Christian 'Zambilfrosh proper' variants (see below). This distinction is likely indicative of a wider typological split between the Christian and Muslim(/Yezidi) versions of this legend. On the other hand, the three 'Zanbilfirosh proper' tales agree that the protagonist grows up as a prince oblivious to suffering and death, until the day when he witnesses death and this turns his life upside down. Shaken to the core because of a sense of vanity of this world, he gives up his wealth and makes a living as a humble basket-seller.

This general similarity notwithstanding, the three 'Zanbilfirosh proper' tales differ on what exactly the prince turns *from* and *towards*. In the ChA. Shaqlawa version by W. Toma, the protagonist simply wants to live a simple life. Since all human successes and pleasures are fleeting and fragile, they are not worth pursuing (§5). In the ChA. Shaqlawa version by A. Sher, Zambilfrosh goes a step further. He desires to replace the vain with something more enduring. He seeks to enter the kingdom of God and worship the Creator (e.g. §23). Still, both stories are explicitly Christian. Zambilfrosh lives with hermit monks and the tales assume a culture in which strict ascetic piety is celebrated. In other words, the response to corruption in society is a life in seclusion from society—which also includes celibacy—and the worship of God.

In the Kurdish-Muslim version, the celebrated value is not strict ascetic piety or a hermit lifestyle, but rather the restoration of justice. Zanbilfirosh leaves his father's house when a mullah tells him that if he remains, he is complicit in his father's unjust policies (§12–13). He then decides to make a living independently, by weaving baskets. This does not mean, however, that he leaves everything behind. On the contrary, he already has a family (§15), and his motivation is to provide for them. The Yezidi versions of Zanbilfirosh likely resemble the Muslim ones in this regard. As mentioned above, the names found at the Lalish temple suggest that the Yezidi Zanbilfirosh had children. This difference highlights the fact that ascetic piety as manifested in hermit lifestyle and celibacy is not valued or institutionalised among the Muslim (and Yezidi?) communities to the extent it is among the (Chaldean-Catholic) Christians (see further the discussion on religious stories (Theme VII) below).

When he has established his new lifestyle, Zanbilfirosh faces a temptation that will prove his moral virtue. One day, a ruler's wife (or daughter) locks the basket-seller inside her palace and tries to seduce him, but he resists. In all the versions of this corpus, this episode closely parallels the Qur'anic story of Joseph and Zulaykha and the Biblical account of Joseph and Potiphar's wife. In the sacred stories and the tales of 'Zanbilfirosh proper', for instance, the woman accuses the young man of assault after her pursuits turn out to be unsuccessful. The motifeme of attempted seduction by a powerful woman is well established,[19] known from the Bible and the Quran, but also in Kurdish folklore. In King Ahmad (Thackston 1991, 91–92), the prince is tempted by his step-mother, who rips his clothes from his back in pursuit of him, as does Zulaykha in the Qur'an.

The protagonist's temptation becomes the ultimate test of his new-found piety. Thus, in the Christian versions, Zambilfrosh must resist a woman's charms as well as the promise of life of luxury and indeed royal status (e.g. ChA. Shaqlawa, *Zambilfrosh* narrated by A. Sher, §36–7 and *Zambilfrosh* narrated by W. Toma, §21). By now, he has experienced both privilege and poverty, life as a royal son and celibacy, and must confirm his dedication to one of these. If he were to yield, he would convey an implicit regret over his conversion. This double temptation (with pleasure in a woman's arms and royal status) occurs also in the ChA. Enishke version. This feature doubtless originates in the folkloristic (or written-poetic) tradition, since there is no mention of the

---

[19] See K1300–K1399 ('Seduction or deceptive marriage') and T481 ('Wife seduces husband's servant') in Thompson's index.

promise of wealth in Joseph and Zulaykha, and Zulaykha is not the queen.

In the end, the Khizava Northern Kurdish version is the most naturalistic one. In the Christian Shaqlawa versions, Zanbilfirosh is miraculously saved from the queen's palace by an angel (the version by A. Sher: §43; by W. Toma: §31). In the Kurdish version, by contrast, he prefers to throw himself down from a tower than succumb to the seduction, and dies as a result of his injuries (§25, 30). Here, the message is, therefore, that virtue is worth pursuing no matter what the cost.

As mentioned above, the 'Zanbilfirosh proper' tales in this corpus are culturally adapted. Most importantly, in the Christian Shaqlawa versions, the protagonist lives with a hermit monk, while in the Kurdish Khizava one, he learns about religion from a mullah. This indicates that the transfer of the story from one community to another most likely took place centuries ago, after which it underwent cultural adaptations.[20] By contrast, the Christian Enishke *Joseph or Zambilfrosh* story draws from a similar religious Joseph narrative, but apparently from the Qurʾanic rather than the Biblical one. For instance, the protagonist is reluctant to share his prophetic dream about his future glory and his brothers' subjugation to him: 'I won't tell, I am not comfortable telling' (ChA. Enishke, *Zambilfrosh*, §3). This parallels the Qurʾanic version where Joseph's father cautions him not to relate his dream to his brothers (12:5) fearing ridicule, and contrasts with the Biblical account, in which Joseph boasts about his dreams to his

---

[20] Contrast this with the unadapted—and therefore likely the more recently 'borrowed'—anecdote *The Two Mullahs*, §4 below.

brothers—all the while knowing that they already despise him (Gen. 37.4–11).

The three stories of Zanbilfirosh proper go to great lengths to emphasise the protagonist's piety, making him an example of modesty, steadfastness and justice or asceticism for all those who tell and hear his story. In the Christian Enishke story, the exemplary pietistic role of the protagonist is arguably less central. For instance, he leaves his house simply because of an argument with his family (ChA. Enishke, *Joseph or Zambilfrosh*, §1).

In general, the story of Zanbilfirosh illustrates the shared nature of the folk literature of northern Iraq as well as the preservation of a distinct cultural-religious imprint on the stories. It also bears witness to the complex and doubtless long-standing interaction with sacred, written and folkloristic traditions. Though the present corpus only includes Christian and Kurdish tales of the pious and humble basket-seller, Yezidi and Jewish versions also exist, as mentioned earlier. Likely, many—if not all—of these communities have claimed Zanbilfirosh as their own.

At the same time, this tale suggests that the communities adapted not only each other's folklore, but sometimes also religious traditions. In this case, both Jews and Christians apparently retold the Qur'anic version of Joseph, or at least used some of its elements.

Finally, the story of a pious (and poor) man resisting the seduction of a powerful woman has likely passed back and forth through oral and written media.[21] Thus, in the Christian Enishke *Joseph* or *Zambilfrosh* story, for instance, an oral and a written source have been merged together to give rise to a new oral tradition.

2.0. The Bridge of Dalale Legend (and Ballad)

Text 8: *The Bridge of Dalale* (ChA. Dure)
Text 9: *The Bridge of Dalale* (ChA. Duhok)
Text 10: *The Bridge of Dalale* (ChA. Zakho)
Text 11: *The Bridge of Dalale* (NK. Zakho)

The Bridge of Dalale/Dalal (also 'The Bridge of Zakho') narrates the story of a builder who sacrifices his female relative (called Dalale) to ensure that the bridge is completed. This legend occupies a unique position in the folklore of northern Iraq. It is bound inextricably to the landscape of region—through one of the local architectural icons, the Bridge of Zakho. It serves as an etiology for this unique construction, which is several centuries old. This, in turn, serves those who tell the story to claim the physical landscape as the habitat of their own cultural life.

Though grafted onto the landscape of northern Iraq, however, *The Bridge of Dalale* bears similarities with stories grouped under 'The Bridge of Atra' (ballad), describing a foundation sacrifice (S261). Versions of 'The Bridge of Atra' are attested from the Balkans all the way to India. This has led scholars such as Shai (1976) to propose that the JA. Zakho ballad 'The Bridge of

---

[21] See further Jakobson and Bogatyrev (1980, 13–14) for the interaction between oral and written literature.

Dalale' which she published is in fact a variant of 'The Bridge of Atra'.[22] This shared origin is possible, but the differences between 'The Bridge of Atra and 'The Bridge of Dalale' also license a hypothesis about independent developments.

In this volume, Christian and Muslim versions of *The Bridge of Dalale* are documented,[23] but as mentioned above, Jewish Neo-Aramaic versions also exist (cf. Shai 1976). A feature that is apparently unique to the Jewish variants is the incorporation of the sacrifice of Jephthah's daughter from the Hebrew Bible (Shai 1976, 307–8). Another Northern Kurdish version in the Zakho dialect is found in MacKenzie (1962, 356–359). Many of the Aramaic versions of 'The Bridge of Dalale'[24] end with a short ballad.

The origin of the Dalale legend is not entirely clear. On the one hand, the ballad that features in some Aramaic versions[25] contains Kurdish expressions, suggesting a Kurdish origin, at least as far as the ballad is concerned. On the other hand, during this project, it has proved impossible to find Kurdish versions of the

---

[22] See Dundes (1989) and the references there. I thank Michael Chyet for drawing my attention to this publication.

[23] Several other Aramaic versions of the ballad have been documented. See, for instance, Talay (2008; a community living today in the Khabur region) and the arrangement by *Mespototamian Fusion*, sung in the dialect of Bohtan (south-eastern Turkey) at
https://www.youtube.com/watch?v=O6Ue4YyH2D4.

[24] See e.g. the ChA. Duhok and ChA. Dure versions in this corpus and the JA. Zakho version in Shai (1976).

[25] For instance, ChhA. Duhok, *The Bridge of Dalale*, 16 and the ChA. Bohtan version at
https://www.youtube.com/watch?v=O6Ue4YyH2D4
with the Kurdish phrase *Dalale brindare*, 'Oh Dalal, you wounded!'

ballad. In fact, the Aramaic (Christian and Jewish) versions of the legend are generally more extensive and poetically developed, which at least suggests that the legend (and the ballad) have been better preserved among the Christians and the Jews, even if they do not originate among them. The Zakho narrator who tells the Kurdish version of the story presented here claims that the Kurds took this story over from the Jews (NK. Zakho, *The Bridge of Dalal,* 24).[26] In any case, there are clear sub-types of the legend (see below), which shows at least that the story has developed in a few separate traditions.

Outside northern Iraq, this legend also possesses a close Mandean parallel from Khorramshahr (south-western Iran; cf. Häberl 2009, 280–89). On the other hand, 'The Bridge of Dalale' is reportedly not known among the Jews of north-eastern Iraq and western Iran (east of the Great Zab), which suggests their relative isolation from the communities in the region west of the Great Zab.[27]

The exact origin of the actual bridge standing Zakho is also somewhat uncertain. There was a bridge in this town likely already in Roman times, but this original construction has since been rebuilt several times. The extent to which the Roman bridge is preserved is uncertain. Some Iraqi archaeologists maintain that most of the modern bridge was erected by one of the Bahdinan princes who ruled the region from the 13th to the 19th centuries (cf. Pavelka 2009).

---

[26] Unfortunately, I was unable to get access to the full legend mentioned in Shai (1976) in order to judge their closeness.

[27] Hezy Mutzafi, personal communication.

A villain, a martyr or a victim? The portrayal of the characters

The versions included in this volume constitute three sub-types that differ in striking ways with regard to the character of the protagonists—Dalale and the builder, and, in one case, also the local *agha*. These points of divergence have implications for the identity of the true hero(s).

Both of the stories from Zakho, the Christian Aramaic one and the Kurdish one, belong to the same category, and they clearly draw from the same source. Here, the builder himself is a victim: his hand had been cut off after he had built another bridge, and now has to work impaired on the Zakho bridge. In the Christian variant, he is also under the threat that his whole family will be killed if he fails. When he sacrifices Dalale, therefore, he does so not to save his reputation as a successful builder, but rather to save his and his family's life. The sacrifice is accompanied by considerable remorse and anguish:

> 'Oh, my God, may it not be my daughter-in-law, because I'll have to put her inside the bridge.' (ChA. Zakho, Text 10: *The Bridge of Dalale*, §34).

The builder, therefore, is a tragic hero forced to murder because it is a lesser evil. Dalale, on the other hand, is a martyr whose death proves redemptive. Her sacrifice is in fact an independent decision taken to save the lives of others, or for the sake of the city:

> 'No, I must be in your stead.' (ChA. Zakho, Text 10: *The Bridge of Dalale*, §35)

The Kurdish version from Zakho differs from its Christian counterpart in the absence of a threat for the builder, but the voluntary and redemptive nature of Dalal's sacrifice remains. In a move of sheer heroism, she refuses to be saved from the bridge by her husband (23), content to be a sacrifice for the sake of the city (18).

In the ChA. Duhok story, by contrast, Dalale undoubtedly holds the moral high ground, while the builder does not shy away from cold calculations. He considers which of his daughters-in-law he should kill for the bridge, so that his reputation in Zakho would suffer the least damage. Dalale is chosen as the least 'harmful' in this regard:

> 'If I put my daughter-in-law Hane,
> her father's family belongs to this community
> and I will be ashamed to sit in their midst.
> If I put my daughter-in-law Hane,
> her family are village chiefs,
> I will be ashamed to sit in the diwan.
> I'll put my daughter-in-law Dalale. Her family come from afar so I'll not be ashamed.' (ChA. Duhok, Text 9: *The Bridge of Dalale*, §3–9).

Dalale, therefore, is unmistakeably the victim, being discriminated against in both actions and language. the other daughters-in-law are introduced through rhymed verse—Dalale is mentioned in simple prose (cf. above—ChA. Duhok, Text 9: *The Bridge of Dalale*, §3–9). The sacrifice of the other daughters-in-law is introduced as a possibility—through a conditional clause. The sacrifice of Dalale is stated plainly using the future tense (ibid.)—her fate is sealed the moment she appears on stage.

When Dalale approaches the bridge unsuspecting, she is seized and killed by her father-in-law. Her life is cut off suddenly, so that she leaves behind a crying baby and bread dough rising (ChA. Duhok, Text 9: *The Bridge of Dalale*, §19). She becomes both the tragic hero and the martyr.

It is also difficult to miss the ironic mismatch between the builder's name and his moral character, which in fact applies to all Neo-Aramaic versions in the corpus. He is referred to as *xəmy-ana*. This word means 'father-in-law', but its lexical root *x-m-y* has the general meaning of protection, reflecting the legal-social protective role of the family patriarch in traditional Middle Eastern societies.

The lexically related verb 'to protect' features in fact in the version of this story as told by the Gargarnaye Christians (southeastern Turkey). There, the builder himself tells Dalale that if she agrees to become a sacrifice for the bridge, he will become the guardian for her son: *ʾana b-xamənne* 'I will protect him.'[28] In a twist of cruel irony, therefore, Dalale is betrayed by the one who should have protected her, and the builder is *de facto* condemned by his own name.

The brief ChA. Dure version in this corpus is more neutral in its portrayal of the builder. Here, it is the local ruler who is asked to make a sacrifice, which he does—we may assume—out of a commitment towards his community. As well as sacrificing one of his seven daughters-in-law, he also has to give up a part of his wealth (one of his seven horses and mills).

---

[28] Source: https://nena.ames.cam.ac.uk/audio/147/ (audio only).

The versions known from other sources such as the NK. Zakho story in MacKenzie (1962) are also less psychologically developed, and do not narrate any inner turmoil of the protagonists. The builders decide to sacrifice the first person whom they see and the girl does not appear to have a choice, just like in the ChA. Duhok version but in contrast to the ChA. Zakho tale. The Zakho Kurdish legend in MacKenzie (1962), however, diverges from the versions in this corpus in that the builders take a considerable risk: the girl whom they choose to sacrifice is the local chieftain's daughter. This is precisely the opposite to the ChA. Duhok version where the girl is chosen because her sacrifice would not pose a risk for the perpetrator. It is likely that all of these points of divergence in the portrayal of the characters reflect different implicit attitudes to particular social groups.

Finally, the motif of a dog—which features in all of the versions included here—arguably also contributes to the moral evaluation of the protagonists. In the ChA. Duhok version, the dog is noble and 'clever', apparently attempting to save Dalale from the builder's trap by getting ahead of her, despite the fact that dogs are generally considered impure or even evil in many traditional Middle Eastern (Muslim) societies. In this way, he would arrive at the bridge first and thus become the sacrifice instead of the girl (ChA. Duhok, *Bridge of Dalale*, 13). The builder, by contrast, lives up to the stereotype of a dog as a curse-worthy being:

'My father-in-law is a black dog,
May the sun never again shine upon him.' (ChA. Duhok,
Bridge of Dalale, 21–22)

3.0. Animal Stories (Animal-Human Relations and Fables)

3.1. 'Man is Wolf to Wolf': Moral Role Reversal of Beasts and Humans

Text 14: *A Man and a Lion* (ChA. Duhok)
Text 15: *A Man and a Snake* (ChA. Duhok)
Text 16: *A Man and a Wolf* (JA. Duhok)
Text 17: *A Woman and a Leopard* (NK. Duhok)

Among the stories with animal protagonists, one distinctive group consists of tales in which the stereotypical attributes of humans and wild animals are reversed. A human behaves in a beastly way, while the beast is noble, caring for the human[29] and in the end imparting to them a moral lesson. The story's message is thus opposite to that conveyed by the European folktales with the ATU 154 motif,[30] where the animal is ungrateful towards a human that shows it kindness.

All four stories in this collection are close and doubtless come ultimately from the same source. Especially close are the Christian and Jewish Aramaic stories *A Man and a Lion* and *A Man and a Wolf,* both of which come from Duhok. It seems, therefore, that the Jews adapted the story from their Christian neighbours or vice versa, rather than from the Kurds. The Christian

---

[29] Like in B530 ('animals nourish men'). The motif of 'man is wolf to wolf' is also akin to—though not identical with—ATU 160, 'Grateful animals; ungrateful men'.

[30] 'The jackal and the farmer'; for instance, 'Man, Snake and fox'.

Duhok story *A Man and a Snake* is also close. All three narratives tell of a poor man who finds an animal that helps him earn a living.

The NK. Duhok story *A Woman and a Leopard* differs from these Neo-Aramaic stories in the identity of its protagonist (a woman) and in the favour performed by the wild animal. In this tale, the favour is not to make a living, but to protect the human from the dangers lurking in a forest. In all four stories, the human hurts the animal, either by haughty words (*A Man and a Lion*, *A Man and a Wolf* and *A Woman and a Leopard*), or by trying to kill the animal for profit (*A Man and a Snake*).

The extent of the overlap between the two Duhok Neo-Aramaic stories, *A Man and a Lion* and *A Man and a Wolf*, is striking (cf. the story summaries). Aside from the animal's identity (lion vs wolf, Christian and Jewish versions respectively), the only significant divergence between them concerns the character of the animal. The lion in the Christian version is philanthropic, but ultimately driven by enlightened self-interest. In the Jewish version, the animal is highly altruistic and forgiving. In the Christian version, the beast agrees to help the human on the condition that the man brings back some food for it (ChA. Duhok, *A Man and a Lion*, 8). By contrast, the wolf in the Jewish variant simply volunteers to give the man a golden coin—on top of the wood which the man cuts to earn his living (JA. Duhok, *A Man and a Wolf*, §4). Similarly, at the end of the Christian folktale, the lion devours the man in revenge (ChA. Duhok, *A Man and a Lion*, §18). The wolf in the Jewish version, on the other hand, forgives the harmful words, but warns the man that he should not come back to the wolf's forest (JA. Duhok, *A Man and a Wolf*, §27).

The three stories *A Man and a Lion*, *A Man and a Wolf* and *A Woman and a Leopard* end with the moral that words can scar more deeply than 'sticks and stones'. In all three tales, the human is commanded to hit the beast with his/her axe/dagger in order to learn a lesson: after some time, the animal heals from the blow, but the disrespect it has suffered still causes pain:

šawpa,	šawp-ət	saypa	g-nàyəx-Ø.ǀ
impact	impact-of	sword	IND-heal-3SG.M

šawp-ət	xabra	là-g-nayəx-Ø.ǀ	
impact-of	word	NEG-IND-heal-3SG.M	

'The impact, the impact of a sword heals. But the impact of words does not heal.' (ChA. Duhok, Text 14: *A Man and a Lion*, §19)

šwir-ət	dəˤrbaǀ	naša	g-naš-è-le.ǀ	šwir-ət
wound-of	blow	man	IND-forget-3SG.M-O.3SG.M	wound-of

xàbraǀ	həˊl	mòθaǀ	naša	là-g-naš-e-le.ǀ
word	until	death	man	NEG-IND-forget-3SG.M-O.3SG.M

'A wound [caused by] a blow [a] man forgets.' [But] a wound [caused by a] word until death [a] man does not forget. (JA. Duhok, Text 16: *A Man and a Wolf*, §25–26)

žē̱	ət-čət	niš-ā	šin-ā	xanjar-à̱ǀ
removed	IND-go.PRS.3SG	sting-EZ.FS	trace-EZ.FS	dagger-OBL.PL

bas	žē̱	nā-č-ītən	šin-ā	xabar-à̱ǀ[31]
but	removed	NEG-go.PRS.3SG	trace-EZ.SG.F	word-OBL.PL

---

[31] I thank Masoud Mohammadirad for providing the Kurdish gloss for this saying.

'The trace of grief caused by daggers will go away, but the grief caused by words will not go away.' (NK. Duhok, Text 17: *A Woman and a Leopard*, §37)

As Michael Chyet has pointed out to me, there is also a Turkish version of this proverb.[32] This suggests that this is a well-known saying throughout the region, as is probably the folktale which it appears in.[33]

The characters in the Jewish version—in contrast to the Christian story of *A Man and Lion*—speak partly in Northern (Bahdini) Kurdish:

> g-emər-ø,   NKxer-a   xudè̀NK   = la,'
> IND-say-3SG.M   NKgoodness-EZ.SG.F   God.OBLNK   = COP.PRS.3SG.F

'He said, 'It is God's favour.'' (JA. Duhok, Text 16: *A Man and a Wolf*, §4)

This phrase could be an innovation to the story, serving to locate it in a Kurdish milieu.

3.2. Anecdotes about Animal-Human Relations

Text 20: *A Family Horse* (NK. Dure)
Text 21: *A Man and his Dog* (CK. Shaqlawa)
Text 22: *A Talking Goat* (CK. Shaqlawa)

---

[32] *Kılıç yarası geçer, dil yarası geçmez.* 'A sword wound heals, a tongue wound does not.'

[33] Masoud Mohammadirad has recorded a story that closely resembles the NK. Duhok tale *A Woman and a Leopard* in Davani (a south-western Iranian language used in the Zagros Mountains area).

These three Kurdish stories also address animal-human relations, but in a more anecdotal way. No directly parallel Aramaic stories were found, but the themes are nevertheless universal.

A Talking Goat, for instance, is an anecdote about a goat that started talking and this drove the man carrying it out of his wits.[34] *A Man and His Dog* resembles in one key aspect the stories of moral 'role reversal' of animals and humans. Here, a dog proves loyal to his master despite the severe and apparently undeserved beating that it receives from him. *A Family Horse* is concerned with family honour. A majestic horse of apparently special strength that is the pride of the family is stolen. The father uses his normal riding horse to pursue the thief, who is fleeing on the special horse. When he is about to reach out for the thief riding the special horse, however, he realises that if the horse is not caught, this will better support the idea of the horse's special strength. This would indicate that it was faster than any other horse and could not be caught. He, therefore, decides to let the horse go to reinforce the myth of the mighty horse. In this way, even though the horse was stolen, its reputation was strengthened, and continued to be a source of pride for the family.

3.3. Fables

> Text 19: *A Ewe and a Wolf* (CK. Shaqlawa)
> Text 18: *A Wolf, a Dog and a Ewe* (ChA. Duhok)
> Text 12: *A 'Pious' Fox* (ChA. Shaqlawa)
> Text 13: *A 'Pious' Fox* (CK. Shaqlawa)

---

[34] This motif bears a distant similarity to ATU 212 ('The lying goat').

The folktales *A Ewe and a Wolf* and *A wolf, a Dog and a Ewe* are two very close versions of the same story, despite the fact that they come from different areas of northern Iraq; the former comes from Shaqlawa within the Central Kurdish area, the latter from Duhok of the Northern Kurdish region.[35] This story also shows similarities with the Arab folktale documented in Algeria 'How the Ewe Outwitted the Jackal' (ATU 154).

Both stories in the present corpus tell of a ewe defended by a dog from a wicked wolf. The wolf wants to devour the sheep (or its lamb), and so brings a fox to swear falsely that the pasture belongs to the wolf and the sheep has no right to graze there, which would legitimise punishing the ewe and killing it (or its young). In the Christian Duhok tale, the relationship between the ewe and the dog is very familial: the two have been living together and the dog looks after the sheep 'like a brother' (ChA. Duhok, *A wolf, a Dog and a Ewe*, §2). In the Kurdish Shaqlawa version, the sheep has lost its flock and is now living alone with its lamb. The dog appears as a helper when the ewe is threatened by the wolf (CK. Shaqlawa, *A wolf, a Dog and a Ewe*, §15–16).

This difference notwithstanding, the two versions exhibit striking overlaps. In both, for instance, the ewe is vindicated when the dog attacks the wolf (ChA. Duhok, *A Wolf, a Dog and a Ewe*, §12; CK. Shaqlawa, *A Wolf, a Dog and a Ewe*, §22).

These two fables as well as several other animal stories in this volume share the theme of trespass on land claimed by a wild

---

[35] Contrast this with the Bridge of Dalale story, which apparently did not spread widely in the Central Kurdish area, or at least did not reach the Jewish communities in this area (cf. §1 above).

animal as their territory. This theme seems to be popular in folktales of northern Iraq, which features here in *A Wolf, a Dog and a Ewe* (ChA. Duhok, §12), *A Wolf, a Dog and a Ewe* (CK. Shaqlawa, §11), *A Woman and a Leopard* (NK. Duhok, §10) and *A Man and a Lion* (ChA. Duhok, §2). Interestingly, in both *A Man and a Lion* (ChA. Duhok, §4) and *A Woman and a Leopard* (NK. Duhok, §11), the human trespasses knowingly, reasoning that even a violent death 'at the incisors of' the beast is better than their current life in misery.

The story of a *A 'Pious' Fox* from Shaqlawa also exists in a Kurdish and a Neo-Aramaic version and both variants are set in Muslim realia. This lack of adaptation to a Christian context along with the strong similarities of the two variants suggest that the Christian version has been adapted from Kurdish relatively recently. The Christian Shaqlawa version even contains a short Kurdish poem calling for repentance (ChA. Shaqlawa, *A 'Pious' Fox*, §8). The main protagonist is a starving fox who assumes the appearance of a religious person—a Sunni cleric—to convince other animals that it is now religious and is, therefore, harmless. The fox convinces two birds of its conversion to Islam and lures them into a trap to eat them. In the Kurdish version, it manages to eat one of the birds while in the Christian tale, the bird escapes.

4.0. Social Status (Marriage, Class, Independence etc.)

Text 23: *The Poor Girl and Her Horse* (ChA. Shaqlawa)
Text 24: *A Woman Builds Her Home* (ChA. Duhok)

Text 25: *As Precious as Salt* (JA. Zakho)

Text 26: *Dindik Hinar—A Girl Called Pomegranate Grain* (NK. Duhok)

Text 27: *The Indecent Neighbour* (CK. Shaqlawa)

The folktales in this category deal with different responses to hardships and interact in several ways with social class and gender. Issues such as social status, poverty, marriage and gender roles are universal to human culture; the differences concern the ways these issues are dealt with. Thus, the question that arises for this analysis is what the folktales discussed here reveal about the values of the community that tell the story.

No direct Aramaic-Kurdish parallels occur in this collection, but they likely exist. In fact, the Zakho Jewish Aramaic tale *As Precious as Salt* is based on the international motif of 'love as strong as salt' (ATU 923). The fact that this motif is especially popular in Central and Western Europe (though attested also in Berber languages and in India)[36] suggests that we are dealing with an ancient Indo-European motif. It is likely, therefore, that the Jews adapted this story from their own Indo-European neighbours, the Kurds.[37]

---

[36] http://www.maerchenlexikon.de/at-lexikon/at923.htm, accessed 14/12/2021 and
http://www.mftd.org/index.php?action=atu&src=atu&id=923, accessed 21/09/2021.

[37] For other original Indo-European themes preserved among the Iranian peoples, see Thackston (1993, i). For a phylogenetic study tracing back a series of Indo-European folktales, see da Silva and Tehrani (2016). They argue that some stories originated as far as 2500–6000 years ago.

The Jewish Aramaic tale *As Precious as Salt* relates—in parallel to, for instance, the German story of 'Princess Mouse Skin'—the story of a princess who tells his father that she loves him as much as salt. The king takes this as an insult and expels her, but she manages to make a living alone. In the end, she becomes wealthy and is vindicated in front of her father, who confesses that it is indeed impossible to eat saltless food (served to him by his daughter herself).

There are three Aramaic stories in this collection that are particularly close: *A woman Builds Her Home*, *As Precious as Salt* and *The Poor Girl and her Horse.* All three tell of girls who in one way or another lose their family, but manage to take their fate into their own hands to turn their situation around. In the first two, moreover, it is the youngest daughter who proves to be more resourceful and wiser than her older sisters (L50 and L61),[38] and marries a poor man whom he eventually lifts to her station (cf. ATU 850–862).[39]

In *A Woman Builds Her Home,* a princess marries a pauper and together with him sets off to prove his father wrong. She shows him that a woman is also capable of providing for her family and for herself. The protagonist in *The Poor Girl and her Horse*

---

[38] Respectively, 'Victorious youngest daughter' and 'Clever youngest daughter'.

[39] 'The man marries the princess'.

disguises as a boy in order to be able to get work as a royal servant.[40] This story features the motif of gender disguise[41] and aid from a magical, talking animal horse (B401). Finally, in the Jewish story *As Precious as Salt*, the princess teams up with a lazy youth to gain wealth and outshine the king in grandeur.

This last tale, *As Precious as Salt*, includes two motfifemes—one akin to *A Woman Builds Her Home*, the other parallel to 'love as strong as salt' (see above). More specifically, the princess in *As Precious as Gold* has two missions, which correspond respectively to the other two aforementioned tales. First, the protagonist has to provide for herself, which she does with the help of a 'servant' boy and of extraordinary luck or magic (cf. *A Woman Builds Her Home*, §36–38 and *As Precious as Salt*, §35). In both stories, in the course of this change the heroin also raises her 'servant' boy from poverty. Her second mission is then to prove to her father that salt is indeed priceless, and therefore that she does love him (*As Precious as Salt*, §55–56).

Dindik Hinar... is a variant of the 'Cinderella' story—an orphaned girl oppressed by her evil step-mother, but eventually vindicated and married to a prince. In this story and in a (partial) contradistinction to the previous three, magic replaces human determination and creativity to help the heroes in overcoming

---

[40] See e.g. the story of a poor boy driven away by an evil stepmother and helped by a talking horse(head) attested in Hungarian (ATU 532).
[41] Compare this also with the theme of sex transformation (D10 and ATU 514), apparently relatively rare cross-culturally, but attested in (at least one) story told by the Jews of Zakho (Aloni 2022, 284–96).

difficulty. When in peril, the orphan Pomegranate Grain is delivered by magical bones that belonged to the girl's beloved cow, previously killed by the evil stepmother.

The 'Cinderella' motif appears in variant forms from Europe all the way to South-East Asia (ATU 510A; cf. Dundes 1988).[42] For instance, the enchanted bones of Pomegranate Grain's dead cow correspond to the magical bones of a beloved fish in the South-East Asian versions.

The final story of this collection, *The Indecent Neighbour* in CK. Shaqlawa, also touches on the issue of social status, but in a much lighter, anecdotal way.[43] In addition, the parameters here are reversed in comparison with the stories in the sense that the protagonist is an ordinary man, not a girl of noble birth (CK. Shaqlawa, 5–7). In this case, moreover, the problem here is not with destitution, but rather its appearances. The protagonist meets a woman bringing his family a gift of fruit. However, the man takes offence, presuming that the woman thinks him poor and in need of her charity. He refuses the gift and drives the woman away.

Yet the story's subtle irony lies in the fact that the man seemed more than happy to receive in another sense (CK. Shaqlawa, §5–7). When he first meets the woman, he is dazzled by her beauty and is apparently expecting an erotic encounter. Soon, it transpires, however, that the woman simply came with

---

[42] A Neo-Aramaic version is also known among the Christians of Urmi (north-western Iran); cf. Khan (2016, 215–18).
[43] Compare this with ATU 1459 ('Keeping up appearances') and W165 ('False pride').

a little gift, but he rejects it, worried that this would make his family appear poor. In its light-hearted way, therefore, this anecdote critiques a culture in which public reputation is valued over actual moral integrity. The man had no problem with the prospect of being unfaithful to his wife, likely as long as this remained a secret, but felt greatly ashamed when thinking that others think him a pauper.[44]

Independent Women in a Patriarchal Culture

In the context of the patriarchal cultures of northern Iraq, the 'emancipation' stories discussed above are noteworthy, at the very least. In the three stories *A Woman Builds Her Home*, *As Precious as Salt*, *The Poor Girl and her Horse* and *The Indecent Neighbour*, the woman is the resourceful and clever one. The male characters, on the other hand, are biased about women (e.g. the king in *A Woman Builds Her Home*), arrogant (*The Indecent Neighbour*) or downright lazy, like the boy who waits for figs to fall into his mouth from the tree (JA. Zakho, *As Precious as Salt*, §11).

The stereotypical gender roles are, therefore, reversed: the woman takes the initiative in providing for herself and for others, even taking on male appearance to legitimise her 'male-like' behaviour (e.g. ChA. Duhok, *A Woman Builds Her Home*, §52–53; ChA. Shaqlawa, *The Poor Girl and her Horse*).

---

[44] For other anecdotes of northern Iraq, often with implicit social critique, see Mutzafi (2008a). For instance, 'A Foolish Pauper' (ibid, 282–285; with audio at https://nena.ames.cam.ac.uk/audio/214/) tells of a thick-headed poor man who drives his wife to insanity.

Interestingly, in *As Precious as Salt,* the princess even takes advantage of her social class to achieve her goals. Initially, she treats the boy whom she finds in her father's vineyard very much as a servant, even punishing him as a servant would be punished (JA. Zakho, *As Precious as Salt,* §12). On her way to what we could call emancipation, therefore, she is still content to rely on a male of a low social class to do the bulk of the hard manual labour.

All in all, such stories remain striking. On the one hand, female resourcefulness, physical strength and entrepreneurship are certainly valued among the patriarchal communities of northern Iraq. Still, their authority and degree of independence has traditionally remained subject to male guidance and benevolence, and their educational and economic opportunities have often been limited.[45]

In their seminal article on the nature of folk literature, Jakobson and Bogatyrev (1980) argue that any folk creation must earn a degree of approval by their community to be passed on because—in contrast to written literature—it relies on the community for its transmission.[46] As a result, folklore production is, according to Jakobson and Bogatyrev, driven by communal values, rather than by a desire to change the *status quo*. As they put it, 'the folk poet (...) does not create a new environment' (ibid, 11).

---

[45] See, for instance, Brauer (1993, 149) for the treatment of women in the Jewish communities, about a century ago.

[46] This is known as 'the preventive censure of the community'.

Still, stories such as those discussed here caution us before oversimplifying the mechanism of folklore transmission. In the vast majority of human societies, the cultural *status quo* is not homogeneous, even though some attitudes might predominate or be considered normative (at least by those with social or political authority). The very existence of folktales such as these means that there must have been space for the diverse attitudes that they represent.

It is possible, for instance, that folktales like those discussed above were created in response to overly rigid gender roles, perhaps by female narrators. They could have been intended for a mixed audience, since female narrators did at times perform for a mixed audience, but this was relatively rare (Allison 2010, 143).[47] Alternatively, the stories of independent women discussed here could have been performed as work stories (see the introductory section) by women for other women.

5.0. Family Relations (Conflict, Intrigue)

Text 28: *Two Mullahs* (ChA. Shaqlawa)

Text 29: *Two Mullahs* (CK. Shaqlawa)

Text 30: *The Girl, Her Evil Stepmother and the Old Witch* (NK. Duhok)

Text 31: *Firyat and Khajija* (NK. Khizava)

---

[47] See Allison (2001) for how the portrayal of women in Kurdish folklore interacts with real-life gender roles etc. See also Ashliman (2004, 148–145) for 'emancipated' women in European folklore. In a minority of cases, which are nevertheless far from exceptions, a female protagonist rebels against a decision imposed on her and perceived to be unjust, and is vindicated (ibid).

Like the previous group of folktales, these stories address social issues—here, in particular, conflict and intrigue within the family.

The anecdote of *Two Mullahs* appears in this corpus in a Christian and a Kurdish Shaqlawa version,[48] once again showing the readiness of the Christian community to adopt a story along with its Muslim setting. This tale warns men against taking a second wife—it causes much strife and tension in the house. While this anecdote is written from the male perspective, narratives with the female viewpoint also exist. For instance, the Jews of Duhok told an anecdote describing the emotional suffering that the second wife experiences.[49]

The story of *The Girl, Her Evil Stepmother and the Old Witch* is similar to *The Girl Pomegranate Grain* (cf. Theme IV above) in that it includes the well-known theme of a girl mistreated by her stepmother (S31).[50] There is also an evil old witch-woman Pirhavir (NK. Duhok, *The Girl, Her Evil Stepmother and the Old Witch*, §28), who conspires with the stepmother to kill Fatma and her brothers.

Firyat and Khajija is a tragic story of love that could not be (T80), because the community of one of the lovers conspires to keep them apart. Khajija's family does not allow her to marry the prince Firyat, because they are from different religions. At first, the girl's community gives Firyat a hope of marriage to Khajija.

---

[48] As demonstrated by Lourd Hanna, this story is also known among the Kurds of Duhok.
[49] My own fieldwork.
[50] It also features motif D150, 'Transformation: man to bird'.

However, this is simply a pretext, used to get him to build a canal for them and thus take advantage of Firyat's wealth (§11–12).[51] In the end, Firyat is made to believe that his beloved Khajija is dead, and dies of despair as a consequence.[52]

Some elements in the story resemble other Iranian tragic love tales of the wider region. Perhaps the most important parallel is 'Khosrow and Shirin', a tragic romance written by the 12th-century poet Nezami Ganjavi. Khosrow and Shirin is a legend, based on the historical romance between the Armenian (Christian) princess Shirin and the Sassanian (Zoroastrian) king Khosrow II (Orsatti 2006). As in *Firyat and Khajija,* the lovers are divided by communal-religious lines. Another obvious parallel is the tragic love-story epic 'Mem u Zin' told by the Kurds of the greater Kurdistan region and their neighbours (Chyet 1991).

6.0. *Mirza Muhammad*

> Text 32: *Mirza Muhammad and the Forty Monsters* (ChA. Duhok)
>
> Text 33: *Mirza Muhammad and the Three Princesses* (ChA. Harmashe)
>
> Text 34: *Mirza Muhammad's Adventures* (NK. Duhok)

---

[51] I thank Masoud Mohammadirad for drawing my attention to 'Khosrow and Shirin'.

[52] This can be seen as a variant of motif N343 ('lover kills himself believing his mistress dead'), though in this case, the death is not actively caused, but rather the result of despair.

Mirza Muhammad is the youngest, but most heroic of three princes who experiences fantastic and heroic adventures.[53] The protagonist Mirza Muhammad is a hero of the 'Hercules' type—an adventurer who goes around slaying monsters and outwitting foes. The number of the adventurous episodes and their character, differ radically across the versions, showing that narrators have often invented new episodes, or perhaps borrowed from other stories.

Despite these differences in the adventures, however, the Mirza Muhammad story is apparently a variant of the widely-attested tale of the three princes-brothers and their quest for the three stolen princesses, occurring also in Europe.[54] This story type is typically categorised under ATU 301 'The three stolen princesses'. This exact description is not entirely fitting for the northern-Iraqi variants of the tale, despite the existence of the parallels. For example, in the NK. Duhok version in this corpus, only one woman—who at the time is already married to the protagonist Mirza Muhammad—is stolen (cf. ATU 400), and this deed is done by a king, rather than by magical creatures. Nevertheless, the *Mirza Muhammad* tales have other points of overlap with the stories of the tree stolen princesses. For instance, the ChA. Duhok version features the motif of defeating monsters (ogres; ATU

---

[53] I thank Paul Noorlander for sharing with me his knowledge of the various forms of the Mirza Muhammad tale, which I drew from in writing this section.
[54] Known as, for instance, 'The Golden Apples' in European folklore.

300),[55] often included within the story of the three stolen princesses.[56] The connection of these stories to the ATU 301 type is corroborated by the existence of tales in which the presence of elements from both tale variants (Iraqi and European) is very explicit. For instance, the ChA. version published by Lazarev (1974)[57] includes the motif of the king's prized apple being stolen (as in European variants), while also sharing the name of the youngest prince ('Mirza Mamed') with the northern-Iraqi variants in the present corpus.

The more specific variant of this international motif is very popular among the communities of the region, including in Armenia.[58] As our Iraqi fieldworker Lourd Hanna has confirmed, however, the protagonist does not always carry the name Mirza. A version in Central Neo-Aramaic[59] has also been published, where the three brothers remain nameless (Jastrow and Talay 2019, 273–281). In this Central Aramaic version, the story of the three princes precedes the story of *Gŭlo Zĭlo Bando*. The hero's

---

[55] For the ogre motif elsewhere in Kurdistani folklore; see, for instance, Mutzafi's corpus of JA. (2008a, 274–277).

[56] On the other hand, the three stories presented in this publication do not include the motif of the golden apples, attested in the European (e.g. Romanian, Bulgarian, French) variants of the related tale.

[57] I could only access the online edition of the publication at https://archive.org/stream/B-001–014–246/B-001–014–246_djvu.txt.

[58] For the Armenian version, see Mouse (2018; page numbers missing in the online PDF).

[59] Ṭuroyo; south-eastern Turkey, Ṭur ʿAbdin, the provinces of Mardin and Şırnak.

(i.e. the wife of the prince otherwise known as Mirza Muhammad) asks for this story before she allows him to marry her. Another Central Neo-Aramaic version recorded in Ritter's collection (1969, Text 61) also closely parallels the ChA. Duhok version (Text 32) with slight differences, for instance the younger hero fights fourteen instead of forty monsters and also collects the ears of lions and foxes in his pocket. A Northern Kurdish version (from Gullī) has been published by MacKenzie (1962, 348–357). A similar story to that of Mirza Muhammad is available in Mohammadirad (2021, text A), a corpus of Central Kurdish of the Sanandaj region.

A key motifeme in most of the stories about an adventurous young prince is the death of the king—the father of the brothers—and/or the issue of his royal succession. This death, moreover, (almost) always coincides with the adventures of his three sons, in all of which Mirza Muhammad clearly excels. Still, the details of this royal succession motif and the role of the king-father differ significantly across the versions.

In the ChA. Duhok version, the last will of the father is for him to be buried in the place where a mare would bring them to (§7–13).[60] The journey to bury their father marks the beginning of their adventures. In the ChA. Harmashe tale, the king's death is only mentioned in passing at the end (§33), and coincides with the marriage of his sons to the three princesses. In a symbolic way, where one life (and apparently one reign) ends, another begins. The princes meet the princesses in the palace of the late

---

[60] This is also the case in the above-mentioned Ṭuroyo version, except that it is a camel that carries the king's body.

king (where Mirza Muhammad had brought them). In the NK. Duhok tale, the father warns his sons to guard his throne after he dies, because the king's brother envies it. Indeed, when the king dies, his brother seizes the opportunity of the time of mourning to usurp his throne. The Armenian version resembles the Kurdish one in this regard; the brother of the late king usurps the throne and expels his nephews (Mouse 2018).

A striking feature of the *Mirza Muhammad* tales is that the hero is the youngest of the brothers, and, therefore, not the rightful heir of his father's throne.[61] At the same time, the adventures of the story demonstrate that Mirza Muhammad is the most resourceful one and the bravest of them, and thus the most 'throne-worthy', as per Thompson's 'Victorious youngest son' motif (L10). In other words, the story deals with the reversal of the law of succession, or at least suggests that it is not always the eldest who excels in his leadership skills and justice.[62] In the ChA. Duhok story, for instance, Mirza Muhammad faces forty monsters and they promise him that if he wins the challenge presented to him, they will consider him 'their older brother' (90–100). In the Armenian variant (Mouse 2018), the brothers themselves present a challenge to Mirza and recognise him as their eldest brother when he succeeds. In the NK. Duhok narrative, Mirza Muhammad is the one who acts like a responsible and just leader, protecting his own brothers as well as victims of war (e.g. 11–20; 38–40).

---

[61] Cf. the Armenian version (Mouse 2018), where—as expected—the oldest brother inherits the throne at first.

[62] Compare this also with the motif of primogeniture reversal, e.g. in the Biblical book of Genesis (Borysov 2020).

As regards the details of the adventures, the ChA. Duhok version contains (at least) one episode with a direct parallel in the Armenian story (Mouse 2018). In both, Mirza Muhammad meets an old person (a woman in the Aramaic and a man in the Armenian variant) who represents the deity Time. This figure causes it to be either day or night by unrolling respectively a white and a black clew (ChA. Duhok, *Mirza Muhammad and the Forty Monsters,* §64–1). In both variants, Mirza Muhammad binds this person in order to lengthen the night, so that he can complete his tasks (ChA. Duhok, *Mirza Muhammad and the Three Princesses,* §72–74). The motif of an encounter with Time is reportedly very popular in Armenian folklore (Abeghyan 1899). This raises the possibility that the tale of *Mirza Muhammad,* or at least part of it, is of Armenian origin. The abduction of Mirza Muhammad's wife by the ruler and the motif of bathing is also reminiscent of ATU 465 ('Man persecuted for his beautiful wife'), attested, for instance, in Armenian.

The protagonist Mirza Muhammad carries the name of a historical figure: a 15th-century Timurid ruler, governor of Samarkand (Woods 1990, 35). This historical Mirza Muhammad married a daughter of the Hakkari Kurd's chief, who had formerly been his adversary. In this way, Mirza Muhammad formed a political alliance with the Hakkari Kurds. Other protagonists of Kurdistani oral literature (of northern Iraq and south-eastern Turkey) were also named after prominent (non-local) political-military leaders.[63]

---

[63] Another example is the Ghaznavid Sultan Mahmud (Thackson 1999), responsible for the wide islamicisation of central-western Asia.

The lives of the historical and folkloristic Mirza Muhammad, however, likely have little in common, except that both have the status of a chieftain/prince who goes on to marry the daughter of another ruler. It is noteworthy that the protagonist of *Mirza Muhammad* is named after the Kurds' former enemy. The motivation for this naming cannot be recovered, but it may have to do with legends that Mirza was a great warrior.

7.0. Religious Legends (and other religious stories)

Text 35: *Mar Yohanan (St John)* (ChA. Shaqlawa)
Text 36: *Mar Giwargis (St George)* (ChA. Enishke)
Text 37: *The Prophet's Horse* (NK. Dure)
Text 38: *The Foul-Mouthed Priest* (CK. Shaqlawa)

Like all religious societies, the Muslims, Jews and Christians of northern Iraq too have stories about pious individuals who set a moral example[64] and stories of miracles. A few of these are represented in this corpus.

Mar Giwargis (ChA. Enishke) tells the legend of Saint George slaying the dragon (F628) and rescuing the princess (see Ogden 2013). The tale of *Mar Yohanan (St John)* celebrates ascetic piety (V462)—one in which life in poverty comes at the expense of everything else. The prince Yohanan is ready to be cut off from his parents despite the grief that it causes them, and to disappoint them over giving up his heirship (ChA. Shaqlawa, *Mar Yohanan*, §8). He leaves them behind and becomes a monk.

---

[64] Though see *The Foul-Mouthed Priest* below for an anti-hero.

Yohanan clings to his vows of poverty even after he becomes ill and is taken back to his parents' palace, refusing to be recognised by them and receive care. He believes that his perseverance until the very end will guarantee him a reward from God (ChA. Shaqlawa, *Mar Yohanan*, §28).

Mar Yohanan's asceticism arguably highlights the difference between Christian (Chaldean Catholic) and Kurdish Muslim saint types. For instance, in the (Chaldean) Catholic church, celibacy is institutionalised (obligatory for priests) and held in high esteem, so the faithfulness of Mar Yohanan to his monastic vows does not surprise us. It is different in the Kurdish Muslim communities, where even among the mystic movements such as the Sufi *derwishes,* celibacy is by no means the norm.[65]

Arguably, this divergence in the ideal of piety is also apparent in the previously discussed story of Zanbilfirosh—the humble basket-seller (which is in fact very popular among Sufi *derwishes*; cf. Sabar 1976, 171, footnote 61). As shown above, the Christian-Aramaic Shaqlawa versions (Texts 4–5) have Zambilfrosh become a monk—in a way that suspiciously resembles the life of Mar Yohanan. In the Kurdish variant (Text 7), there is no mention that Zanbilfirosh lived as a hermit or a monk.

The story of *The Prophet's Horse* (NK. Dure) is a Kurdish variation on the Muslim story of Muhammad and his flying horse Buraq. Here, the Prophet's miraculous journeys are deliberately placed in the realia of northern Iraq. The narrator also says that

---

[65] https://www.britannica.com/topic/celibacy/Islam-Judaism-and-Christianity.

the horse Dildil left a hoofprint near the village of Sararo (north-western Iraq).

In the anecdote *The Foul-Mouthed Priest* (CK. Shaqlawa), the religious figure—the priest—is an anti-hero; an impatient, unkind and rude religious leader.[66] In the end, his malice is exposed—perhaps deliberately—by a simple woman. She offers him hospitality, but he is too impatient to receive it. The tale is told by Muslim Kurds, but set in a Christian environment.

---

[66] See ATU 1725–1849 ('Jokes about Clergymen and Religious Figures') and ATU 831 ('The Dishonest Priest').

3. NARRATIVE STYLE AND DISCOURSE IN KURDISH AND NEO-ARAMAIC ORAL LITERATURE[1]

Paul M. Noorlander and Masoud Mohammadirad

Northern Iraq is the homeland of a wide range of linguistic minorities with closely intertwined traditions transmitted orally over numerous generations of bi- and multilinguals. The Neo-Aramaic speaking communities—both Jews and Christians—used to be an integral part of this once vibrant, multilingual oral culture, now disappearing rapidly. The resulting commonalities of their coexistence with the Kurdish speaking communities can be found in almost every aspect of linguistic structure (e.g. Noorlander 2014; Haig and Khan 2018), including their oral literature and its stylistic features.[2] Thus, the shared folkloristic traditions of the Kurds, Jews and Christians of Northern Iraq are also reflected in the parallel style of storytelling and use of idioms. This chapter provides a succinct overview of some of the stylistic and linguistic devices found across the Kurdish and Neo-Aramaic oral

---

[1] We are grateful to Dorota Molin and Geoffrey Khan for their helpful comments on an earlier draft of this chapter.

[2] E.g. Garbell (1965), Chyet (1994), Coghill (2009, 2020a), Khan (2009). See also Molin, Chapter 2 in this volume.

narratives in this collection, and demonstrates how these devices can converge in genetically distinct languages.

The Neo-Aramaic and Kurdish stories were transmitted orally and thereby exhibit characteristic features of oral literature. While the linguistic devices used by the storytellers are thus sometimes typical of orality in general, they are also indicative of shared traditions through areal diffusion, sometimes spanning the whole of West Asia and even extending beyond it. Among them are the shared opening and closing traditions (Section 1), including the insertion of the moral lesson before the concluding formula.

Various discourse connectors can be used in the organisation of the narrative (Section 2), such as conjunctional adverbs as well as various other discourse markers are at the narrator's disposal to. The event linkage through the inchoative verb 'to rise', the additive particles and tail-head recapitulation demonstrate striking areal parallels. Storytellers also embed parallel songs, proverbs and idioms into their oral narrative (Section 3). Figurative language and symbolism are common literary and rhetorical devices (Section 4), of which sound symbolism is typical of oral narratives *par excellence.*

Repetition (Section 5) in general is a stylistic device and/or discourse strategy found throughout stories and oral literature. It comes in different types and may involve individual lexical items as well as whole sentences. Some functions of repetition are also discussed under the relevant sections, notably clause linkage in narrative discourse (Section 2.4. and 7.1.1.), to serve as a figure of speech (Section 4.1.3), as well as to express verbal aspect (Section 7.2.1). Deictic elements and characterise the narrative style and discourse structure (Section 6), and the same holds true for devices on a syntactic level, such as word order changes and verbal syntax (Section 7). Finally, we conclude with a few remarks on storytelling techniques (Section 8).

1.0. Opening and Closing Formulae

Neo-Aramaic and Kurdish speaking storytellers have similar introductory and concluding formulas.[3] In what follows we offer a few examples of such formulas found in our collection.

1.1. Opening Formulae

1.1.1. There Once Was / There Was One

Introductory formulas involving an existential construction and the numeral 'one' or an adverbial phrase 'once' are similar to the well-known opening expressions of fairy tales like Danish *der var engang* and Dutch *er was eens* conveying 'there was once'. This type occurs in both Neo-Aramaic and Kurdish texts, for instance in the Christian Neo-Aramaic dialect of Harmashe and the Central Kurdish dialect of Shaqlawa:

(1) ʾamriwa ʾəθwa xàʾa,ˈ xa malka ʾə́θwale t̮laθà bnone.ˈ
 They said there was one, a king who had three sons. (ChA. Harmashe, Text 33: *Mirza Muhammad and the Three Princesses*, §1)

---

[3] See e.g. Chyet (1995, 237) and Coghill (2020a, 2020b, 394).

(2) got=ī zamānē xò=yᶦ qašàk ha-bū,ᶦ aw qaša zəmān=ī galak pìs bū.ᶦ

It was said that there once was a Christian priest. He was a very foul-mouthed priest. (CK. Shaqlawa, Text 38: *The Foul-Mouthed Priest*, §1)

1.1.3. There Was, There Was Not

The affirmative and negative past existential are generally used together as opening formula typical of the region:[4]

(3) ʾətwa=w làtwaᶦ xa màm-telona ʾətwa.ᶦ
There was and there was not, there was an Uncle Fox. (ChA. Shaqlawa, Text 12: *A 'Pious' Fox*, §1)

(4) a-rē ha-bū na-bū Mām Dzardàk ha-bū.ᶦ
It is said that once upon a time (lit. there was and there was not) there was [a man called] Uncle Jarda. (CK. Shaqlawa, Text 22: *A Talking Goat*, §2)

1.1.4. There was None Greater than God

The existential phrase 'there was there was not' can be expanded by a phrase asserting the maximal greatness of the one God. For example:

(5) aḷē ha-bo na-bòᶦ kas la xwāy gawratər nà-bo.ᶦ
It is said that there was and once there was not, but there was no one greater than God. (CK. Shaqlawa, Text 29: *Two Mullahs*, §3)

---

[4] See §2.4.

In the Neo-Aramaic stories of this collection, this is only attested in the narrative of *Two Mullahs*, where the storyteller adds a distinctly Christian dimension:

(6) ʾətwa=w lə̀twa| mən bāb ʾAlaha=w ʾoda Maryam bəš raba lətwa=w qàt=iš la k-awe.|
There was, there was not, there was no one greater than Father God and Mother Mary and there never shall be. (ChA. Shaqlawa, Text 28: *Two Mullahs*, §2)

This formula can also be further extended in Kurdish with a phrase about humanity or sometimes the storyteller being a liar.[5]

(7) ha-bū na-bū kas šə xudē maztə̀r na-bū| kas šə banīyā dərawīntə̀r na-bū.|
Once there was, once there was not, there was no one greater than God, no bigger liar than man. (NK. Duhok, Text 26: *Dindik Hinar—A Girl Called Pomegranate Grain*, §2)

1.1.5. Impersonal Use of 'to say'

The above examples (1)–(2) and (4)–(5) also illustrate the impersonal use of the reporting verb 'to say' for story openings. The reporting structure suggests to the reader that the storyteller repeats a story as handed down to them without revealing the identity of the source.

---

[5] See Chyet (1994, 237) for more examples, some taken from Mackenzie's (1962) collection.

1.1.6. Blessing of the Parents

Another common opening and closing formula[6] consists of a blessing on the listeners' parents, which presupposes a younger audience:

(8) *jārakē əž jārā řahmat əl day bāv-ēt gohdārā*ˈ
 Once upon a time—blessings on the listeners' parents. (NK. Duhok, Text 17: *A Woman and a Leopard*, §2)

1.1.7. Sung Introduction

In one of the stories, the introduction consists of a rhyme that is sung by the storyteller, e.g.

(9) *maṣitun ya xanwàta.*ˈ *maḥkənoxun da qəṣə̀tta,*ˈ *bər màlka,*ˈ *bronət ʾazùta,*ˈ *tiwa=wewa l-kursi ʾət malkùta.*ˈ
 Listen, oh brothers. I am going to tell you the tale of a prince, a child of power, who sat on a kingdom's throne. (ChA. Shaqlawa, Text 4: *Zambilfrosh by A. Sher*, §1)

1.2. Closing Formulae

1.2.1. It is finished

The originally Arabic verb خلص *xalaṣa* 'to be finished' or interjection خلاص *xalāṣ* 'enough; it is over' is generally used in concluding formulas:

---

[6] See §1.2.3.

(10) Dǎlale mə̀θla,ˈ ʾu ʾayi qaṣṣa diyyaḥ xlə̀ṣla.ˈ
Dalale died, and her story ended. (ChA. Duhok, Text 9: *Bridge of Dalale*, §24)

(11) babay məθle; xlə̀ṣla.ˈ
Their father died; the story is over. (ChA. Harmashe, Text 33: *Mirza Muhammad and the Three Princesses*, §47)

(12) amn=ı̀š hātm-awˈ hı̀ts=əm pē na-bəřā.ˈ xalās=ū řoy.ˈ
I came back, nothing was given to me. It is finished (lit. It is finished and gone.) (CK. Shaqlawa, Text 19: *A Ewe and a Wolf*, §22)

1.2.2. I have come back from there

A common closing formula, especially in the CK. Shaqlawa tales of our collection, has the narrator take part in the story, as if they returned from the events of the tale but were not given the opportunity to attain the protagonists' happy ending.

(13) am gahəštīn=a dumāhı̆kā čīrokā xoˈ az hātm-ava čə̀ na-dā mən.ˈ
We have arrived at the end of our tale. I have come back, but they (i.e. the protagonists in the tale) gave me nothing. (NK. Duhok, Text 17: *A Woman and a Leopard*, §37)

(14) amn=ı̀š gařām-awa=ū hı̀ts=əm pē na-bəřā.ˈ
As for me, I have come back [from these events] and they [i.e. the characters of the story] have given me nothing. (CK. Shaqlawa, Text 22: *A Talking Goat*, §10)

This formula occurs also in the ChA. Shaqlawa stories in the corpus:

(15) *'ana=š 'itèli* tsə́ məndi la wəlu qati.|
I have come back, but they have given me nothing. (ChA. Shaqlawa, Text 12: *A 'Pious' Fox*, §38)

This closing formula is also shared by the neighbouring community that speaks Gorani, spoken in the Iran-Iraq border east of Sulaymaniyah:

(16) *wa mən=ič āmānē, hič=šā na-ḍānē.*
And I too have come, they gave me nothing. (Gorani Luhon; MacKenzie 1966, 78)

In one of the Neo-Aramaic texts, the storyteller receives three apples that belong to the storyteller and usually two members of the audience, a typical feature of Iraqi oral literature but also found in Kurdish and Azeri Turkish (Garbell 1965, 176) and Armenian (Surmelian 1968),[7] for example:

(17) *m-tama θèli,| məθeli ṭlaθa xabùše,| xa ta Màdu,| xa ṭali 'u xa tad mera ḥakkòθa.|*
I have come from there with three apples, one for Madu,[8] one for myself and one for the storyteller. (ChA. Duhok, Text 24: *A Woman Builds Her Home*, §54)

---

[7] See the discussion in §1.4.
[8] The narrator's name.

1.2.3. Blessing of the Parents

Another common closing formula is the blessing of the listeners' parents.[9] This is, for instance, attested at the end of both the Kurdish and Aramaic version of the Mirza Muhammad epic:

(18) *kut šmele raḥmaθa gawət yəmmeḥ.*
Mercy on the mother of whomsoever listened. (ChA. Duhok, Text 32: *Mirza Muhammad and the Forty Monsters*, §235)

(19) *o řahmàt əl day bābēt gohdārā*
May blessing be on the audience's parents. (NK. Duhok, Text 34: *Mirza Muhammad's Adventures*, §113)

This is also attested in the Kurdish tales collected by Mac-Kenzie (1962):

(20) *hazār řaḥmat la tū ū la dāy-bābē tū. xalās.*
A thousand blessings on you and your mother and father. It is finished. (NK. Surchi, MacKenzie 1962, 238)

The audience themselves may also be blessed, see line 12 of *A Dog, A Ewe and A Wolf* narrated in ChA. Duhok.

1.2.4. Ballad

The Neo-Aramaic versions of *The Bridge of Dalale* story end with a ballad:

Text 8: *The Bridge of Zakho* (ChA. Dure)
Text 9: *The Bridge of Dalale* (ChA. Duhok)

---

[9] Blessings of listeners are also found in Azeri Turkish (see Garbell 1965, 176) and Arabic (e.g. Talmon 2001, 216).

1.3. Moral Lessons

The moral of the story is sometimes added at the end, occasionally in the form of a proverb.[10] Several stories convey moral lessons, including:

> Text 12: *A 'Pious' Fox* (ChA. Shaqlawa)
> Text 14: *A Man and a Lion* (ChA. Duhok)
> Text 16: *A Man and a Wolf* (JA. Duhok)
> Text 17: *A Woman and a Leopard* (NK. Duhok)
> Text 19: *A Ewe and a Wolf* (CK. Shaqlawa)
> Text 28: *Two Mullahs* (ChA. Shaqlawa)

For example, in the Neo-Aramaic narrative the *Two Mullahs* from Shaqlawa, the storyteller adds the following moral of the story before the closing formula:

(21) ʾăya ḥŭčita[|] k-əmrila qa daw našət rešu là hawe mara=w[|] rešu mamrèle.[|] ʾawdza ʿàbra mən de naša k-šaqlìla.[|] k-əmrila qa dàn naše[|] ʾaxtsa gu qŭsət naše là ate=w ʾazəl,[|] gu moxət jànu ʾawəd,[|] ʾaxtsa gu tănayatət naše la qayəm=u yàtu.[|]

> This story is told about those who do not have a headache but cause themselves to have a headache, so that people will learn a lesson from the story of this man. The story tells people that one should not act[11] according to what other people say, but one should act using one's own wit, rather than stand and sit according to what other people say. (ChA. Shaqlawa, Text 28: *Two Mullahs*, §20)

---

[10] See Section 3.3.
[11] Lit. come and go.

Similarly, in the Kurdish narrative *A Ewe and a Wolf* from Shaqlawa the narrator elaborates on Kurdish culture:

(22) jā a-rē law hāḷatay dā ūdzāġ awanda pīròz boa| la nāw ko-maḷgāy kurdī| yaʿnī sùnd꞊ī pē xorā꞊ya.| har loya꞊š a-bīnīn haqāyata kurdīyakàn baw amānjay a-ban.|

It is said that the clan was so holy in Kurdish society that one took an oath on it. That is why we see that it has been referred to in Kurdish tales. (CK. Shaqalwa, Text 19: *A Ewe and a Wolf*, §22)

1.4. Discussion

Some of the formulas such as 'there once was' are found across the world, and others such as 'there was, there was not' are part of standardised story openings in Asian and Eastern European folklore occurring in Persian as *yeki bud yeki nabud* 'there was one, there was not one', in Turkish as *bir varmış bir yokmuş* 'there was one, there was not one' (Zeyrek 1993, 169) and in Azeri as *bir varmış bir yoxmuş* (Garbell 1965, 175), and in Armenian, Georgian and Romani (Matras 2014) and languages of the Balkans (Sandfield 1930), as well as Czech and Hungarian. The latter opening also has a more elaborate version with an affirmation of faith in the one God and his maximal greatness, as in the Arabic *Takbīr*, i.e. اَللّٰهُ أَكْبَرُ *ʾallāhu ʾakbaru* 'God is greater', and the magnifications of Yahweh above all other gods found in the Hebrew Scriptures.[12]

---

[12] For example, מֵאֵין כָּמוֹךָ יְהוָה גָּדוֹל אַתָּה 'There is none like you, O LORD, you are great' (Jer. 10.6), גָּדוֹל יְהוָה מִכָּל־הָאֱלֹהִים 'The LORD is greater than all gods' (Ex. 18.11).

It is unclear where this formula originated. Sandfield (1930, 162), referring to an article by M. Östrup in 1925, considers it to be a calque from the Arabic *kān mā kān*[13], which could be rendered either '(there) was, (there) was not' or '(there) was what (there) was', rhyming with other common Arabic words ending in *-ān* such as *fī 'awwal* or *qadīm z-zamān* 'in the past' (Ferguson and Rice 1960; Ingham 2005, 173). Asmussen (1968; Marzolch 2010, 220) also assumes it made its way into Persian folklore as *yeki būd yeki nabūd* 'there was one, there was not one' via Arabic. Incidentally, one finds the formula with the existential construction *fī* 'there is' typical of Colloquial Arabic also in Anatolian Arabic:

(23) *kə-fi mə-kə-fi* < **kān fīh mā kān fīh*
There was, there was not. (Anatolian Arabic; Akin, Jastrow and Talay 2020, 89)

Ingham (2005), however, traces this introductory phrase back to Sanskrit poetry found in the so-called *Hymn of Creation* in the Rigveda, which reads *nāsad āsīn no sad āsīt* conveying something in the vein of 'the nonbeing is not nor the being is'. The connection with this Sanskrit verse, however, seems questionable. Since the poem ponders the unknowable origin of the cosmos, and plays with a whole series of negations of antitheses,

---

[13] See also Coghill (2020b, 394). Variants of this Arabic formula are *kān wa-mā kān* 'there was and there was not' with coordinator *wa* 'and' and *kān yā mā kān* 'there was or there was not' using the coordinator *yā* 'or' of ultimately Iranian origin. The latter would be identical to the vocative particle *yā*, which would often also follow the opening formula addressing the listeners *yā mustamiʿīn* 'Oh, listeners!'.

the style and genre cannot be equated with the aforementioned story openings. The structure of the formula is also different in that it involves double negation, i.e. *nāsad* < *na a-sat*[14] 'not non-being' vs. *no sad* < *na u sat* 'nor being'. Moreover, as far as we know, the formula is not common to Indo-Aryan folklore.

Be that is it may, the core commonality between Kurdish and Neo-Aramaic is the use of a dedicated existential construction involving an existential element and past tense marking derived from the past tense form of the verb 'to be' (Stilo and Noorlander 2015, 470).

The use of the existential 'there was' in the opening coincides with the general use of existential expressions to introduce new information, and thereby serve to introduce one of the main protagonists in the story (*There once was someone who* etc.). The formula 'there was, there was not' also signals to the audience the beginning of the oral narrative set in an alternative reality about to unfold, featuring someone somewhere sometime. The negated counterpart like the English phrases *in the middle of nowhere* and *Never Neverland* convey spatial, temporal and epistemic distance between this world and that of the story. The narrator remains noncommittal to the truth of their story (Zeyrek 1993, 169), i.e. the narrated events may or may not be fictional,, thus expressing the narrator's prerogative to guide the listeners' imagination and narrating events that are half true, half lie.[15]

---

[14] The words *asat* 'nonbeing' and *sat* 'being' are related to Latin *absent-*.
[15] The same type of syntagm occurs with verbal predicates 'they did and did not do X', see §7.2.7, meaning 'whatever they did'. Thus, the opening formula could also be understood to mean 'whatever there was'.

The opening and closing formulas may also involve the blessing of the parents of the audience, suggesting this was once part of a widespread repertoire of blessings at the beginning and end of children's stories. These and other closing formulas are also presumably more widespread through Eurasia, being also attested at least in Armenian folklore (Mouse 2018), Iraqi Arabic children's rhymes (Ferguson and Rice 1960) as well as Italian (Beckwith 1987) and Serbo-Croatian folktales (Bošković-Stulli 1966). The use of the Arabic verbal root *xlṣ* 'to finish, to be over' in proclaiming the end of the narrative presumably betrays its Arabic source.

Finally, the mentioning of the storyteller's return with three apples—usually one for the storyteller—is one of the key elements of concluding formulas in Iraqi folktales (Ferguson and Rice 1960), but also occurs in Kurdish and Azeri (Garbell 1965, 176) and Armenian (Surmelian 1968). Beckwith (1987) mentions several closing rhymes in folktales collected by Italo Calvino that involve the phrase 'they gave me nothing', referring to the narrator not having been able to join in their happy ever after. This same phrase is part of closing formulas recorded in a collection of Serbo-Croatian folktales (Bošković-Stulli 1966, 312), where the narrator attended the festival at the end as a guest, but was given nothing. Thus, these concluding formulas add a relativising touch of humour and element of playfulness, sometimes also involving members of the audience.

2.0. Discourse Dependency and Clause Linkage

Narrative discourse can be organised into connected thematic units called paragraphs or episodes. As the narration progresses, the storyteller may draw attention to the shift from one scene to the next. While transitions generally need not be marked by specific formulas or discourse connectives, there are several linguistic expressions in particular that seem to be geared towards the organisation of narrative structure into interdependent parts while maintaining coherence.

2.1. The Verb 'to Rise'

The change of position verb conveying 'to rise, to stand up, to get up' is used in a type of serial verb construction where it functions as a subordinate verb conjoined with often an immediately following verb of motion, indicating the beginning of a new action, for example:

(1) *qəmle plə̀ṭle mən beta.*ǀ
     He rose and left the house. (ChA. Shaqlawa, Text 4: *Zambilfrosh by A. Sher*, §19)

(2) *řā-bī dàr-kat.*ǀ
     He rose and left the house. (NK. Khizava, Text7: *Zanbilfirosh—The Basket Seller*, §15)

This initiation of a new action often coincides with a new scene in the chain of events, establishing event cohesion. The verb can thus be stripped of its original lexical meaning of a change of position and undergo semantic bleaching into a more abstract discourse connective much like conjunctional adverbs such as English *then* and *thereupon*, for example:

(3) qəmle ʾay masəqθa kùlla šitale b-reše dànne ḥambušaye.|
Then he threw the entire torch over the heads of these monsters. (ChA. Duhok, Text 32: *Mirza Muhammad and the Forty Monsters*, §80)

(4) ř̄ā-ṭ-bən awē žənē āzȧ̀d ət̯-kan| ū ət-gal xo ət̯-ban=a əškaftḕ.|
Then they freed the woman and took her with them to the cave. (NK. Duhok, Text 30: *The Girl, Her Evil Stepmother and the Old Witch*, §83)

These constructions are found across our collection of tales, except for those narrated in the Kurdish of Shaqlawa.

The integration of the verb 'to get up' in a serial verb construction is widely attested across Semitic languages including Biblical Hebrew where it is said to express ingressive aspect (e.g. Dobbs-Allsopp 1995; Chrzanowski 2011, 356ff.)[16]. Whether this is motivated by a shift in event viewpoint thereby focusing on the beginning of the event, e.g. *He got up to go*, or by pragmatics to mark consequent action, e.g. *Then off he went*, the construction is characteristic of Semitic languages in general and a hallmark of oral narratives. The cognate of the Neo-Aramaic verb *qym* 'to rise' has the same function in several Arabic dialects, notably Egyptian, Levantine and Mesopotamian Arabic (e.g. Fischer and Jastrow 1980, 76; Lahdo 2009, 170), where this verb in the suffix conjugation—with dialect-specific variants such as *qām*, *ʾām*, *gām* etc.—precedes another verb as a preverbal modifier. It is also attested in Ṭuroyo, the Neo-Aramaic dialects of Ṭur ʿAbdin (e.g.

---

[16] For example, וַיָּ֥קׇם וַיֵּלַ֖ךְ *wayyā́qom wayyélek* 'he arose and went'.

Jastrow and Talay 2019, 16), closely related to NENA. The use of this serial verb construction in Northern Kurdish is therefore likely ultimately of Semitic origin, possibly Aramaic and/or Arabic.

Furthermore, in both Arabic and Ṭuroyo, the same verb has further grammaticalised to an invariant particle based on its past form without agreement, often coinciding with the 3sg.m. form with a ∅ morpheme. This is also attested in our NENA corpus, where the subject agreement marked by the L-suffix of the past perfective of the verb *qym* 'to rise' is elided, e.g.

(5)   *qəm hàm aw zəlle dməxle.*|
      Then he also went and fell asleep. (ChA. Duhok, Text 32: *Mirza Muhammad and the Forty Monsters*, §37)

The Neo-Aramaic verb *qym* and its phonetically reduced variant can also indicate unexpectedness in NENA dialects such as ChA. Harbole (SE Turkey; Khan 2021, 169–72) as well as the progressive aspect in yet other dialects such as JA. Bəjil (NW Iraq; Mutzafi 2002, 70).

Finally, the same verb has been suggested as one of the possible etymologies of the preverbal TAM modifier *qam* and its dialectal variants—ranging from *qām, qəm, gəm, kəm* to *tam*—shared by the majority of NENA dialects to construct a transitive past perfective verbal form, e.g. *qam-šaql-a-le* 'she took him', which possibly first emerged on the Nineveh Plains partially due to Arabic influence.[17]

---

[17] See Noorlander (2021, 211–14) for a discussion and further references.

2.2. Additive Particles (*ži* / *=š*)

The Kurdish particles *žī* (NK) and *=īš* (CK) generally placed after a (pro)nominal element, sometimes after a verbal element, have been fully integrated into NENA discourse. In her typological study of additive markers, Forker (2016) distinguishes between several prototypical functions, which also capture the use of the particles *ži* or *žī* and *=(ī)š* or *=ž* in Kurdish and Neo-Aramaic.

2.2.1. Additive Focus ('too')

(6) ʾiba ʾarbi ḥàmbušaye.│ ʾu yə̀mmay **ži** ʾīθ tama,│ yəmmət ḥambušàye.│
There were forty monsters inside. And their mother was there **too**—the mother of the monsters. (ChA. Duhok, Text 32: *Mirza Muhammad and the Forty Monsters*, §76)

(7) aw āgəray la mārē tù bū│ da mārē mə̀n=**īš**=ət bar-dā!│
The fire that existed in your house, you threw it at my house **too** (meaning: Your life was hell and you inflicted the same hell upon me!) (CK. Shaqlawa, Text 29: *Two Mullahs*, §12)

2.2.2. Scalar Additive ('even')

(8) tsə məndi lìtən.│ ʾixalàne=**š** litən.
There was nothing. There was not **even** food. (ChA. Shaqlawa, Text 12: *A 'Pious' Fox*, §5)

(9) gotī, 'awa bo ma hḕ **ži** bāštər.'│
They said, 'It's **even** better for us. (NK. Duhok, Text 26: *Dindik Hinar—A Girl Called Pomegranate Grain*, §145)

2.2.3. Concessive ('even if')

(10) ʾu g-ə̀bət **ži**,ˈ ʾana hun ʾəθya m-majburùθiˈ d-máʿyəšən ʾắyằl diyi.ˈ

Even if you want to eat me, know that I have come out of the need to feed my children. (ChA. Duhok, *Man and Lion*, §7)

(11) *agar az hatā hatāyè̱ **ẕ̌ī**ˈ ət kuḷkī-va bə-nəvə̀mˈ bo mən nà məškīla=yaˈ bo mən ʿādì=ya.*ˈ

Even if I live till the end of my life in the barn, it is no issue for me. It is fine by me. (NK. Duhok, Text 26: *Dindik Hinar— A Girl Called Pomegranate Grain*, §94)

2.2.4. Topicalisation

Contrastive:

(12) ʾaniži qə́mlayˈ drelay ʾixala ṭḷaθá yomaθa ṭḷaθá lelawaθa l-xaṣət sùstay.ˈ ʾu bàbay **ži** gəm-markəwile xa xə̀rta,ˈ xa susta xə̀rta.ˈ

So they put food for three days and three nights on the back of their mare, **but** their father they mounted on another mare. (ChA. Duhok, *Mirza*, §8)

(13) *amə̀n la mārē d-ēm=a darē=o ba āsānī=oˈ atò=š har la mārē=y=o taʾxìr a-bī.*ˈ

I'm already out of the house heading towards the mosque, but you keep being delayed. (CK. Shaqlawa, Text 29: *Two Mullahs*, §6)

Switch of topic:

(14) *aw pīražə̀na čū=a žorē,ˈ har dar-nà-hātˈ har dar-nà-hāt.ˈ zor=ī pē čù̀.ˈ maṭrān=īš tahamùl=ī kərd.ˈ*
The old woman went inside. She did not come out of the house for a while (lit. she did not come out; she did not come out). It took her a lot of time (lit. a lot went to/with her). The bishop tolerated her delay. (CK. Shaqlawa, Text 38: *The Foul-Mouthed Priest*, §8)

Topic reactivation:

(15) *ʾila xaze hola tòta,ˈ yəmmət ḥambušáye **ži** hola tàma.ˈ*
Look, he sees the old woman there, the mother of the monsters is there. (ChA. Duhok, Text 32: *Mirza Muhammad and the Forty Monsters*, §136)

(16) *wàxtakī sah tə-kat=ēˈ bərāyē wī hatā nīvaḵā šavē yē hằt=o čo.ˈ pəštī hingē aw **žī** čù̀ sar jəhē xoˈ ū nəvə̀st.ˈ*
At one moment he realised that his brother had kept watch (lit. came and went) only until midnight, and after that had gone to bed and slept. (NK. Duhok, Text 34: *Mirza Muhammad's adventures*, §16)

2.2.5. Constituent Coordination

The additive particle can also function as a coordinator. It can appear only once within the coordinating phrase (17), or separately on each constituent (18).

(17) ṭlaha qupyàta=wˈ xa ʾawa=š qa de baxta xṣùṣi wədwale.ˈ
He made three baskets, **as well as** one special mat for the woman. (ChA. Shaqlawa, Text 5: *Zambilfrosh* by W. Toma, §18)

(18) ū žənbābē wē **žī** ū kəčē wē **žī** čə jārā̀ əš wērē dar-nā-xītən.ˈ
Also, he decided not to set free **either** the stepmother **or** her daughter from the prison at all. (NK. Duhok, Text 26: *Dindik Hinar—A Girl Called Pomegranate Grain*, §120)

2.2.6. Conjunctional Adverb

While their basic function is the expression of additive focus equivalent to that of English *too* and *also*, one of the functions most relevant for narrative style and discourse organisation is that of a conjunctional adverb, linking one discourse unit with the preceding. This is an optional effect of additive markers common to several languages across the world (Forker 2016), and also characteristic of additive markers in the languages in the area. This function, however, is not easily distinguished from other pragmatic functions, such as topicalisation where the particles are added to a clause-initial noun phrase to indicate a contrastive topic, a switch of topic or to reactive a topical referent.

(19) kamər: 'psu gawət baṭrət ʾurxət duglana hàl xazəx l-eka g-maṭpelux.'ˈʾàmər.ˈ kălăbāb=**iš** xa ʾaqla=w xa qàma bizale=le xa ʾaqla bədʾare=le qa bàṭra.ˈ
Uncle Fox said, 'Go down the road of the liar until we see where he will lead you.' So he said. **Then** the rooster went one step forwards and one step backwards. (ChA. Shaqlawa, Text 12: *A 'Pious' Fox*, §17–18)

(20) k-ìmər,ˈ 'yaba, ʾàtiˈ kăbira lè maḥkət.ˈ hayyu ʾàxxaˈ ʾu mṣàpuxla ʾana w-ati m-uxðaðe.ˈ ʾàwa žiˈ zəlleˈ nxətle laxù gəra.ˈ

He said, 'Fellow, don't talk so much. Come here and let's settle it, I and you together.' **So** he went down towards the bottom of the hill. (ChA. Duhok, Text 32: *Mirza Muhammad and the Forty Monsters*, §26–27)

(21) ət-bēžt=ē, 'wara sarì!ˈ wara sarī hagar dē ta pərčē xəsīnəmˈ ū dē ta īnm=a sarì!'ˈ Dəndək Hənārē **žī** zīkā manjalokā xo ət-hāvēžīt=a wērè.ˈ ū ət-k̯at=a ġārè čīt=a dafˈ

She said, 'Come upstairs! Come upstairs, otherwise I will crumple your hair and bring you upstairs myself!' So Dindik Hinar immediately threw away her milk-pail, ran towards her. (NK. Duhok, Text 26: *Dindik Hinar—A Girl Called Pomegranate Grain*, §45-46)

(22) got=ī, 'wā hēwāra dā hàtˈ aw jā waxtī nūstənì=ya.ˈ bas kas kas iz'āj nà-kāˈ čūnka řē=n dūr=a hatā gayn=a hadžè.'ˈ karabāb=ū kotər=**īš** gotī=yān, 'basar hàr dū čāwān!'ˈ

The fox said, 'It's getting near evening; it's time to sleep. But no one should disturb anyone since we've a long way ahead of us until we reach Mecca.' Then the rooster and dove said, 'All right! (lit. on both eyes)' (CK. Shaqlawa, Text 13: *A 'Pious' Fox*, §10)

The same generally holds for the additive particle *ham* in NENA—ultimately from Persian and found throughout the area, which precedes the focal referent:

(23) ḥàrəs| hole kəlya=w hole ṭwiʾa.| **ham** ʾawa qəmle mà-wədle?| gəm-tayəpla xòrta.|

A guard was standing though asleep. **So**, he, then what did he do? He bent the poplar. (ChA. Duhok, Text 32: *Mirza Muhammad and the Forty Monsters*, §122–123)

2.3. Other Adverbials and Discourse Conjunctions

Temporal adverbials can also serve as a device to structure the narrative and mark episode transitions. Their usage is pragmatically motivated to connect discourse units rather than grounded in the clause itself. Adverbials like 'once' and 'one day' are a case in point, where the start of a new day coincides with the start of a new thematic unit and thereby a type of opening formula, as illustrated in (24)–(25) below.

(24) **xà yoma**| mălà xa ʾizəle l-xəlmət raʾisət dèṛa.|
   One day an angel appeared in a dream of the abbot of the monastery. (ChA. Shaqlawa, Text 35: *Mar Yohanan*, §14)

(25) **řožak la řožằn**| malāy yakàm la malāy duam=ī pərsi,|
   One day, the first Mullah asked the second Mullah. (CK. Shaqlawa, Text 29: *Two Mullahs*, §4)

Other conjunctional adverbs that may be used in NENA are *naqla, ʾənnaqla, ʾannăqa* 'now, then', composed of the near deixis demonstrative *ad* and dialectal Arabic *naqla* 'round, trip', and *žnu*, composed of originally Kurdish *žə* 'from' and *nū* 'now', e.g.

(26) ʾay xona zora là maḥkele ču məndi,| Mərzá Mḥàmmad.| ʾənnaqla pə̀šla yoma kulle.| mġudelay, mʿušelay, xənna pəšle θàni yom| b-làyle.

The youngest brother did not say anything—Mirza Muhammad. **Then** the whole day passed. They had dinner and had supper. It was the second night of holding watch. (ChA. Duhok, Text 32: *Mirza Muhammad and the Forty Monsters*, §33–34)

(27) qṭilili ṭlaθá ḥambušaye t-θelay l-qawrət bàbi,ˈ šaqlíwalan qawrət bàbi.ˈˈ **žnu** ðelay xunwaθeḥ Mərzá Mḥămad hole qṭilay ḥambušaye tàma.ˈ

I killed the three monsters who came to my father's grave; they would take us to my father's grave. Mirza Muhammad's brothers **now** knew that he had killed the monsters there. (ChA. Duhok, Text 32: *Mirza Muhammad and the Forty Monsters*, §224–225)

Both adverbials also occur in the Neo-Aramaic dialects of Ṭur ʿAbdin, but, as far as we are aware, are not found in Arabic or Kurdish as such.

The Kurdish conjunctional adverb *vējā, ijā* 'now, then' has the same linking function:

(28) *az꞊ē bə řēkē dā čəm dā b-čəm꞊a māḷā bābē xò.ˈ **vējā** hamā haga tu žī dē mə xòyˈ dē təštakị̄ lə mə k̲ạ̀y,ˈ hamā mən bə-xò!ˈ*

[The woman said,] 'I'm on the road to my father's house. Now, if you intend to eat me or do any harm to me, then go ahead eat me! (NK. Duhok, Text 17: *A Woman and a Leopard*, §11)

In addition, in the Kurdish Mirza Muhammad tale, the particle *inā*,[18] is used to link the narrative unit with the preceding:

(29) *aw haspē xo dē bələ̀nd kət꞊o| dē pəšt꞊o pəšt zəvəř̀ət.| āvē nà-va-xot.| īnā řožakē duā hàr av hāla bo.| īnā sulṭānī aw haspē sulṭānī꞊ya.| īnā sulṭān ət-bēžt꞊ē, 'būč̀ī av haspa yē lāwāz꞊a꞊w| yē bē-xòlk꞊a꞊w?'|*

On seeing the hair, the horse rose to his feet and reared up; it did not drink the water. **Then** for one or two days it went on like this. **Then** the sultan—the one-eyed horse belonged to him—**then** the sultan said to him, 'Why is this horse weak and left without care?' (NK. Duhok, Text 34: *Mirza Muhammad's Adventures*, §63-64)

2.4. Tail-Head Linkage

In the unfolding story line, the final clause of the preceding chain can be partially or completely repeated as the first clause of the next chain to connect an unbroken series of events.[19] This is arguably a conventionalized technique of clause linage for the sake of thematic continuity and event cohesion.[20] For example:

---

[18] This particle is presumably demonstrative in origin (cp. English *then* with the same historical base **tha-* as in *this* and *that*), the proximal demonstrative base *in* being found in, for instance, *īnā* 'this' in the Gorani of Gawraju (Bailey 2018, 156, 559) and *in* in Persian, or derived from the past form of the Kurdish verb *īnān* 'to bring'.

[19] See Thurman (1975) and de Vries (2005).

[20] See the discussions on repetition in Khan's grammars, e.g. C. Barwar (Khan 2008, 943–945). See also Coghill (2009, 277) and Molin and Noorlander (2022, 247).

(30) *qām-šaqəla=w matula baθrət xaṣeu=w* **nàbəla 'aya.**ˈ **nabəla,** *ḳum-darela gu xà ġurfa.*ˈ
He lifted her, put her on the horseback and **took her along**. **After he took her**, he put her in a room. (ChA. Harmashe, Text 33: *Mirza Muhammad and the Three Princesses*, §10)

(31) *zə̀lle yoma*ˈ *θèle yoma*ˈ—*là g-əbən marxənna ʾəllawxun*ˈ—*ḥakəm mə̀θle.*ˈ *ḥakəm màtle,*ˈ *yale zòre*ˈ *k-əmri,*
As the days passed by—I do not want to make it too long for you—**the ruler died**. **After the ruler died**, his little children said, (ChA. Duhok, *Mirza*, §6)

(32) *damē t-dan=a bar xanjarà*ˈ *P̂irhavīr nà-mərītən.*ˈ **wakī həndak paṟēt qalařaškē ət nāv hawāyē dā barzà ṭ-bīt-ava.**ˈ *ət nāv hawāyē dā barzà ṭ-bīt-ava.*ˈ *ṭə-bēžītən, 'o, ava čə̀ čē bū?*'ˈ
They stabbed Pirhavir with daggers but she did not die. She disappeared into the sky in the form of something like feathers of a black raven. She disappeared into the sky. They (the brothers and Fatma) said, 'Oh, what has happened?' (NK. Duhok, Text 30: *A Girl, her Evil Stepmother, and the Old Woman*, §79)

(33) *paštī bəhorīnā sē čār řožaḳà*ˈ *Hənār žī bə sar kàft*ˈ *barē xo datē māl yā čòl=a.*ˈ *māl yā čòl=a*ˈ *bə tənè*ˈ *xəškàḳā wē yā ž qasr hāzər.*ˈ
After three, four days, Hinar went upstairs, looked around and saw **the house was empty. The house was empty.** Only one of her sisters was home. (NK. Duhok, Text 26: *Dindik Hinar—A Girl Called Pomegranate Grain*, §71)

3.0. Poetic and Formulaic Language

Kurdish and Neo-Aramaic share similar phraseology in other formulaic language and poetic techniques. After a discussion of a selection of idioms and fillers, this section offers a few examples of proverbs, end rhyme and parallelism and alliteration found in the corpus.

3.1. Idioms and Phraseology

Among the manifold idioms are:

There is Fire in Your House

The idiomatic expression 'there is fire in your house' describes that the person's life is hellish and that he has trouble in his house.

(1) aw āgəray la mārē tù būˈ da mārē mə̀n=iš=ət bar-dā!ˈ
 Your life was hell and you inflicted the same hell upon me (lit. The fire that existed in your house, you threw it at my house too.) (CK. Shaqlawa, Text 29: *Two Mullahs*, §12)

(2) ʾāt betux nura ʾitən gu betux ʾarqətwa mənə ʾăna šə̀ne,ˈ
 Your home was like hell (lit. There is fire in your house) from which you fled all these years. (ChA. Shaqlawa, Text 28: *Two Mullahs*, §17)

A Day Came A Day Went

The idiomatic expression 'a day came and a day went' or the equivalent in the plural is found in both Kurdish and NENA to denote the passage of time:

(3) řož hàtən=o řūž čòn[|]

Several days passed by (lit. days came and days went). (NK. Duhok, Text 26: *Dindik Hinar—A Girl Called Pomegranate Grain*, §16)

(4) zə̀lle yoma[|] θèle yoma[|]

As the days passed by (lit. a day went a day came). (ChA. Dohok, *Mirza and the forty monsters*, §6)

Coming Going

Combinations of the verbs 'to come' and 'to go' provide background to the following foreground action, denoting preparation, both physical and mental, before doing an action. Interestingly, the order of the verbs 'go' and 'come' is reversed in the two languages, i.e. Kurdish *hāt=o čo* 'came and went' and NENA *zəle=w θele* 'went and came', compare:

(5) hāt=o čò[|] hāt=o čò.[|] nà-ẓānī dē čə katən.[|] bar-av xārḕ va čū.[|]

She went back and forth. She did not know what to do. She went downstairs. (NK. Duhok, Text 26: *Dindik Hinar—A Girl Called Pomegranate Grain*, §74)

(6) zəle=w θèle[|] zəle=w θèle=w[|] šitàle ganeu l-aw bara xəna.[|]

He went back and forth, back and forth, and flung himself to the other side. (ChA. Harmesha, *Mirza and the three Princess*, §24)

It Is Not in My Hands

This formula expresses inability to do something in facing of an unpleasant situation.

(7) b-idati lèwa?ˈ
    I cannot help it? (lit. It is not in my hands.) (ChA. Shaqlawa, Text 12: *A 'Pious' fox*, §34)

(8) ma čə̀ dastē ma dā ni꞊na!ˈ
    We—we cannot manage it! (lit. there is nothing in our hands.) (NK. Duhok, Text 34: *Mirza Muhammad's Adventures*, §109)

Fall in Love

Falling in love is rendered literally by the phrase 'one's heart fell' and/or 'something fell to one's heart'. Examples:

(9) jəhē dā viyānā ku̱řkī kat dəlē ḳəčkè̱.ˈ
    She was filled with love for the boy (lit. The longing for the boy fell into the girl's heart.) (NK. Khizava, Text 7: *Zanbilfirosh—The Basket Seller*, §19)

(10) har dzwān pešàwaˈ har har ləbu pə̀le.ˈ
    She grew more and more beautiful and he fell in love with her (lit. his heart fell.) (ChA. Shaqlawa, Text 23: *The Poor Girl and her Horse*, §27)

3.2. Fillers

Narrators also have linguistic expressions that are used repetitively, often to signal hesitation or pause, or to mark salient points in the story. NENA and Kurdish speakers have a wide range of fillers at their disposal, most of which ultimately go back to Arabic such as *yaʿni*, *yăʿăni* or *yani* from يعني *yaʿnī* '(he/it) means', which fulfils a wide range of pragmatic functions, for instance indicating that the speaker seeks to offer clarifications, modifications or corrections equivalent to English *I mean*, *that is* or *in other words*. Also common are the connector ʾəlla from إلا *ʾillā* for 'but, except', which introduces a contrast or exception, and the interjection *waḷḷa* or *waḷā* 'by God' from والله *wallāhi*, which generally adds assertive force or expresses surprise.

A frequent substitute for when a speaker cannot think of the word is *hənna* or *ʾənna* cognate with Arabic هن *han* (or هنة *hanah* 'thing'), which can be equivalent to English *thingy* or *what's-it-called*. It can be inflected like a noun and even be converted into a verb, i.e. *hnele* 'he Xed'.

(11) *ʾaw hole qìma*ˈ *xəzya gu* **hə̀nna,**ˈ *ḥawš díyeḥ꞊ila.*ˈ **ʾə̀nna.**ˈ

He is already up and has seen what is in—**what's-it-called**—his garden. **The thing.**

The cognate *hno* occurs in the Neo-Aramaic of Ṭur ʿAbdin (Jastrow and Talay 2019, 15–16). The Kurdish narrator from Khizava uses *awādī*, which is most likely a combination of demonstrative *aw* + ezafe feminine form *_ā* + *dī* 'other', 'lit. the other one', as an equivalent to NENA *hənna*.

(12) *əš bənamālā* **awādī** *bī* ... *Bahninè bī.*ˈ *əš bənamālā Faq əbrāhīmì bī.*ˈ

She was from that **so-and-so** family in Bahnin; she was from Faq Ibrahim's family. (NK. Khizava, Text 31: *Firyat and Khajija*, §6)

Furthermore, NENA and Kurdish dialects also have the particle *flān* or *flan* from Arabic فلان *fulān*,[21] which can serve as a noun substitute or nominal attribute when the referent is unknown.

(13) ʾăna jŭlu šmə̀ṭṭe=wan mənu' **flan** dukta mtù tu=wan.'

The clothes that I have taken from them, put them in **such-and-such** a place. (ChA. Shaqlawa, Text 35: *Mar Yohanan*, 33)

In the following Kurdish example, the particle *fəlān* has been combined with *kas* 'person' to substitute the nominal.

(14) ȩ̌k šə wānā t-bēšt=ē,' 'arē **fəlānkas** mā ta čə zārok nằ-bən?'

One of them said, 'Hey **so-and-so**! Won't you have any children? (NK. Duhok, Text 26: *Dindik Hinar—A Girl Called Pomegranate Grain*, §3)

A typical narrator-oriented discourse marker in Neo-Aramaic is the fossilised imperative form of the stem II verb of the root *hym* 'believe', which can occur as *mhaymən* or *mhemən* 'believe!'. It adds assertive force and emphasises salient events.

The particles ʾ*e* in NENA and *a* in Kurdish, otherwise expressing affirmation, agreement or approval like English *yes*, may be used in the narrative to express assertiveness and thus intensification or rhetorical salience, especially when it occurs in its own intonation unit. The particle can also fulfil the function of a sentence connector and indicate the end of a paragraph, as for instance in the concluding sentence of the story given below.

---

[21] Compare Syriac *plān*.

(15) *'e, qày,| šawpa, šawpət saypa g-nàyəx.| šawpət xabra là g-nayəx.| xabra nàxwaš, nàxwaš꞊ile, 'e.|*
Indeed, therefore, the impact of a sword heals, but the impact of words does not heal. Words can be very evil, **indeed**. (ChA. Duhok, Text 14: *A Man and a Lion*, §19)

(16) *xarək ba kārwānḕ safar꞊ī kərdīya.| dzā kārwānakān zīyātər ba payā̀n būwa,| wa zəyātər꞊iš ba kàr būwa.| à!|*
People would travel with caravans. The caravans were mostly on foot, but also with donkeys. **Yes!** (CK. Shaqlawa, Text 22: *A Talking Goat*, §3)

An impersonalised form of the narrative or reporting verb 'to say' literally conveying 'he says' can be used as a reportative or quotative particle, which is usually added at the beginning of a new clause but can also be placed at the end. The particle can permeate an entire story between and across narrative units, and arguably functions as a filler. There is a subtle difference from the above fillers in that this seems to be particular to narrative discourse rather than part of everyday use of language. It is possible this is an emergent evidential strategy, but this would require further investigation. Examples:

(17) *'amər xà yoma| 'izəle 'àwa| kàrta qam-ṭa'əna l-xàṣu.| mxuškunta 'azəl zambilu mzabə̀nu.| 'amər bax màlka| qam-xazyàle.|*
It is said that one day one day he went off carrying a load on his back. He went at dawn to sell his baskets. **It is said that** a king's wife saw him. (ChA. Shaqlawa, Text 4: *Zambilfrosh by A. Sher*, §29)

(18) *a-rē řož hāt=ū řož řòy| mař har pərsyārī a-kə̀rd, 'da-bī| šāhēd-ī gurgʸī kʸè̱ bī?'|*

It is said that dawn broke [lit. the sun came and the sun went]. The ewe kept asking herself, 'Who is going to be the wolf's witness?' (CK. Shaqlawa, Text 19: *A Ewe and a Wolf*, §15)

The same filler occurs in Anatolian Arabic, where *qāl* literally 'he said' can permeate a story, for example in the text from Qarṭmin in Mardin (SE Turkey) recorded by Jastrow and Fischer (1989: 165–169).

3.3. Proverbs

(19) *šwirət xàbra| là k-eθe nšaya.|*
šwirət ḍə̀rba| naša g-našèle.|
šwirət xàbra' ḥə̀l mò̱θa| naša la g-našele.|
A wound caused by words is not forgotten.
A wound caused by a blow a man does forget.
But a wound caused by words—a man does not forget it until death. (JA. Duhok, Text 16: *A Man and a Wolf*, §24–27)

(20) *šawpət saypa g-nàyəx.| šawpət xabra là g-nayəx.|*
The impact of a sword heals, but the impact of words does not heal. (ChA. Duhok, Text 14: *A Man and a Lion*, §19)

(21) *žē ət-čət nīšā šīnā xanjarà̱| bas žē nā-čətīn šīnā xabarà̱.|*
The trace of grief caused by daggers will go away, but the grief caused by words will not go away. (NK. Duhok, Text 17: *A Woman and a Leopard*, §37)

3.4. End Rhyme

(22) ʾurxət marya ta=t malpilè=w|
ʾurxət malkuta maxwilè=w|
ʾadi ʿalma ta=t šawqilè.|

to teach him the path to the Lord and
to show him the path towards the heavenly kingdom and
so that they may abandon this world.
(ChA. Shaqlawa, Text 4: *Zambilfrosh by A. Sher*, §52)

(23) Fāt Fātokè![22]|
təl mēžūkè!|
yān ži bərākožūkè! |

O little Fatma!
Your fingers to be sipped blood from!
Or your brothers to be killed!
(NK. Duhok, Text 30: *The Girl, her Evil Stepmother and the Old Witch*, §61)

(24) muhabtè ḵəč mubtalā ḵər.|
səř lə jārīyē āškərā ḵər,|
ʿlāwaḵè qalb=əm jədā ḵər.|
mən žə ʿašqā̀n xaw na-tē'|

Love overtook the girl.
She disclosed her story to her maid:
'The boy broke my heart
I cannot sleep because of [his] love.'
(NK. Khizava, Text 7: *Zanbilfirosh—The Basket Seller*, §39)

---

[22] The ending *-kē* consists of the diminutive suffix *-k* followed by the oblique affix *-ē*.

(25) *Atmān! sīyārē Dəndəlè!*
pāžo hara Müsəlè!
Atman! The rider on Dindil!
Ride it, go to Mosul!
(NK. Dure, Text 37: *The Prophet's Horse*, §9)

3.5. Alliteration

(26) *kma iwat **šar=u šapàle** … xəmyani **kalba kòma**.*
How **weary and worn out** you are… My father-in-law is **a black dog**. (ChA. Duhok, Text 9: *The Bridge of Dalale*, §17, §21)

(27) *gundak yē bḕ-**dang**=a nà **dang**=a nà dūr=a.*
It was a silent village. It was not full of sound, nor was it remote (from civilization). (NK. Duhok, Text 34: *Mirza Muhammad's Adventures*, §35)

4.0. Figurative Language

Certain figurative uses of language are common stylistic devices of oral narratives, especially the mimicry of sounds. Narrators can also transform ordinary sentences into questions as figures of speech. This section lists examples of figures of speech typical of the Kurdish and Neo-Aramaic oral literature found in our collection, starting with onomatopoeias and ideophones as well as the use of repetition, lengthening and reduplication.

4.1 Sound Symbolism

4.1.1. Onomatopoeias

(1) *θele xa xənna **mnahmòre**.| kepət ṭura hole b-qale **mzarzòye**,| làyt?|*
'Another came **blustering**. The rocks of the mountain were already **shaking** at the sound of his voice, weren't they?' (ChA. Duhok, Text 32: *Mirza Muhammad and the Forty Monsters*, §40)

(2) *dītī꞊yān kotərak lasàr dārē bū| **bərġa bə̀rġ꞊ī** bū.|*
They saw a dove was in the tree. He was **cooing**. (CK. Shaqlawa, Text 13: *A 'Pious' Fox*, §7)

(3) *řəp řəp*
'clip-clop of horses' (NK. Duhok, Text 34: *Mirza Muhammad's Adventures*, §71)

(4) *qəṛ qəṛ*
'cracking noise' (NK. Duhok, Text 34: *Mirza Muhammad's Adventures*, §60)

4.1.2. Ideophones

(5) *ṣŭpurta ʾàmra:| **wəj wəj wə̀j!**|*
The sparrow said, '**Chirp, chirp, chirp!**' (ChA. Shaqlawa, Text 12: *A Pious Fox*, §35)

(6) *xəre ʾəla xandaq xpə̀rta.| zəle xðə̀re xa, tre čarxe| xðə̀re,| xðə̀re| ʾu꞊**fiiiit** šitàle ganeu l-aw bara xə̀na.| k̭um-šawə̀ra.|*
He looked at the trench that had been dug. He went and walked round one, two times, walked round and round, and **woosh** he flung himself to the other side. He had jumped over it. (ChA. Shaqlawa, Text 12: *A Pious Fox*, §35)

(7) mxèle,ˈ **taq, tàq.**ˈ wele dewa ... hənna, ʾàrya k-šame qala g-nàxəθ ʾəlle.ˈ

He started cutting, **crack, crack,** and a wolf... I mean, lion heard the sound and came to him. (ChA. Duhok, Text 14: *A Man and a Lion*, §6)

(8) ʾowà!ˈ mux məlxa g-əbatti bàs?!ˈ ... ʾanya tre bnási=lu, ʾahat leat bràti,ˈ **wiii!**ˈ

'Oh! You love me only as much as salt?!' ... Those two are my daughters, you are not my daughter, **oh!**' (JA. Zakho, Text 25: *As Precious as Salt*, §7)

(9) gāzē mərišk=ū barxàk,ˈ dū sē bàrx=ī ha-būn:ˈ **t̂p, t̂p, t̂p, t̂p, t̂p**=ū, ʘ²³, ʘ, āwā=y kərd: **t̂p, t̂p, t̂p,** 'warə̀n!'ˈ mərišk hātən àw lā.ˈ

He called for the hens and sheep—he had two, three sheep: **Cluck! Cluck! Cluck! Cluck! Cluck! Ba! Ba!** He did this, **Cluck! Cluck!** 'Come!' The hens came to eat the berries. (CK. Shaqlawa, Text 27: *The Indecent Neighbour*, §6)

(10) **ns! ns!** bèhn tə-k̂atən.ˈ

Sniff! Sniff! She smelled. (NK. Duhok, Text 30: *The Girl, her Evil Stepmother and the Old Witch*, §53)

(11) qomāšaka=y har-a-dāt-awa a-bīnī **tûf!**ˈ tù wəḷāhī!ˈ ʿasabì bū.ˈ

She removed the cloth on the tray to show him what was in the tray. He said (lit. he saw), '**Wow!** Indeed the tray was full of berries!', he became furious. (CK. Shaqlawa, Text 27: *Indecent Neighbour*, §4)

---

[23] That is, a bilabial click.

4.1.3. Repetition

Repetition stands in an iconic relationship to the extensive amount, size or distance of the activity or property:

(12) **psèle**ˈ **psù,**ˈ **psù,**ˈ **psù,**ˈ **psù,**ˈ **psù,**ˈ **psù.**ˈ ʾani ʾan qămàye ʾamriwa, k-amri, l-Bàġdad.ˈ
He **went off, on and on and on and on**—to Baghdad, as they, the old folks, used to say. (ChA. Shaqlawa, Text 4: *Zambilfrosh* by A. Sher, §20)

(13) rkule l-xaṣət susa xwàra.ˈ ga ʾərta **zəle=w zəle=w zəle=w**, qam-šawə̀ra ga ʾərta xandaq.ˈ
He rode on the back of a white horse. Once more **he went on and on** and then jumped over the trench again. (ChA. Harmashe, Text 33: *Mirza*, §14)

(14) har bənamā̀ḷaḵēˈ hàspaḵē makənē,ˈ jəhēlə̄ˈ **galà gala gala gala** lāv ha-bū.ˈ
Each family had a young, reliable horse that was **very very** strong. (NK. Dure, Text 20: *A Family Horse*, §2)

(15) **hēdī hēdī hēdī hēdī**ˈ qūnāxā dārəstānē darbā̀s ḵər.ˈ
Slowly, slowly, slowly, slowly, they crossed the wild forest. (NK. Duhok, Text 17: *A Woman and a Leopard*, §14)

(16) baḷằmˈ kotər **zor zor zor zor** la řiwī zīraktə̀r bū.ˈ
The dove, however, was **much much** cleverer than the fox. (CK. Shaqlawa, Text 13: *A Pious Fox*, §14)

4.1.4. Lengthening

Similarly, the prolongation of the pronunciation of a consonant or vowel coincides with intensification and rhetorical salience, thus symbolising the larger extent to which the relevant semantic content applies.

(17) ʾən ʾamruxle, **bəšššš** b-àwux ʾàzat.ʾ|

If we tell him, we are going to be **far more** free. (ChA. Duhok, Text 32: *Mirza Muhammad and the Forty Monsters*, §107)

(18) gūtī, '**harềēē**!ʾ|

She said, '**Come on!**' (NK. Duhok, Text 26: *Dindik Hinar— A Girl Called Pomegranate Grain*, §73).

Such lengthening can also be combined with repetition, as illustrated below, to build up suspense. Often the stressed vowel of the last element of the repeated word is lengthened.

(19) kŭlay hune **bizàla,| bizàla=w,| bizàaala,|** lène biyara.|

Everybody **was going back and forth**, but they did not dare to jump. (ChA. Harmashe, Text 33: *Mirza Muhammad and the Three Princesses*, §5)

(20) inā aw pə̀rčā we| aw ā dārkē ālāndī̀| āv **ət-bat ət-bat ət-bàaat**| **ət-bat** ət-čət=a bəṛkā sultānakī̀ dā.|

Her (Gulizar's) hair—the one which was twisted onto the stick—the water **took it away and took it away, took it all the way** to the lake of a sultan in another city. (NK. Duhok, Text 34: *Mirza Muhammad's Adventures*, §61)

4.1.5. Reduplication

Reduplication is the repetition of a word or a part of a word in the formation of a lexeme or idiom. The full reduplication is typical of onomatopoeias consisting of closed syllables.. Complete and partial reduplication is thus a regular process in the lexicalisation of animal cries such as 'bleating' (of sheep) Kurdish *bāřabāř* and NENA *mbarbore* as well as 'wailing, barking' (of dogs) Kurdish *čalačal*[24] and NENA *mčalwole*. In the Kurdish examples, reduplication serves both to augment the quantity of a word, and to intensify the meaning expressed by it.

(21)   Total reduplication:

a.   *got-got*

'sayings' (lit. said-said) (NK. Zakho, Text 11: *The Bridge of Dalal*, §13)

b.   *pəšt=o pəšt*

A continuous backward movement (lit. back and back) (NK. Duhok, Text 34: *Mirza Muhammad's Adventures*, §63)

In the partial reduplication, the word's initial consonant is replaced by another consonant, usually labial like /m/, to express the continuation of an indefinite number of the same set with a similar effect to English *and so forth*, *etcetera* or *whatever*, e.g. NENA *xabuše mabuše* 'apples and so forth'. This *m*-reduplication ultimately originated in Turkic languages, e.g. Turkish *gözüne mözüne* 'eyes and so forth', and spread to Persian, Kurdish, NENA,

---

[24] See Chyet (2003, 103).

Ṭuroyo and local Anatolian Arabic dialects, e.g. Mardini Arabic *ṛās-māṣ* 'heads and other body parts' (Grigore 2007, 319–330).

(22) Partial reduplication

a. *hāl=o māl*
    '(mental) state and such' (NK. Duhok, Text 34: *Mirza Muhammad's Adventures*, §41)

b. *lat=ū pat*
    'torn and destroyed' (CK. Shaqlawa, Text 19: *A Ewe and a Wolf*, §17)

In many NENA dialects total reduplication involves adding the particle *ma* between reduplicated forms. An equivalent construction with the particle *mā(n)* occurs in Kurdish:

c. *xabuše ma xabuše*
    'apples and so forth'

d. *dūr mān dūr / dūr mā dūr*
    'surroundings, all around' (NK. Duhok, Text 34: *Mirza Muhammad's Adventures*, §6, §82)

4.2. Use of Questions

Questions can be used for various literary effects and engagement with the audience without expecting an answer, often to express a character's state of mind.

4.2.1. Rhetorical Questions

A statement can be put in the form of a question to prompt a debate, for example:

(23) ʾè,ʾ| k-imər, "ăla kùllən, de qumu!| ma ftàrta ᴬhawnᴬ?| xo là maṛəšə́nnawxun hēš layle?"|

'Yes,' he said. 'Anyway, come on wake up! Isn't breakfast here? Should I not have woken you up while it was still night?' (ChA. Duhok, Text 32: *Mirza Muhammad and the Forty Monsters*, §30)

(24) yaʿnī čūnko az žənə̀k=am| hīn mə bə čāvakī nērīnì əl mə ət-fəkərən?"|

Just because I am a woman, do you have a false belief in me (lit. You think of me through a negative eye? (NK. Zakho, Text 11: *The Bridge of Dalal*, §18).

4.2.2. Question in the Narrative

The narrator can highlight an event by introducing it in the form of a question, as if to refresh the audience's memory, for example:

(25) **mì k-iwə́ðwala ta Dălale?**| g-nabə́lwala kùdyum laxma=w mìyya.

What did he used to do for Dalale? He would bring her bread and water every day. (ChA. Duhok, Text 9: *The Bridge of Dalale*, §15)

(26) **bərāyē mazən čə̀ t̪-bēžt=ē?** ət̪-bēžt=ē, ʾna bərà!| bəlā àz avroka bə-mīnəm.ʾ|

What did the elder brother say to him? He said, 'No, brother! Let me stay home today.' (NK. Duhok, Text 30: *The Girl, her Stepmother, and the Old Witch*, §31)

The narrator of *The Bridge of Dalale* story in the Christian Neo-Aramaic of Zakho adopts this strategy several times to switch to one of the leading characters, i.e. the prince, putting him in the spotlight and giving prominence to his actions, for instance:

(27) ʾokey, ʾə́nnuhu b-zale=w ʾati=w šula palxi b-rəš jə̀sr,ˈ fa-**mà wədle ʾamír?**ˈ ḥatta ʾə́nnuhu ʾawedwa xa hădiya ṛabta ṭa ʾawwa muhàndəs,ˈ Tòma,ˈ mkarə̀mwale,ˈ **mà wədle biyu?**ˈ

OK, then people were coming and going, working on the bridge. So, **what did the prince do?** Instead of giving this architect Toma a huge gift, in order to honour him, **what did he do to him?** (He summoned him to his side and cut off his right hand.) (ChA. Zakho, Text 10: *The Bridge of Dalale*, §12–13)

4.2.3. Expression of Doubt

A question can describe a character's state of mind, as if they were prompting for help.

(28) mere **mà b-awðən?**ˈ ma t-ile bədraya hole mpàla.ˈ

'**What shall I do?**', he thought. 'Whatever he puts there, it falls down.' (ChA. Duhok, Text 9: *The Bridge of Dalale*, §2)

(29) žənəkē žī həzrā xo ḳər, '**az čə̀ b-ḳam?**ˈ čə nà-ḳam?ˈ kī-và bə-čəm?**ˈ az žənkaḳ=ā b tanèˈ ət vān čol=ū čīyà ṛā!ˈ dē bar=av kī-và čəm?**'ˈ

The woman thought, '**What should I do? Where can I go?** I'm a lonely woman in this wilderness, in these mountains! **Where can I go?**' (NK. Duhok, Text 17: *A Woman and a Leopard*, §4)

5.0. Repetition

Repetition is a common stylistic device of oral literature as well as a common storytelling technique. Not only individual words, phrases and clauses can be repeated, but also entire sentences and even whole episodes that encapsulate the main theme or a recurrent theme as the so-called *Leitsätze* (Pinault 1992: 21; see §8.1.). This section provides a brief typology of repetition found in the NENA and Kurdish texts with illustrative examples. Neo-Aramaic and Kurdish narrative discourse can seem highly repetitive. The particular function of recapitulation can vary from one case to the next, and is sometimes chiefly a matter of style. Some of these are also mentioned in the relevant sections, see Section 2.4 on tail-head recapitulation, Section 4.1.3. on symbolism, Section 7.1.1. on inverted word order and 7.2.1. on aspect. As a discourse strategy, repetition can be used to recapitulate, to keep track of major themes in the story, to give the speaker time to think, and/or to establish a bridging linkage between core events for the sake of event cohesion.

5.1. Thematisation

The successive occurrence of the same word, as illustrated in (1)–(2) below, can be characterised as an instance of thematisation, the development of a thematic unit around a core and highly topical constituent.

(1) nĭhàye,ˈ ṭămăʿuθət barnàša,ˈ xzi hàtxa=yla.ˈ yaʿni ʾawa kud yoma b-yawəllux trày lireˈ ʾu šwaqa labole qàysux.ˈ ʾe, ṭămăʿùθaˈ g-əbe, hənna, šaqəlwala xăzəntət hənna, ʾe.ˈ yaʿni ʾay ṭămàʿhum qaṭəllu,ˈ dàx k-əmrila.ˈ

In the end, **the greed** of mankind, see what it is like. This is to say, he gives you two coins every day and even lets you take some wood. Indeed, **greed**: he wanted to take the whole treasure. That is, it is **their own greed** that kills people, as they say. (ChA. Duhok, Text 15: *A Man and a Snake*, §7)

(2) bāb gala galak **ʾājə̀z** bītən.ǀ Sorā Čavšīn žī husā xo dīyằr ət-katən ǀ ʾalasās yā **ʾājə̀z**=a.ǀ xuškēt wē žī husā xo dīyār ət-kan ʾalasās yā **ʾājə̀z**=ən.ǀ

The father was very **upset**. Sora Chavshin pretended to be innocent, as if she was **upset**. Her sisters too pretended to be innocent, as if they were **upset**. (NK. Duhok, Text 26: *Dindik Hinar—A Girl Called Pomegranate Grain*, §146)

5.2. Stylistic Variation

The successive occurrence of the same word at the beginning of a sentence for stylistic variation is known as anaphora and at the end of a sentence as epiphora. Anaphora and epiphora can be combined, as in the follow case in Neo-Aramaic where the repetition seems to be a matter of style:

(3) qam-darilu gu day ʾàrxe.ǀ **kma d-qam**-taxnìle ǀ **là mətle**,ǀ **kma d-qam**-mazwerile **là mətle**.ǀ

They put him in that mill. **No matter how hard** they made him grind, **he did not die**. **No matter how hard** they made him spin the millstone, **he did not die**. (ChA. Enishke, Text 36: *Mar Giwargis*, §6)

5.3. Event Cohesion

Recapitulation can also serve as a bridge between constituents for event cohesion. In the following example from Kurdish, for instance, the adverbials are added successively and the verb is repeated to maintain event cohesion, thus conveying 'They went secretly in a group to the bishop'.

(4) *čūn ba jamā'àt,*ˈ *čūn ba dəzî̀,*ˈ *čūn=a kən maṭrằn.*ˈ
They went in a group, **they went** secretly, **they went** to the bishop. (CK. Shaqlawa, Text 38: *The Foul-Mouthed Priest*, §2)

It is common for the narrator to repeat the last word or phrase at the beginning of the next sentence for the sake of event cohesion. This type of reiteration is a general strategy to organise narrative discourse and connect clausal chains through so-called tail-head linkage (see §2.4.).

5.4. Foregrounding

A duplicate can be placed both at the beginning and at the end creating, as it were, a frame around particular clause(s), as the head and tail clause are the same. This type of recapitulation seems to be used to return to the foreground after having switched to background information. For example:

(5) *ʾəθwa xa ʾarya mṣíṭera wewa l-ṭùra.*ˈ *là qabəlwa čù barnašət zə̀lwale l-ṭura,*ˈ *maxewa qàyse*ˈ *ʾu ʾawəðwa xà məndi.*ˈ *hàr zə̀lwale,*ˈ *g-naxəθwale, k-ìxəlwale.*ˈ *là qabəlwa ču xa zawale.*ˈ
There was a lion who controlled a mountain. **He did not allow any humans to enter** the mountain to cut wood or

to do anything else. If someone went there, he would come down on them and eat them. **He did not allow anyone to go there.** (ChA. Duhok, *Man and Lion*, §2)

(6) *řā-bī čo got, 'tə-vēt hīn vē kəčê bə-dən mən.| mən nāv=ū dangē wē gò lē bī.| kəčakā yā pēškēš=ū barkatî=ya.| tə-vēt hīn vê kəčē bə-dən mən.'|*

He rose and went to Khajija's family and said, '**You must give me this daughter of yours in marriage.** I have heard about her fame. I have heard that she is a beautiful and gifted girl. **You must give me this daughter of yours in marriage.**' (NK. Khizava, Text 31: *Firyat and Khajija*, §6)

5.5. Synonymous Repetition

In the NENA texts it is not uncommon for the multilingual speaker to repeat a Kurdish loanword with its Arabic equivalent. One could analyse this type of synonymous repetition as an instance of codeswitching, inserting a word from among the multilingual repertoire into the Neo-Aramaic frame for the sake of clarification. In (7) below, for instance, the speaker first says *dargăvana* adapted from Kurdish *dargavān*, i.e. *dergevan* or دەرگەوان in Kurdish orthography, meaning 'gatekeeper, guard', then immediately repeats the same concept through the Arabic equivalent *ḥarəs*, i.e. حارس *ḥāris*, meaning 'guard, guardian'. The speaker does not do this only once, but several times in the story whenever he uses the word *dargăvana*.

(7) *man manxətle dargăvana, ᴬḥarəsᴬ, mən š-xòrta?'| làỳbe manxətle,| ʾàyka manxətle?|*

Who gets down **the gatekeeper, the guard**, from the poplar? He could not get him down. Where would he get him down? (ChA. Duhok, Text 32: *Mirza Muhammad and the Forty Monsters*, §193)

The NK Duhok example below reflects a similar phenomenon. The storyteller, a native speaker of Badini Northern Kurdish from Duhok, first uses the more prestigious Central Kurdish *dəḷnīya* 'sure, certain' then switches to the equivalent Northern Kurdish *pištřāst*.[25]

(8) bərāyē wē yē **dəḷniā̀=ya**,ˡ yē **pəštřā̀st=a**ˡ Fātmā sababī bo nà-bēžītənˡ

The brother was sure and certain that Fatma would not tell him the cause of her wounded hand (NK. Duhok, Text 30: *The Girl, Her Evil Stepmother and the Old Witch*, §69).

Similarly, in (9) the bilingual speaker from Zakho repeats the Arabic loanword *ʿarrāf* 'fortune teller' with its Kurdish equivalent *xēvzānk*.

(9) got=ē, 'ḥāl=ū masalēt ʿarāfī yēt xēxzānkī avà=naˡ ət-vēt az tà bə-kəm haykalē pərē dā.'ˡ

He said, 'The fortune-teller's saying is like this; I must put you into the construction of the bridge.' (NK. Zakho, Text 11: *The Bridge of Dalal*, §17)

---

[25] See Haig & Mustafa (2019) for a sociolinguist study of Bahdini Kurdish in Duhok.

6.0. Demonstratives, Indefinites and Deictic Particles

6.1. Indefinite Suffixes and Particles

Indefiniteness is expressed by the prenominal *xa* derived from the numeral 'one' in NENA, e.g. *xa malka* 'a certain king', and the suffix *-ak* derived from *yak* 'one' in both Northern and Central Kurdish varieties, e.g. *sag-ak* 'a certain dog'. Indefinite marking tends to be associated with specific nominals that have a prominent role in the discourse structure, especially when first introduced in the narrative, e.g.

(1) k-amər ʾətwa **xa malka** gu de màta.[|]
It is said there was **a king** in the village. (ChA. Shaqlawa, Text 5: *Zambilfrosh by W. Toma*, §2)

(2) got⸗ī zamānē xo⸗y **qašàk** ha-bū.[|] aw qaša zəmān⸗ī galak pìs bū.[|]
It was said that there once was a Christian priest. The priest was very foul-mouthed. (CK. Shaqlawa, Text 38: *The Foul-Mouthed Priest*, §1)

The indefinite suffix tends to be absent on nominals which have an incidental role in the discourse, cf. Neo-Aramaic *ʾida* 'hand' in (3) and Kurdish *musalaḥà* 'police car' in (4).

(3) **ʾida** waṛe l-adya ʾələt ṣŭpurta gòrīn.[|]
He stretched out **a hand** to the sparrow. (ChA. Shaqlawa, Text 12: *A 'Pious' Fox*, §18)

(4) *suwārī* **musalaḥà**⸗*yān kərd*⸗*ū lo Hawlērē.*ǀ
They put him into a **police car**, and headed towards Erbil.
(CK. Shaqlawa, Text 21: *A Man and His Dog*, §4)

6.2. Near Deixis Demonstratives

Near deixis demonstratives can be used anaphorically to refer to the main protagonist in the tale, in addition to the deictic function, i.e. pointing to referents in the extra-linguistic situation. The forms are given in Table 10. below.

Table 10. Near demonstrative pronouns in NENA and Kurdish

	NENA		NK.		CK.
	NOM	GEN	DIR	OBL	
sg.m.	ʾawwa	dawwa		vī	aw
sg.f.	ʾayya	dayya	av	vē	
pl.	ʾanna	danna		vān	(a)wān

As anaphora, the near deixis demonstratives forms are used for nominals whose referents are the centre of attention at a particular point in the discourse, for example *ʾăna* (<* *ʾanna*) in ChA. Shaqlawa:

(5) *ʾətwa trè malaye.*ǀ *ʾăna tre malàye,*ǀ *malayət xà mata*⸗*wənwa,*ǀ *xa məzgaft*⸗*u xa màta.*ǀ *ʾăna tre malàye*ǀ *xəzmətət dè məzgaft ʾudiwa*ǀ *gàwət*ǀ *masròxe*ǀ *qatət msalòye*⸗*w*ǀ *gu ḥdarət gu taziye*⸗*w məndyàne.*ǀ

There were two mullahs. **These** two mullahs were mullahs serving the same village, the same mosque and the same village. **These** two mullahs served the mosque by calling to prayer, attending funerals and so on. (ChA. Shaqlawa, Text 28: *Two Mullahs*, §2–3)

(6) āwān žī nà-vīyāt bə-də=yē,ˈ dīyānatā wān nà ēk̬ bī.ˈ **av** lə Bahnīnē bəsəlmằn bī.ˈ **avē** dītərē —nə̀-zānəm—,ˈ ījā ān ān masīhī̀ bīˈ ān zaradaštī̀ bī.ˈ

They did not want to give her to him in marriage, since their religion was not the same. **The one** from Bahnīn was Muslim. As for **the other one**—I do not know [for sure]—he was either Christian or Zoroastrian. (NK. Khizava, Text 31: *Firyat and Khajija*, §7).

In CK. Shaqlawa the forms singular *aw* and plural *(a)wān* are used for both near and far demonstrative, thus having a similar function, as shown in (7) below, and contrasting with NK. *av* (near deixis) and *aw* (far deixis).

(7) got=ī zamānē xo=y qašàk ha-būˈ **aw qaša** zəmān=ī galak pìs bū.ˈ

It was said that there once was a Christian priest. **This/that priest** was very foul-mouthed. (CK. Shaqlawa, Text 38: *The Foul-Mouthed Priest*, §1)

6.3. Zero Anaphora

Throughout the Kurdish and Neo-Aramaic the main characters of the story and thus highly topical arguments are often reduced to zero anaphora, as they are presupposed to be easily retrieved from the context. The majority of subject referents in the narratives, especially in dialogues, are only marked on the verb via person indexes and agreement, and thus verbal person marking is the core morphological device to construct referential coherence. This reflects universal bias against lexical NPs in A (transitive subject) function (Du Bois 1987), and their low referential density (Bickel 2003). The verb with its generally obligatory subject inflection constitutes the core around which the discourse is organised, while the other arguments can be considered more or less optional.

The following passage from *A Girl Called Pomegranate Grain* narrated in the Kurdish dialect of Duhok contains a dialogue between an evil stepmother and her daughter, which illustrates the use of zero anaphora. The switch in referents, i.e. the stepmother and the daughter, is generally not indicated and zero anaphora are used instead. Only once the ambiguous independent pronoun *aw* is used in combination with the additive marker *ži*, but the pronoun itself is ambiguous.

(8) damē dā dad=a kùr̄ē xo| žənbābē dastē kəčā xo gə̀rt got=ē,| 'həstoyē ta bə-škētə̀n!| mā ava šūl bū tà ḳərī?| mā ava ta čə̀ bə sarē ma īnā!| mā ava čə darmāna tà ināy?| **gūt=a** kəčā xo yā žə r̄ə̀st r̄ā.| **gūt=ē**, 'ava har àw=a awē ta š| Hənār̄ə̀ sətāndī.'| **gūt=ē**, 'na na ava na àw=a!'| **gūt=ē**, 'balē bāwar ḳa àw=a'| **gūt=ē**, 'awa čə̀ bū?'|—hāšārē wa—**gūt=ē**, 'pīsātī bū.'| aw ži galà gala ʾājəz bū.| har tə wē damī dā damē wa **gotī=ē**| wakī gēžbūnaḳə̀ bū čēk **bū**| ū hə̀l əf ʾardī **kàt**.|

When he gave the medicine to his son, the stepmother grabbed her daughter's hand and said, 'May your bones be broken! What have you done? Why did you do this to us? What is this medicine that you've brought?' **She said** these words to her real daughter. **She (i.e. the daughter) said**, 'This is exactly the one you took from Hinar.' **She (i.e. the stepmother) said**, 'No, this is not the one!' **She (i.e. the daughter) said**, 'Yes, believe me this is the one!' **She (i.e.**

the daughter) said, 'What was that then?'—May it be far from you the audience—**She (i.e. the stepmother) said**, 'It was animal's dirt.' Then **she** (i.e. the daughter) got very troubled. As soon as **she** (i.e. stepmother) **said** those words, **she** (i.e. her daughter) **experienced** some dizziness and **fell** to the ground. (NK. Duhok, Text 26: *Dindik Hinar—A Girl Called Pomegranate Grain*, §63-64)

The same holds for the following dialogue between a father (the king) and his son (the prince) from the Christian Neo-Aramaic dialect of Shaqlawa, where the narrative verb is expressed by means of ʾamər lit. 'he says' and the only indication of a switch, e.g.

(9) har yeksar mən tằ ṛa wəre,ǀ babu tele b-qàmu.ǀ mən rằw bitáye=le.ǀ *ʾamər*: yà babi,ǀ ʾaxtsi janux gu fắhì ma=wǀ ʾadya mutwe=wət.ǀ *ʾamər*: mà bəxdare=wət?ǀ *ʾamər*: madam baṛ naša gənsakŭ la mayù te=le,ǀ tsə̀ ṭəma lət gu de dùnye.ǀ xaye lə̀t gawaw.ǀ *ʾamər*: ya brònìǀ qamà ʾatxa səhla lux?ǀ mdiwə̀ne?ǀ mà =ile?ǀ brònìǀ *ʾamər*: ʾitùǀ xur ʾàta.ǀ kursìyi čyawəna qàtux.ǀ malka k-udənux l-dùki.ǀ ʾàtxa k-udən qatux,ǀ ʾàtxa k-udən qatux.ǀ *ʾamər*:ǀ kŭle be fàyde=na ʾăna.ǀ là g-nafʿili.ǀ *ʾamər*: matənux bàxta,ǀ mustàqbal.ǀ yàle k-awelux.ǀ gu yàle k-paṣxət,ǀ gu bèta k-paṣxət.ǀ

The moment he entered through the door, his father came to meet him. He was coming back from hunting. **He said**, 'Father, you consider yourself to be a wise person.' **He (the king) said**, 'What are you wondering about?' **He said**, 'Since all the human race is mortal, this world has no longer any taste. There is no life in it.' **He (the king) said**, 'My son, why has this feeling come over you? Has he gone mad? Or what?' 'My son,' **he said**, 'sit and look here. I shall give my throne to you. I shall make you a king in my place. I shall do such and such things for you.' **He said**, 'These things are all without benefit. They are no use'. **He (the king) said**, 'I shall bring you a woman and a future. You will have children. You will have joy in your children. You will have pleasure in a family.' (ChA. Shaqlawa, Text 4: *Zambilfrosh* by A. Sher, §12-15)

6.4. Deictic Particles and Copulas

The Neo-Aramaic dialects—as well as the *qəltu*-Arabic dialects of the region— have developed various presentative copulas out of presentative particles and/or deictic elements combined with the (pronominal) copula. The third person singular forms of such presentative copulas can, in turn, further grammaticalize into invariant particles. In the Neo-Aramaic texts in our collection, such presentative copulas can be used to express mirativity, for example in (10) below, and are often combined with verbs of perception either before the verb, as shown in (11), or after it, as shown in (12). The presentative copula and its related particles can thus be used by the narrator for the purpose of suspense sometimes through their identification with the surprise of the unsuspecting character, adding a sense of anticipation at crucial moments in the story.

(10) *qam-šarela mən ʿaqə̀le,ˈ* **wela trə̀sta.**ˈ
 He untied it from its bandages and **look, it has** healed! (JA. Duhok, Text 16: *A Man and a Wolf*, §21)

(11) **wele k**-xaze b-ʾaynət ʾə̀nna,ˈ ʾaynət kàlbaˈ mbalboṣe gawət kèpa
(So he went to tap the rock with his hand) and **look,** he saw the dog's eyes glinting under the rock (ChA. Duhok, Text 18: *A Dog, a Ewe and a Wolf,* §12)

(12) xəre ʾ**ila** xa ʾaqə̀rwaˈ hola bənxata kùmta,ˈ ʾəš-malka dədnasàle.
He looked and—**lo and behold!**—a scorpion was coming down—black—onto the king to bite him. (ChA. Duhok, Text 32: *Mirza Muhammad and the Forty Monsters,* §124)

In Christian Neo-Aramaic dialect of Shaqlawa, the deictic copula based on *wəl-* or *wăl-*, targeting the addressee in a dialogue, can express impatience and irritation:

(13) **wə̀lux** yəmu!ˈ bratət mà ʾəl ʾurxət ʾalaha?ˈ
Come on, my son! What girl for God's sake?! (ChA. Shaqlawa, Text 23: *The Poor Girl and her Horse,* §19)

In Kurdish tales the presentative particles *ā*, and *ahā* are used to express mirativity. They convey the speaker's surprise upon experiencing an unexpected situation. In the tales these particles also serve as an attention-drawing strategy.

(14) barē xo dat꞊ē wērī galakā bē-sar-ū-bàr꞊a.ˈ **ahā**, bərāyak̀ī ṯ-bīnītən,ˈ sar ēk̲ šə wān taxtā yē nəvəstī꞊ya.ˈ
She looked around the cave and saw that it was very messy. **Lo**, she saw a brother sleeping on one of the beds. (NK. Duhok, Text 30: *The Girl, her Evil Stepmother and the Old Witch,* §14)

(15) bərāyē mazə̀n jo ṭ-kavītən.| əṭ-bēžt=ē, 'ā ava čan təštakī sàyr=a čē boy!|

The eldest brother bludgeoned his way through his brothers and said to them, '**Oh, what has been happening here is indeed surprising!**' (NK. Duhok, Text 30: *The Girl, her Evil Stepmother and the Old Witch*, §19)

7.0. Syntactic Stylistics

7.1. Word Order

7.1.1. Repetition and Inversion

As a stylistic device, an entire clause or part of the clause can be repeated in the reverse order. One of its effects is to draw attention to a certain event in the narrative and establish event cohesion with the preceding clause through tail-head linkage.[26]

(1) *bắle šqulle nắra dìdox!| nắra dìdox šqùlle,| g-emər, mxìle go reši,| kmà ʾibox!| ʾu tùrre reši bət nắra.|*
'But **take your axe! Take your axe**,' he says, 'and hit my head with it as hard as you can. And crack my head with the axe.' (JA. Duhok, Text 16: *A Man and a Wolf*, §17)

(2) *fa-mà wədle ʾamír?| ʾămír mà wədle?| ʾamər...|*
So, **what did the prince do? What did the prince do?** He said... (ChA. Zakho, Text 10: *The Bridge of Dalale*, §19)

---

[26] See §2.4.

(3) **babay màθle.** babət Mərzá Mḥä́mad=u ʾAḥmád Čä́läbi=w Mḥämad Čä́läbi, **məθle bàbay.** malka **màθle.**
   Their father died. The father of Mirza Muhammad, Ahmad Chalabi and Muhammad Chalabi—**their father died.** The king **died.** (ChA. Harmashe, Text 33: *Mirza*, §17)

(4) šīr=o matāḷēt xo ř̀ā-t-kan=o t-hēn=a šařē xo t-kàn. tə-hēn=a šař̃ı ət-kan=o šařē xo t-kàn=o. ... ət wī šař̃ı dā ... xə̀škēt wī ... **t-ēn=a koštə̀n, t-ēn=a koštə̀n xə̀škēt wī.** hatā də-zəvřət=a qasrè̃ aw yē dargàhē pəštē řā čoyn.
   They picked up their swords and shields and went (lit. came) to fight. They went and fought. They fought their fight. In that battle **his sisters were killed. His sisters were killed.** By the time he came back to the palace, the ones from the back gate had gone away. (NK. Duhok, Text 34: *Mirza Muhammad's Adventures*, §78-79)

7.1.2. Word Order in Kurdish

In Kurdish the word order is by default SOV. In the following example, the direct object moves from its default position to the post-verbal slot to create a link with the following relative clause of which it is the head:

(5) kāfərà̃ gərt **av payxambara=w,** awē lə sīyàrē Dəndəlī=ya.
   The villains waylaid **the prophet,** the one who was riding Dindil. (NK. Dure, Text 37: *The Prophet's Horse*, §6)

A change in the position of O relative to S is triggered by factors such as topicalisation. In the following example, the SOV order is observed in the first clause. In the second clause though, the order changes to OSV due to the topicalisation of the direct object, marked by the additive particle *žī*.

(6) *tu dē īšāra darmānì bēžī=ya ma| ʾardižī tē bū mà dastnīšān ḳay|*
You shall tell us about the whereabouts of the medicine. In addition, you shall show us the exact place in which you have hidden the medicine. (NK. Duhok, Text26: *Dindik Hinar—A Girl Called Pomegranate Grain*, §106)

7.1.3. Word Order in NENA

In the majority of NENA dialects of northwestern Iraq and southeastern Turkey,[27] word order is relatively more flexible and more sensitive to pragmatics than word order in Kurdish. The clause-initial slot or left periphery is generally used for topicalisation. Thus, the most frequent position of independent personal pronouns is clause-initial, which coincides with their high topicality. In (7) below, however, rather than occurring in its more frequent clause-initial position, the independent personal pronoun *ʾana* is postposed to clause-final position, as a stylistic variant to show event cohesion with the preceding and draw the listener's attention to it.

(7) *ʾàmər:| ʾana măḥammàd=iwən.| ʾe gət mare măḥammád=iwən, kəmu ptəxle| ṣŭpurta ʿərə̀qla.| ʾawhù!| ʾana qa mà məri măḥammadi?| hawənwa mira járjəs=iwən ʾàna...|*
He said, 'I am Muḥammad.' When he said, 'I am Muḥammad', he opened his mouth and the sparrow fled away. 'Oh! Why did I say I was Muḥammad? If I only had

---

[27] See Noorlander and Molin (2022) for a comparison of word order typology in NENA dialects.

said I was George...' (ChA. Shaqlawa, Text 12: *A 'Pious' Fox*, §37)

Since the most common order is topic-comment, SVO order is characteristic of these NENA dialects. There is, however, a tendency for discourse-new subjects to follow the predicate, especially in thetic sentences, e.g.

(8) *qəmle θele xà qala.| mère,|*
'Then a voice came and said,' (ChA. Duhok, Text 9: *The Bridge of Dalale*, §3)

In NENA dialects where indefinite objects are generally postverbal, preverbal position, i.e. OV, is an optional stylistic variant of definite object placement. In the example below, for instance, the object *xanjart ʾaqərwa* 'the dagger of the scorpion' is placed before the verb *gəm-garəšle*, which takes the L-suffix *-le* and indexes the object. Fronting as such serves to provide event cohesion with the preceding and draws attention to the fronted object.

(9) *ham ʾawa gəm-mapə̀qle xanjar diye.| malka gəm-yawəlle ṭàleḥ,| ʾu xanjart ʾaqərwa gəm-garə̀šle.| ʾaqərwa npəlla tàma məθta.|*
So he drew his dagger. The king gave it to him and he pulled off **the dagger of the scorpion**. The scorpion fell down dead right there. (ChA. Duhok, Text 32: *Mirza Muhammad and the Forty Monsters*, §216)

There is a far stronger tendency for OV word order in the Christian Neo-Aramaic dialect of Shaqlawa (NE Iraq), however, which converges with the word order in the local Kurdish variety. Even discourse-new arguments, such as indefinite objects and newly introduced protagonists in the story, will tend to be placed before the predicate, e.g.

(10) *m-xúška qădamta qə̀mle.*ˈ **xa karta** *wədwale qàtu.*ˈ *ṭlaha qupyàta=w*ˈ **xa ʾawa=š** *qa de baxta xṣụ̀ṣi wədwale.*ˈ

He woke up early next morning. He made **a load of baskets** for himself. He made **three baskets and a special mat for the woman.** (ChA. Shaqlawa, Text 5: *Zambilfrosh* by W. Toma, §18)

7.2. Verbal Syntax

7.2.1. The Narrative Function of Verb forms

As will be seen in this section, the following table shows the convergence between NENA and Kurdish in the functions the verb forms express. The 3sg. form of the verb 'to go' in Kurdish and the verb 'to take' in NENA has been given for ease of comparison:

Table 11. Main discourse functions of verbal forms in Kurdish and NENA

	NK	CK	NENA	Function
Present	ət-čə-t	a-čē-t	k-šaqəl or y-šaqəl	Narrative present
Past Perfective	čū	čū	šqəlle	Narrative past
			qam-šaqəlle	Transitive narrative past (NENA only)
Present Perfect	čūy	čū-a	šqíla=yle	Evidential (Kurdish only); Anterior
Imperative	hař-a	bə-řo	šqūl	Narrative imperative (NENA only)

7.2.2. Narrative Present

Narrative (or historical) present is the use of present tense forms to refer to past events. It is a common device in oral narratives, and its use is linked with making past events vivid and increasing the dramatic impact of the story (Schiffrin 1981). The narrative present has the same referential function in Kurdish and Aramaic narratives. In so doing, it can alternate with the past tense, mainly to foreground special events with respect to other events. In the following example from Neo-Aramaic, for instance, a surprise triggers the use of present tense forms:

(11) nxə̀tle ʾəl darta.| ʾila xàze| darga bằra;| **hole kəlya** qam-tằra,|
yaʿni ḥàrəs.| **hole kəlya**=w **hole ṭwìʾa.**|

He went down into the garden. Look! He **saw** (lit. he sees) a front door; he **was** (lit. is) **standing** at the gate, I mean, a guard. He **was** (lit. is) **standing** though asleep. (ChA. Duhok, Text 32: *Mirza Muhammad and the Forty Monsters*, §122)

In the Kurdish excerpt below, the narrative present expresses new information. In other words, it foregrounds the events expressed earlier by the narrative past:

(12) Mīrzằ Məhamadī šīr=ū matāḷēt xo **īnān=a darē.**| o əš ... pīčakē š wān **dīr kat**=o lə wārā har **hằt**=o čo.| **dīt** du sề sīyārakē t-ēn=o.| yē b-sar **t-ền.**|

Mirza Muhammad **took out** his sword and shield. He **went some distance** from them and kept walking around (lit. He **came** and **went**) there. He **saw** that two or three riders came (lit. come). They **came** (lit. come) to him. (NK. Duhok, Text 34: *Mirza Muhammad's Adventures*, §17-18)

In NENA, the indicative present form, i.e. *k-šaqəl* or *y-šaqəl*, and occasionally also the unmarked form, i.e. *šaqəl*, can be used instead of the past perfective, i.e. *šqəlle* and *qam-šaqəlle*, to express the narrative past (Khan 2009, 171–172). This is especially common with the reporting or narrative verb 'to say', e.g. *'amər*, *k-imər* or *y-amər* for 'he said', where generally the form that would express the imperfective present in conversational speech is used in the narrative to denote a punctual event completed in the past.

Likewise, the narrative present in Kurdish is common with reporting and narrative verbs. The use of the narrative present is excluded from subordinate clauses, which typically express background events.

7.2.3. Narrative Imperative

The so-called Narrative Imperative is only attested in the NENA texts of the present collection. The narrator, as it were, commands the character in the story and typically adopts this technique with verbs of motion (Khan 2009, 172).[28] This notwithstanding, verbs of motion are also the more frequent ones to occur in the imperative in general.

---

[28] The narrative imperative also occurs in Arabic folktales, e.g. Talmon (2001, 224–225).

(13) *psèle*| *psù,*| *psù,*| *psù,*| *psù,*| *psù,*| *psù!*|
   He went off. Off you go and on and on and on! (ChA. Shaqlawa, Text 4: *Zambilfrosh by A. Sher*, §20)

7.2.4. Evidentiality

In the Kurdish dialect of Shaqlawa, the perfect can also express a habitual situation in the past which the speaker knows about through hearsay, i.e. the speaker has not witnessed the event themselves, for example:

(14) *aw jā xarkakà **dā-ništī=na**.| šaw=īš dərȇž **būa**.| ba tāybatī šaw-ē hāwĭn-ȃn.| **dā-ništī=na** hatā dawrī saʿȃt da=ū yāzday.| la īš=ū kārī **hātī=na-wabàw**| aw jā sawzà=w mīwà=w masalan| qaysī=ū məšməša=w aw xwārnȃnay ka **ha-būa**.| **dȃ=yān-nāy-aw** haqāyat=yān gȇřāy=n-awa*| *hatā řoyīštī̀=ya.*|
   Back then, people **would sit together**. The nights **were** long. They **would sit around**, especially during summer nights until 10 p.m., 11 p.m. People **would come back** home from their daily work. It **was** the custom that vegetables and fruit, such as dried apricot, apricot, and such **would be put** in front of the guests while they **would narrate** the tales until they **would leave** the party. (CK. Shaqlawa, Text 19: *A Ewe and a Wolf*, §6)

This evidential function of the perfect is also attested in NENA (Khan 2012, 2020) and other languages in the region such as Turkish, Persian and West Armenian (e.g. Lazrad 1999).

7.2.5. Repetition of Motion Verbs

Individual motion verbs can be repeated to indicate that the action denoted by the verb reiterated or continued for some time.

(15) ga ʾərta **zəle=w zəle=w zəle=w**, qam-šawə̀ra ga ʾərta xandaq.|
Once more he **kept going** (lit. he went and went and went) and then he jumped over the trench again (ChA. Harmashe, Text 33: *Mirza*, §14)

(16) ū **hāt=ū hāt=ū** mantaqa hatā hātī kalhā šằbānīyē.|
He **kept coming** (lit. he came and he came) until he arrived at the gate of the Shabani citadel. (NK. Khizava, Text 7: *Zanbilfirosh—The Basket Seller*, §16)

The following examples with the repetition of the motion verb have the same durative function.

(17) **dı̀v dā čītən** bərāyē wē.| **dīv dā ṭ-čī, dīv dā ṭ-čī, dīv dā ṭ-čī**, barē xo dat=ē p̂īražənàḳ ā lə wērē.|
Her brother followed her. He **kept following her** all the way and noticed that an old woman was there. (NK. Duhok, Text 30: *The Girl, her Evil Stepmother and the Old Witch*, §70–71)

(18) aw p̂īražə̀na čū=a žorē,| **har dar-nà-hāt**| **har dar-nà-hāt**.| zor=ī pē čừ.|
'The old woman went inside. **She did not come out of the house for a while** (lit. She did not come out; she did not come out.) (CK. Shaqlawa, Text 38: *The Foul-Mouthed Priest*, §8)

7.2.6. Negation of the Predicate

Both Neo-Aramaic and Kurdish make use of a construction that conjoins an affirmative and negative polarity of the same predicate, literally meaning 'he did and did not do X'. The context in which this idiom is generally used is that of a failed attempt or uncertain outcome.[29]

In Kurdish this idiom indicates incomplete action equivalent to English *not yet*, as in the following case:

(19) *nānē xo ḵar ḵə̀r ḵar na-ḵər| sībarà̱ḵ꞊ā gala galak꞊ā ṃazən p̂əž dīyār ḵər|*

She had not completely cut the bread into pieces yet (lit. **she cut her bread into pieces; she did not cut her bread into pieces**), when a very big shadow appeared from behind. (NK. Duhok, Text 17: *A Woman and a Leopard*, §8)

In NENA, the same idiom expresses an indefinite series of events without delivering the desired results,[30] for example:

(20) *mà θele| ʾu là θele| là wədla b-xabreḥ.|*

Whatever happened (lit. **what came and did not come**), she did not listen to him. (ChA. Duhok, Text 32: *Mirza Muhammad and the Forty Monsters*, §72)

This feature also occurs in narratives recorded in the Neo-Aramaic dialects of Ṭur ʿAbdin (e.g. Jastrow and Talay 2019, 24).

---

[29] This syntagm also occurs in Arabic where it expresses dilemma (Talmon 2001, 222).

[30] This function of a similar construction is a typical trait of the languages of the Balkans (Joseph 1992).

7.2.7. Modal Particle *de*

Both Kurdish and Neo-Aramaic can use the particle *dā, da, de* or *də* to intensify an imperative verb, for example:

(21) *b-kèpux,ˈ də sì!*
As you wish, go **then**! (ChA. Duhok, Text 18: *A Dog, a Ewe and a Wolf*, §5)

(22) *dằ řa-bin žə vē rē bə-čin!ˈ*
Let us rise and leave this place! (NK. Duhok, Text 34: *Mirza Muhammad's Adventures*, §30)

8.0. Notes on Storytelling Techniques[31]

8.1. Repetition as Storytelling

Thus far we have observed that recapitulation is both a stylistic device and a discourse strategy. Repetition can also be a storytelling technique, for instance to create a pattern within the tale, as in a repetitive tale like the *The Three Little Pigs*. Consider for instance the Mirza story in the Christian Neo-Aramaic dialect of Harmashe (Text 33). Once upon a time there were three princes and three princesses. This already establishes a base for the pattern that the narrator will develop in his short tale. Mirza, the youngest of the princes, claims the three princesses for himself and his brothers by meeting the challenge set forth by their father, the king. The overall plot of the story is thus based on the reiteration of the same event for each princess, with only slight variation, such as the colour of Mirza Muhammad's horse (black,

---

[31] On thematic patterning, see Molin, Chapter 2, this volume.

white, red) and the fact that Mirza, the youngest brother, gets to marry the youngest princess.

Repetition, however, can also serve to designate objects or characters which appear insignificant when first mentioned but reappear frequently and or intrude suddenly in the narrative (Pinault 1992: 16). To illustrate, in the Kurdish Mirza tale (Text 34), Gulizar, Mirza Muhammad's wife, has beautiful golden hair. The old woman who hosts Mirza Muhammad's family, advices Gulizar to tie her hair strands, which fall out while taking a bath in the river, to a stick. The recurring statements about her hair create a background for its later significance in the tale, where the rain washes away Gulizar's hair strands to a lake in a neighbouring region, and the hair strands make the lake golden. Upon seeing the golden hair strands, the sultan of that region orders the owner of the hair to be found in order to marry her to his son. This triggers later events in the narrative, including the sultan's men attacking the old woman's castle, Gulizar's abduction by sultan's men, Mirza Muhammad's bid to bring back his wife, who has been married to the sultan's son, etc.

Another example comes from the Mirza epic narrated in the Christian Neo-Aramaic dialect of Duhok (Text 32). Every time Mirza killed a monster, he took their ears and put them in his pocket. At first, this recurring event seems random and insignificant, but later it turns out that this is the one piece of evidence he could show to the king as well as his brothers to prove that he was the one who had killed them and saved everyone.

The principle of *Leitworstil*, i.e. intentional repetition of a core word or word root key to unlock the meaning of the story, which has been applied in Biblical studies, can also be applied to other narratives such as *The Arabian Nights* (Pinault 1992: 18). By extension, the principle of *Leitsätze* involves the repetition of entire phrases, clauses or sentences for a similar purpose (Pinault ibid. 21). In introducing the Mirza story, the narrator announces he will tell a story from the time when people used to be *mar ġirətta*,[32] where *mar* goes back to the construct state of the Aramaic word *mare* 'master, owner' and *ġirətta* to Arabic غيرة *ġayra* from the root *ġyr* 'to be jealous'. The phrase *mar ġirətta* can be rendered as 'possessor of zeal', which captures the hero prototype. The hero is brave, virtuous, fearless, and devoted to the cause. The phrase *mar ġirətta* recurs with respect to Mirza and provides the rationale for his actions. He is not simply a hero who is powerful and clever enough to overcome all challenges, but he also acts with dignity. For instance, carrying out his father's last wishes was a matter of honour. When it was his turn to keep watch, there was no more fire and he could not get the fire started again. He was afraid to wake his brothers and asked them for help, as this would make him, the youngest, come across as the weakling. At the same time, when he wanted to take the fire from the monsters' cave, his dignity did not allow him to steal the fire stealthily, since stealing is wrong. He also did not want to leave the old woman, the goddess Time, tied up, but intended to untie her as soon as he got the fire, as this would not be honourable etc. etc. His heroic qualities are a recurring theme and the repetition of the word *ġirətta* thus epitomises this.

---

[32] The cultural significance of this term was pointed out to me by Lourd Hanna.

8.2. Dramatic Visualisation

Dramatic visualisation is one of the devices used in folktales through which an object or a character is described in detail in order to make the scene 'visual' and tangible to the audience (cf. Pinault 1992, 25–29), for example:

(1) *barē xo dat=ê.| barē xo dat=ē čə̀ t̯-bīnītən?| p̂īražənàk̯=a.| pəštā wē yā xằr.| dəfnā wē yā mazə̀n.| xəzēmak̯ ət dəfnā wē dằ=ya,| kū həndī təblak̯ā mərūvı̂ tēdā=ya.| həndī təblakā mərovī yā va-k̯arī̀=ya xəzēm.| ū gala galak yā kərèt=a.| yā za῾îf=a.| nūkēt wē dərễž=ən.|*

She looked around. She looked around; what did she see? There was an old woman there. She was a hunchback. Her nose was big. A nose-ring was on her nose, on which there were some human fingers. The nose-ring was the size of a human finger. She was very ugly. She was very thin. Her fingernails were long. (NK. Duhok, Text 30: *The Girl, her Evil Stepmother and the Old Witch*, §51)

9.0. Conclusion

In this chapter we have presented an overview of the common features of the oral narrative style found in the texts in this collection, the main ones listed in Table 12. below. Our primary aim has been to show that this collection of Kurdish and Neo-Aramaic narratives proves a fruitful starting point for further investigation of the convergence between the languages not only in terms of shared linguistic structures, but also in terms of common traits of oral narratives, including stylistic devices, discourse strategies and storytelling techniques. Some of these features we have seen are common to many other communities in the world, such as the opening formulas, some of which are paralleled by introductory formulas in the Balkans, the Caucasus and beyond. A number of features, such as repetition, the use of fillers and sound symbolism can be considered typical of oral narratives in general. Tail-head linkage—for instance, an areal pragmatic feature of New Guinea (de Vries 2005)—may be a more common trait of oral literature throughout the world, e.g. it is also found in Amazonian languages (Guillaume 2011). Other features tend to group Kurdish and Neo-Aramaic with immediately neighbouring languages such as Arabic, Azeri and Armenian. Some of these are typical of Semitic oral traditions, such as the use of the verb 'to rise' in discourse linkage, which spread into the Kurdish narrative style. Many fillers, idioms and phrases ultimately come from Arabic. The concluding formula involving the three apples is a typical trait of Iraqi Arabic narratives, but also occurs in Kurdish, Aramaic, Azeri and Armenian.

Table 12. Overview of some shared narrative hallmarks

	Feature	Section
Formulas	There was there was not	§1.1.1.
	There was none greater than God	§1.1.4.
	Impersonal use of 'to say'	§1.1.5.
	Blessing of parents	§1.1.6.
	It is finished	§1.2.1.
	I came back from there	§1.2.2.
	They gave me nothing	§1.2.2.
	They gave me three apples	§1.2.2.
Repetition	Recapitulation and tail-head linkage	§2.4.
	Repetition and inversion	§7.1.
	Repeated motion	§7.2.5.
Sound symbolism	Reduplication in onomatopoeia	§4.1.5
	m-Reduplication	§4.1.5
Discourse markers	The verb 'to rise'	§2.1.
	Additive particles *ži* and *=š*	§2.2.
	ʾe / a 'yes'	§3.2.
	yaʿni 'it means'	§3.2.
	wallā 'by God'	§3.2.
Verbal syntax	Narrative Present	§7.2.2.
	Narrative Imperative	§7.2.4.
	Modal particle *de/ dā*	§7.2.7.
	V not-V	§7.2.6.
	Evidentiality	§7.2.4.

GLOSSED TEXTS

CHRISTIAN ARAMAIC OF DURE
TEXT 8: §1–9

Geoffrey Khan

Speaker: Dawid Adam

Audio: https://nena.ames.cam.ac.uk/audio/231/

(1) gu   Zàxo| bnaya   wɛ-wa   xa   gə̀šra,|
    in   Zakho build.INF COP.3PL-PST one   bridge

In Zakho, they were building a bridge.

gəšra   y-amr-əx-le   gəšr-ət   Dalàle,| b-zon-ət
bridge   IND-say-1PL-O.3SG.M bridge-of   Dalale   in-time-of

ʿAbbasìye.| kəmət   ban-í-wa-le   ta-t   qaṭər-∅-wa
Abbasids   how.much   build-3PL-PST-O.3SG.M   to-SBR   arch-3SG.M-PST

We call the bridge the bridge of Dalale. [This was] in the time of the Abbasids. However much they built the bridge in order for its arch to be completed,

ʾo   gə̀sra,| là   qaṭər-∅-wa.| yaʿni   la
that.M   bridge   NEG   arch-3SG.M-PST   it.means   NEG

maxe-∅-wa   l-ġðàðe.|
hit-3SG.M-PST   to-each.other

its arch was not completed, it was not put together.

(2) | xa | yòma | ʾo | gòra, | ʾàġa, | xze-le
    | one | day | that.M | chief | agha | see.PFV-3SG.M

b-xə̀lm-e
in-dream-his

One day, the chief, the agha, saw in his dream

ʾaw | zàngīn=we-wa, | xɛlàn-a. | ʾíθ-wa-le | šawwà
he | rich=COP.3SG.M-PST | powerful-SG.M | EXIST-PST-3SG.M | seven

ʾarxaθa, | ʾíθ-wa-le | šawwà | kalaθa. | ʾíθ-wa-le
mills | EXIST-PST-3SG.M | seven | daughters.in.law | EXIST-PST-3SG.M

šawwà | susyaθa.
seven | mares

that he was rich and powerful. He had seven water mills. He had seven daughters-in-law. He had seven mares.

malaxa | mər-e | ʾəll-e | dìye, | 'mən | kul | xa
angel | say.PFV-3SG.M | to-him | OBL.3SG.M | from | every | one

mən | dànna | lazəm | xa | mbàṭl-ət.
from | OBL.these | necessary | one | eliminate-2SG.M

An angel said to him (in the dream), 'You must get rid of one of each of these.

mən | kalaθ-ux | ða | kalθ-ux | qàṭl-ət.
from | daughters.in.law-your | one.F | daughter.in.law-your | kill-2SG.M

mən | susăwaθ-ux | xa | susta | qàṭl-ət.
from | mares-your | one | mare | kill-2SG.M

mən | ʾarxaθ-ux | xa | ʾarxe | màkl-ət.'
from | mills-your | one | mill | stop-2SG.M

You should kill one of your daughters-in-law. You should kill one of your mares. You should stop one of your water-mills.'

(3) 'anna malaxa mər-e 'əll-e diye ta
these angel say.PFV-3SG.M to-him OBL.3SG.M to

ṯ-awə̀d-∅-la| ta-t 'o gə̀šra| maxe-∅ l-ġðàðe,|
SBR-do-3SG.M-O.3PL to-SBR that.M bridge hit-3SG.M to-each.other

qàṭər-∅.|
arch-3SG.M

The angel told him to do these things, so that the bridge would come together and its arch would be completed.

mara 'o gə̀šra| b-šə̀nne,| b-šə̀nne,| šurye-la
say.INF that.M bridge for-years for-years begin.PFV-3PL

bnaya ta-t maṭe-∅ l-ġðàðe,|
build.INF to-SBR reach-3SG.M to-each.other

lεle mə̀ṣy-a.|
NEG.COP.3SG.M be.able.PTCP-SG.M

Indeed, they had started building the bridge (and had been working on it) for years and years in order for it to come together, but it could not (be completed).

(4) qìm-ε=le| xa 'arxe
rise.PTCP-SG.M=COP.3SG.M one mill

mbùṭl-ə-l-la.| 'u xa mən susyaθ-e
stop.PTCP-SG.M=COP.3SG.M-O.3SG.F and one from mares-his

qṭìl-ə-l-la.| 'u Dalàle,| kalθ-e
kill.PTCP-SG.M=COP.3SG.M-O.3SG.F and Dalale daughter.in.law-his

diye zur-ta šəmm-a Dalàle-we-wa,|
OBL.3SG.M small-SG.F name-her Dalale=COP.3SG.M-PST

He went and stopped a water-mill and killed one of his mares. Now, Dalale—his youngest daughter-in-law was called Dalale—

ʾɛ	Dalàle	qím-ɛ=le	mšùdr-a	mənn-a
that.F	Dalale	rise.PTCP-SG.M=COP.3SG.M	send-PTCP-SG.M	with-her

ʾixala	ta-t	nábl-a	ta-palàxe	ṭ-ila	plàxa
food	to-SBR	take-3SG.F	to-workers	SBR-COP-3SG.F	work.INF

rəš	gə́šr-ət	Dalàle.
on	bridge-of	Dalale

he sent food with Dalale for her to take to the workers who were working on the bridge of Dalale.

(5)
ʾanna	mìr-ə=l-la,	'ku	nə̀šma
they	say.PTCP-SG.M=COP.3SG.M-O.3SG.F	every	soul

t-màṭy-a	rəš	gəšr-ət	Dalàle	ʾɛ	nəšma
SBR-arrive-3SG.F	on	bridge-of	Dalale	that.F	soul

bəd-pèš-a	prìm-ta,	qṭìl-ta.'
FUT-become-SG.F	slaughter.PTCP-SG.F	kill.PTCP-SG.F

They said to her, 'Any soul that comes onto the bridge of Dalale— that soul will be slaughtered, killed.'

ʾit-la	kalba	mə̀nn-a.	ʾən	hawe-∅-wa	kalba
EXIST-3SG.F	dog	with-her	if	be-3SG.M-PST	dog

zil-a	qămày-a,	qaṭl-i-wa	kàlba.
go.PTCP-SG.M	first-SG.M	kill-3PL-PST	dog

She had a dog with her. If the dog had gone first, they would have killed the dog.

là	qaṭl-í-wa-la	Dalàle.
NEG	kill-3PL-PST-O.3SG.F	Dalale

They would not have killed Dalale.

qìm-e-la	kalba	šqil-le	rìxa	t-xa	kàlləš.
rise.PTCP-PL=COP.3PL	dog	take.PFV-3SG.M	smell	of-one	carrion

But the dog picked up the scent of carrion.

kalləš	yăð-ət	mòdi=la?ˈ	xa	ʾərba	mìθ-a.ˈ
carrion	know-2SG.M	what=COP.3SG.F	one	sheep	dead-SG.M

Do you know what a carrion (*kalləš*) is? It is a dead sheep.

(6)	zil-le	kalba	rəš	dè	kalləš.ˈ
	go.PFV-3SG.M	dog	on	OBL.that.F	carrion

The dog went to the carrion.

ʾayya	Dalale	piš-la	qam-èθa.ˈ	zìl-la,ˈ
this.F	Dalale	become.PFV-3SG.F	first-SG.F	go.PFV-3SG.F

Dalale became the first one. She went,

mṭe-la	l-gəšra,ˈ	qəm-dawq-ì-la.ˈ
arrive.PFV-3SG.F	to-bridge	PFV-seize-3PL-O.3SG.F

she reached the bridge and they seized her.

qəm-parm-ì-la.ˈ	matt-i-la	gu	gə̀šra.ˈ
PFV-slaughter-3PL-O.3SG.F	place-3PL-O.3SG.F	in	bridge

and slaughtered her. They put her in the bridge.

gəšra	qṭìr-re.ˈ	mxe-le	l-ġðàðe.ˈ
bridge	arch.PFV-3SG.M	hit.PFV-3SG.M	to-one.another

The arch of the bridge was completed. It came together.

bena	y-àmr-i:ˈ
so	IND-say-3PL

So, they say:

(7)	Dalal,	Dalal,	Dalale,
	Dalal	Dalal	Dalale

Dalal, Dalal, Dalale,

gəšr-ə	Zaxo	raman-a
bridge-of	Zakho	high-SG.M

The high bridge of Zakho

sel-ət	*xoθ-e*	*milan-a*
river-SBR	under-it.M	blue-SG.M

The river under it is blue (with grief).

Dalle	*dwiq-a*	*l-xəmyan-a.*
Dalle	seize.PVF-3SG.F	by-father.in.law-her

Dalle (= Dalale) has been seized by her father-in-law.

(8)
gəšr-ət	*Zaxo*	*daqiq-a*
bridge-of	Zakho	narrow-SG.M

The narrow bridge of Zakho,

'u	*sel-ət*	*xoθ-e*	*raqiq-a*
and	river-SBR	under-it.M	narrow-SG.M

The river under it is narrow.

'u	*Dalle*	*l-xəmyan-a*	*dwiq-a.*
and	Dalle	by-father.in.law-her	take.PFV-SG.F

Dalle has been seized by her father-in-law.

(9)
m-o	*kalb-ət*	*p̂ərruš*	*we-le*
from-that.M	dog-SBR	treacherous	be.PFV-3SG.M

On account of that dog which was treacherous.

ṣle-le	*rəš*	*kalləš*	*kle-le*
go.down.PSV-3SG.M	upon	carrion	stand.PFV-3SG.M

It went down and stood over carrion.

xəmyan-ət	*Dalle*	*bxe-le.*
father.in.law-of	Dalle	weap.PFV-3SG.M

The father-in-law of Dalle wept.

CHRISTIAN ARAMAIC OF SHAQLAWA
TEXT 28: §1–21

Geoffrey Khan

Speaker: Seran Sher

Audio: https://nena.ames.cam.ac.uk/audio/230/

(1) ʾana šəm-i Serán ʾAdday Šèr=ile.ˈ
    I name-my Seran ʾAday Šer=COP.3SG.M

My name is Seran Adday Sher.

brāt Ḥane ʾÀwdu=iwan.ˈ naš-ət Šaqlàwe=wan.ˈ
daughter.of Ḥane ʾAwdu=COP.1SG.F people-of Shaqlawa=COP.1SG.F

I am the daughter of Hane Awdo. I am [one of the] people of Shaqlawa.

šāt ʾalpa=u təša ma=u ʾə̀šti=u xamša
year.of thousand=and nine hundred=and sixty=and five

hwè-te=wanˈ gu Šàqlawa.ˈ
be.PTCP-SG.F=COP.1SG.F in Shaqlawa

I was born in 1965 in Shaqlawa.

(2) ʾət-i xa ḥŭčita šəm-aw trè malaye=le.ˈ
    EXIST-1SG one story name-its.F two mullahs=COP.3SG.M

I have a story called 'The Two Mullahs'.

ʾət-wa=u	lə̀t-wa	mən	bāb	ʾalaha=u	ʾoda
EXIST-PST=and	NEG.EXIST-PST	than	father	God=and	mother

Maryam	bəš	rab-a	lət-wa=u	qàt=iš	la
Mary	more	big-SG.M	NEG.EXIST-PST=and	never=also	NEG

k-awe-∅,
IND-be-3SG.M

There was and there was not, there was no one who was greater than God the Father and Mother Mary and shall never be,

ʾət-wa	trè	malaye.	ʾăna	tre	malàye,	malay-ət
EXIST-PST	two	mullahs	these	two	mullahs	mullahs-of

xà	mata=wən-wa,	xa	məzgaft=u	xa	màta.
one	village=COP.3PL-PST	one	mosque=and	one	village

there were two mullahs. These two mullahs were mullahs serving the same village, the same mosque and same village.

(3)
ʾăna	tre	malàye	xəzmət-at	dè	məzgaft
these	two	mullahs	service-of	OBL.that	mosque

ʾud-i-wa	gàwət	maṣròxe	qatət	mṣalòye=u
do-3PL-PST	in	call.INF	to	pray.INF=and

gu	ḥdar-ət	taziye=u	məndyàne.
in	attend.INF-of	funerals=and	things

These two mullahs served the mosque by calling to prayer, attending funerals and so on.

(4) xa   mən   dăna   malàye,   qămət   waxt-ət   ṣlot-ət
    one   from   OBL.these mullahs   before   time-of   prayer-of

xuškənta   hawe-∅-wa,   baraw   băyani   ʾawa   ʾəl
dawn   be-3SG.M-PST towards   morning   he   at

məzgăft   hawe-∅-wa.   hawar   maṣrəx-∅-wa=u   qù
mosque   be-3SG.M-PST   call   call-3SG.M-PST=and   rise.IMP

mṣaloye=u   məndi=u   bằng   yawəl-∅-wa.
prayer.INF=and   thing=and   call   give-3SG.M-PST

One of these mullahs used to be in the mosque at dawn before the time of morning prayer. He would make a call to prayer crying 'Rise to pray' and so forth.

(5) ʾaw   malà   xət   gălak   mətʾàsər   payəš-∅-wa.
    that.SG.M mullah   other   very   upset   become-3SG.M-PST

The other mullah used to get very upset.

ʾamər-∅-wa   maʿqúl=ila   ʾằt   qămet-i   l-ṭàma
say-3SG.M-PST   possible=COP.3SG.F   you   before-me   to-there

haw   -ət?
be   -2SG.M

'How is it possible for you to be there before me?'

naše   lòm   wəd-lu.   ʾamr-i   ʾāt   ʾəl   ma   məndì
people   blame   do.PFV-3PL say-3PL   you   for   what   thing

People began to blame him saying 'Why

ʾaxni   ʾəty-e=wət   lăxa?   la   xəzmət-an
we   come.PTCP-SG.M=COP.2SG.M   here   not   service-our

k-ud-ət
IND-do-2SG.M

have you come to us here? You do not offer us service

la	bằng	č-aw-ət.		ʾe	qa	tsə̀	məndi
not	call	IND-give-2SG.M		yes	for	no	thing

bāš	lew-ət.|
good	NEG.COP-2SG.M

nor do you call to prayer. You are not good for anything.'

(6)
fà|	gălak	mətʾàsər	pəš-le.|	xə̀r-e|
and	very	upset	become.PST-3SG.M	look.PST-3SG.M

So, he became very upset. He thought to himself (lit. he saw).

ʾamər-∅:	ʾaz-ən	baqr-ən	mən	de
say-3SG.M	go-1SG.M	ask-1SG.M	from	OBL.that

xàwr-i|	ʾaw	mən	didi	qəṣa	haya	k-àte-∅.|
friend-my	he	than	OBL.1SG	little	early	IND-come-3SG.M

He said, 'Let me go and ask my colleague, who comes before me a little earlier.

ʾana	kut	tira	də̀rang,|	gu	tsə̀	məndi
I	every	time	late	in	no	thing

la	g-maṭp-ən.|
NEG	IND-reach-1SG.M

I am late every time, I do not catch up with anything.

(7)
ʾàmər-∅:|	măla.|	ʾamər-∅:	hà	ʾaxoni-i,|
say-3SG.M	mullah	say-3SG.M	yes	brother-my

mà=ila?|
what=COP.3SG.F

He said, 'Mullah.' He said, 'Yes, brother, what is the matter?'

ʾamər-∅:	mur	qàt-i,	gu	mà	məndi	ʾāt	qămət
say-3SG.M	say.IMP.S	to-me	in	what	thing	you	before

waxt-ət	mṣaloye	lằxe=wət?	ʾamər-∅:	qa	mà?
time-of	pray.INF	here=COP.2SG.M	say-3SG.M	for	what

He said, 'Tell me, how is it that you are here before the time of prayer?

ʾamər-∅:	hemən	naš-ət	ʾawayi	lèw-u
say-3SG.M	believe.IMP.SG	people-of	village	COP.PST-3PL

mən-i	razi.
with-me	happy

He said, 'Believe me, the people of the village are not happy with me.

k-əmr-i	àt	dràng	k-at-ət=u	qat	qal-ux
IND-say-3PL	you.S	late	IND-come-2SG.M=and	to	voice-your.SG.M

là	k-šăm-əx-le.
NEG	IND-hear-1PL-O.3SG.M

They say "You come late and we never hear your voice.

dyara	la	yan	qal-ux	băsim-a	lèw-e
seems	NEG	either	voice-your.SG.M	pleasant-SG.M	NEG.COP-3SG.M

yan	ṭàmbal=iw-ət,	là	k-at-ət.
or	lazy=COP-2SG.M	NEG	IND-come-2SG.M

It seems you do not come either because your voice is not good or because you are a lazy person."

(8) 'àmər-∅:| mhèmən,| 'ana xà məndi
    say-3SG.M believe.IMP.S I one thing

'amr-ən-ux 'àxon.|
say-1SG.M-O.2SG.M brother

He said, 'Look, let me tell you one thing, brother.'

'amər-∅: čăd-ət mà?| 'ana trè 'išunyata 'ət-i.|
say-3SG.M know-2SG.M what? I two wives EXIST-1SG

He said, 'Do you know what? I have two wives.

(9) 'ăna tre 'išunyàta| xa har màye g-mašxən-a
    these two wives one always water warm-3SG.F

qat-i,| xa pəštumàḷ g-dawq-a-la qat-i,|
for-me one cushion IND-hold-3SG.F-O.3SG.F for-me

These two wives, one of them always warms water for me [to bathe], one holds a cushion for me,

xa gòr-i g-matw-a-lu qat-i,| xa jə̀le
one sock.PL-my IND-put-3SG.F-O.3PL for-me one clothes

ḥazər k-ud-a-lu| xa qundə̀r-i=š ṣŭbuġ
ready IND-make-3SG.F-O.3PL one shoes-my=also polish

k-ud-a-lu.|
IND-make-3SG.F-O.3PL

one puts out my socks for me, one prepares my clothes, one polishes my shoes.

qa hàdax| xa=u tre 'ana ḥàzər k-peš-ən.|
for thus one=and two I ready IND-become-1SG.M

qa hadax qằmet-ux k-ṭap-ən.|
for thus before-you.SG.M IND-reach-1SG.M

That is why I get ready in a moment, and this is why I get here before you.'

(10) ʾamər-Ø: màtu?|
     say-3SG.M how?

He said, 'But how?'

ʾàmər-Ø| yaʿni   raʾy-ux   mà=ile?|
say-3SG.M it.means   view-your.SG.M   what=COP.3SG.M?

He said, 'I mean, what is your advice?'

ʾàmər-Ø:| raʾy-i=le   ʾawd-ət-u   trè   ʾišunyata.|
say-3SG.M view-my=COP.3SG.M   do-2SG.M-O.3PL   two   wives

'My advice is for you to have two wives.'

ʾamər-Ø: matʾàkkəd=iwət?| ʾamər-Ø: ma   de   mdzàrəb!|
say-3SG.M sure=COP-2SG.M?   say-3SG.M well well try.IMP.SG

He said, 'Are you sure? He said, 'Just give it a try!

ʾaxon-ux   mà   mare=le   qat-ux?|
brother-your.SG.M   what   say.INF=COP.3SG.M   to-you.SG.M

ʾamər-Ø: ha   halʿàn   k-az-ən.|
say-3SG.M well   now   IND-go-1SG.M

This is your brother's advice to you.' He said, 'I shall go immediately [and marry another woman].'

(11) har   pləṭ-le   mən   məzgàft| ʾizəl-e
     just leave.PFV-3SG.M   from   mosque   go.PFV-3SG.M

xa   baxta   mte-le.|
one   woman   bring.PFV-3SG.M

As soon as he left the mosque, he went and married another woman.

ʾite-le   qam-yawəl-Ø-a| qam-matù-Ø-la   l-beta.|
come.PFV-3MS   PFV-give-3SG.M-O.3SG.F   PFV-put.3SG.M-O.3SG.F   at-house

He came and put her, he helped her settle at the house.

ʾamər-∅:	ʾàna	ṣloθ-ət	ʾaṣə̀rte=la,	b-izàl=ən
say-3SG.M	I	prayer-of	evening=COP.3SG.F	in-go.INF=COP.1SG.M

qa	məzgaft.
to	mosque

He said, 'It is time for the evening prayer. I am going to the mosque.'

(12)	hătà	dər-e	qàl-ət	ʾăna	tre	ʾišunyàt-u
	until	return.PFV-3SG.M	voice-of	these	two	wives-his

l-dàw	bal-ət	Zaba	ṭape-∅-wa.
to-OBL.that	side-of	Zab	reach-3SG.M-PST

By the time he returned home, the cries of these two wives were reaching the other bank of the Zab River.

xà	ʾamr-a-wa:	kalba	xəry-ət	mǎla.
one	say-3SG.F-PST	dog	defecated.PTCP.SG.M-of	mullah

One said, 'May a dog shit on the mullah!'

ʾaw	xə̀t	ʾamr-a-wa:	ʾatxa	ʾələt	riš-ət	mǎla.
that.M	other	say-3SG.F-PST	thus	on	head-of	mullah

Another said, 'May this [dog's shit] be on the head of the mullah.'

ʾe	xət	ʾamr-à-wa:	kalba	l-qawr-ət	mǎla
that	other	say-3SG.F-PST	dog	on-grave-of	mullah

xare-∅.
defecate-3SG.M

Another said, 'May the dog shit on the mullah's grave.'

bejəga	mən	xatwat-u=u	ʾòd-u,
besides	from	sisters-his=and	mother-his

Besides his sisters and his mother,

ʾani	kŭl-u	qam-mat-i-lu	l-gor.
those	all-them	PFV-bring-3PL-3PL	to-situation

they included them all in their curses.

(13)
ma	ʾằwəd-∅?	wə̀r-e	ʾamər-∅:
what	do.3SG.M	entered.PFV-3SG.M	say-3SG.M

mà=ila?
what=COP.3SG.F

What could he do? He entered [the house] and said, 'What is the matter?'

ʾamər-∅:	bằš=ila,	ʾaxtun	qa	mà	ʾəli
say-3SG.M	good=COP.3SG.F	you.PL	for	what	me

mṣawore=witun?
curse.INF=COP.2PL

He said, 'All right, why are you swearing at me?

ʾana	mà?	ʾamr-i:	xer	ʾằt	muty-an=iwət?
I	what	say-3PL	but	you	bring.PFV-O.1PL=COP.2SG.M

What have I done?' They said, 'But it was you who brought us [here].'

(14)
ʾàl-mŭhəm	là	ʾide-le	màtu	tre
the-important	NEG	know.PFV-3SG.M	how	two

tlaha	sằʿát	fət-lu.
three	hours	pass.PFV-3PL

Well, he did not know how the next two or three hours passed by.

qăm<u>ə</u>t	yoma	bàyəz-∅,	ʾərə̀q-le	mən	qam	ʾidắt
before	day	pour-3SG.M	flee.PFV-3SG.M	from	before	hands.of

dan	trè	ʾišunyata	ʾət	mara	qat-u:
OBL.those	two	women	SBR	say.INF	to-him

Before dawn broke, he fled from the hands of the two women as they were saying to him,

ʾằt	ʾatxa	wəd-lux	ʾằt	ʾatxa	wəd-lux,
you	thus	so.PFV-2SG.M	you	thus	do.PFV-2SG.M

'You did this, you did that',

b-e	ga	mṣawoṛe	l-ʾəġdàde.	reš-u
at-that	time	swear.INF	at-each.other	head-his

gălak	gălak	mrè-le.
much	much	hurt.PFV-3SG.M

at the same time swearing at each other. He had a big headache.

(15)
ʾizə̀l-e.	lèle=le,	lebe	tsə	məndi
go.PFV-3SG.M	night=COP.3SG.M	cannot.3SG.M	any	thing

ʾawəd	gu	mə̀zgaft.
do.3SG.M	in	mosque

He went away. It was night time and he could do nothing in the mosque.

la	ʾib-e	màṣrəx-∅	la	ʾib-e	mǎla
NEG	can-3SG.M	call-3SG.M	NEG	can-3SG.M	mullah

bang	ʾawəd-∅.
call	make-3SG.M

He could not call to prayer. The mullah could not make a call [to prayer].

la	tsə	mendi	lèb-e	ʾawəd-∅.	ʾizəl-e	tăṛa
NEG	any	thing	cannot-3SG.M	do-3SG.M	go.PFV-3SG.M	door

qam-patəx-∅-le.	ʾitù-le	ʾələl.
PFV-open-3SG.M-O.3SG.M	sit.PFV-3SG.M	above

He cannot do anything. He went and opened the door. He sat on the upper floor.

(16)
ʾitu-le	ʾələl.	ʾamər-∅	qatət	măla,
sit.PRF-3SG.M	above	say-3SG.M	to	mullah

He sat on the upper floor. He said to the mullah,

ʾàmər-∅,	waxt-ət	mṣalòye=le.	xaz-əx	mən-u
say-3SG.M	time-of	pray.INF=COP.3SG.M	see-1PL	with-him

mən	jàn-u	maḥčoye=le	măla.	k-àmər-∅:
with	self-3SG.M	talk.INF=COP.3SG.M	mullah	IND-say-3SG.M

waxt-ət	mṣalòye=le?
time-of	pray.INF=COP.3SG.M

It is said that it was prayer time and the mullah began to talk to himself saying 'Is it prayer time?

la	waxt-ət	mṣaloye	lèla.	ʾe	ga	xa	ġàfwa
no	time-of	pray.INF	NEG.COP.3SG.F	that	time	one	nap

šaql-ən-i	xantsa	ʾèn-i	matw-ən-u.
take-1SG.M-O.1SG	a.little	eyes-my	put-1SG.M-O.3PL

No, it is not prayer time. So let me take a nap and close my eyes for a bit.'

(17)
k-àmər-∅:	xzè-le	xa	ṭăpăṭap	ʾitè-le.
IND-say-3SG.M	see.PFV-3SG.M	one	tapping	come.PFV-3SG.M

It is said that he heard some footsteps coming.

xze-le	ʾe	màla	xət	ʾitè-le.ǀ
see.PFV-3SG.M	that	mullah	other	come.PFV-3SG.M

ʾàmər-∅:ǀ	ʾitè-lux?ǀ
say-3SG.M	come.PFV-2SG.M

He saw the other mullah come. He said, 'Have you come [already]?'

ʾàmər-∅:ǀ	naša	xoš	nàša!	madam	ʾāt	bet-ux
say-3SG.M	man	good	man	if	you.SG	house-your.SG.M

mṣuṭə̀m-wa-le,ǀ	qa	mà	bet-i	qam-mṣaṭm-ət-e?ǀ
ruin.PFV-PST-3SG.M	for	what	house-my	PFV-ruin-2SG.M-O.3SG.M

He said, 'My friend, if your life was ruined, why did you ruin my own life?

ʾāt	bet-ux	nura	ʾitən	gu	bet-ux
you.SG	house-your.SG.M	fire	EXIST	in	house-your.SG.M

ʾarq-ət-wa	mən-e	ʾăna	šə̀ne,ǀ	qa	mà	bet-i
flee-2SG.M-PST	from-it.M	these	years	for	what	house-my

qam-awd-ət-e?ǀ
PFV-do-2SG.M-O.3SG.M

Your home was like hell from which you fled all these years, so why did you make my home [the same]?'

(18)
ʾamər-∅:	qa	ma	bas	ʾàna	mər-ux?ǀ
say-3SG.M	for	what	only	me	say.PFV-2SG.M

He said, 'Why have you blamed me?[1]

ʾāt	la	ṭləb-lux	mən-i	məsàʿăda?ǀ
you.S	NEG	ask.PFV-2SG.M	from-me	help

Did you not ask for help from me?

---

[1] Lit. why have you said [this] only to me?

ʾay	məsaʿădä	dəx	lèw-ət	bəxzaya?	qằmet-i
this	help	how	NEG.COP-2SG.M	IN-see.INF	before-me

l-məzgaft=iw-ət,	hăta	par-ux	ḥălằl
at-mosque=COP-2SG.M	so.that	money-your.SG.M	legitimate

ʾawdət-u.	
do.2SG.M-O.3SG.M	

Do you see how I have helped you? You are at the mosque before me, so you will legitimately earn your money.'

(19)	wəlux	ʾamər-∅	ʾāt	bet-i	nura
	DEIC.2SG.M	say-3SG.M	you.SG	house-my	fire

qam-awd-ət-e.	ʾamər-∅:	bas	bèt-i	k̀àwla
PFV-do-2SG.M-O.3SG.M	say.3SG.M	only	house-my	ruin

payəš-∅,	mà?	ʾăye=la	ʿeš-an	weta	xà,
become-3SG.M	what?	this=COP.3SG.F	life-our	be.PTCP.SG.F	one

'But you,' he said, 'have turned my home into a hell.' He said, 'Should only my house be in ruins? So our life has now become the same.'

(20)	ʾăya	ḥŭčita	k-əmr-i-la	qa	daw	naš-ət
	this	story	IND-say-3PL-O.3SG.F	to	OBL.that	man-who

reš-u	là	(ha)we-∅	mara=u	reš-u
head-his	NEG	be-3SG.M	ache.INF=and	head-his

mamrè-∅-le,		ʾawdza	ʿàbra	mən	de	naša
cause.to.ache-3SG.M-O.3SG.M		thus	lesson	from	OBL.this	man

k-šaql-ì-la.	
IND-take-3PL-O.3SG.F	

This story is told about those who do not have a headache but cause themselves to have a headache, so that people will learn a lesson from [the story of] this man.

k-əmr-i-la		qa	dàn	naše[|]	ʾaxtsa	gu	qŭsət
IND-say-3PL-O.3SG.F		to	OBL.those	people	thus	in	story.of

naše	là	(a)te-∅=u	ʾazəl-∅,[|]	gu	mox-ət
people	NEG	come-3SG.M=and	go-3SG.M	in	mind-of

jàn-u	ʾawəd-∅,[|]	ʾaxtsa	gu	tănayat-ət	naše
self-3SG.M	do-3SG.M	thus	in	speeches-of	people

la	qayəm-∅=u	yàtu-∅.[|]
NEG	stand-3SG.M=and	sit-3SG.M

[The story] tells people that one should not act[2] according to what other people say, but one should act using one's own mind, rather than stand and sit according to what [other] people say.

(21)	ʾawdza	ʾite-li	ʾitè-li[|]	tsə̀	məndi=š
	so	come.PFV-1SG	come.PFV-1SG	no	thing=also

la	wəl-u	qa-ti.[|]
NEG	give.PFV-3PL	to-me

So, I came back [from the scene of the story], but they gave me nothing [to prove that I saw it].

---

[2] Lit. come and go.

CHRISTIAN ARAMAIC OF DUHOK
TEXT 14: §1–19

Dorota Molin

Speaker: Yawsep Elisha Ishaq

Audio: https://nena.ames.cam.ac.uk/audio/224/

(1) ʾana   Yawsəp   ʾEliša   ʾIsḥàq   mən   Dǔhok=iwən.|
    I   Yawsep   ʾEliša   ʾIsḥàq   from   Duhok=COP.1SG.M

I am Yawsep Elisha Ishaq, from Duhok.

yəmm-i   naš-ət   Mar   Yàqo=la,| šəmm-aḥ   Maryam
mother-my   people-of   Mar   Yaqu=COP.3SG.F   name-her   Maryam

Toma   Jubrằʾəl.|
Toma   Jubrằʾəl

My mother is from Mar Yaqo her name is Maryam Toma Jubrail.

g-əb-ən   ʾamr-ən-nux   xa   maθalǔke=la,|
IND-want-1SG.M   tell-1SG.M-O.2SG.M one   tale=COP.3SG.F

d-àrya| ʾu barnằša.|
of-lion   and man

I'd like to tell you a story, about a lion and a man.

(2) ʾəθ-wa   xa   ʾarya
    EXIST-PST   one   lion

There was a lion

mṣíṭer-a	wewa	l-ṭùra.'
rule.PTCP-3SG.M	COP.PST.3SG.M	on-mountain

[who] controlled a mountain.

là-qabəl-∅-wa	čù	barnaš-ət	zəl-wā-le	l-ṭura,'
NEG-accept-3SG.M-PST	no	human-SBR	go.PFV-PST-3SG.M	to-mountain

māxe-∅-wa	qàyse'	ʾu awəð-∅-wa	xà-məndi.'
cut-3SG.M-PST	wood.PL	and do-3SG.M-PST	some-thing

He did not allow any humans to enter the mountain to cut wood or to do anything [else].

hàr	zəl-wā-le,'
if	go.PFV-PST-3SG.M

g-nāxəθ-∅-wa	ʾəll-e	k-ìxəl-∅-wā-le.'
IND-descend-3SG.M-PST	on-him	IND-eat-3SG.M-PST-O.3SG.M

If someone went there, he would come down on them and eat them.

là-qābəl-∅-wa	ču	xa	zəl-wā-le.'
NEG-accept-3SG.M-PST	no	one	go.PFV-PST-3SG.M

He did not allow anyone to enter.

(3)
ʾu xa	faqìra	ʾəθ-wa.'
and one	poor.man	EXIST-PST

There was also a poor man.

pəš-le	majbūr	d-za-le	maθe-∅
become.PFV-3SG.M	desperate	SBR-go-3SG.M	bring-3SG.M

qàyse'	d-mzābən-∅-nay	gyan-e'
wood.PL	SBR-sell-3SG.M-O.3PL	self-3SG.M

He had to go and get wood to sell it

d-ʿayəš-∅	b-gàw-ay.ˈ
SBR-live-3SG.M	in-with-them

in order to make a living through it.

ʾe, là-k-əθy-a	mənn-eˈ	xāze-∅-le	dáʾəman
yes NEG-IND-come-3SG.F	with-him	see-3SG.M-O.3SG.M	always

yala	zor-a	bə-myaθa	m-kəpna	barqul-eḥˈ
child	little-SG.M	in-die.INF	from-hunger	before-him

He was not able to see [his] little child dying of hunger in front of him.

ʾu la-t-te	čʾu məndi	d-māxəl-∅-lay.ˈ
and NEG-EXIST-3SG.M	nothing	SBR-feed-3SG.M-O.3PL

And he had nothing to feed them.

(4)	k-imər-∅	ʾana	mḍăḥ-ən
	IND-say-3SG.M	I	sacrifice-1SG

'I shall sacrifice [myself].

b-za-li	l-day	ṭura
FUT-go-1SG	to-OBL.that.F	mountain

d-ile	ʾarya	gaw-e	d-āxəl-∅-li,
SBR-COP.3SG.M	lion	inside-it.3SG.M	SBR-eat-3SG.M-O.1SG

I shall go to the mountain where the lion is and might eat me.

nayx-ən	mən	xày-i.ˈ
rest-1SG.M	from	life-my

I will be spared [the burden of] my life.

bə̀š ṭu	mət	xaz-ən	yale	zor-e	myaθa	m-kəpna."ˈ
better	than	see-1SG.M	children	little-PL	die.INF	from-hunger

It is better than seeing [my] little children dying of hunger.'

šqəl-le	*xmar-eḥ*	*ʾu məndi*	*dìyeḥ,*	*xàwl-eḥ,*'
take.PFV-3SG.M	donkey-his	and thing	his	rope.PL-his

So he took his donkey and his equipment, his ropes.

(5) *qəm-le   ham   ʾaw*
    arise.PFV-3SG.M also he

ʾu zəl-le   d-awəð-∅   qayse   ʾu àθe-∅.'
and go.PFV-3SG.M SBR-do-3SG.M wood and come-3SG.M

He got up and went to get wood before going back.

θe-le,   là-θe-le,   b-nayəx-∅   m-gyan-e.'
come.PFV-3SG.M NEG.come.PFV-3SG.M FUT-rest-3SG.M of-self-his

Whether or not [the lion] would come, he would find relief.

mhàymən-∅,'   zəl-le,   mṭe-le   l-ṭura
believe.IMP-SG go.PFV-3SG.M arrive.PFV-3SG.M to-mountain

ʾu nàr-eḥ'   d-qaṭe-∅   qàyse.'
and axe-his SBR-cut-3SG.M wood

Believe it, he went and climbed the mountain [with] his axe to cut wood.

mxè-le,   taq,   tàq.'
hit.PFV-3SG.M crack crack

He started cutting, *crack, crack*.

wele   dehwa...   hənna   ʾàrya
DEIC.COP.3SG.M wolf thing lion

k-šame   qala   g-nàxəθ-∅   ʾəll-e.'
IND-hear-3SG.M voice IND-descend-3SG.M to-him

Look, a wolf... I mean, a lion heard the sound and came to him.

(6) 'ha, barnàša,'
    ha   human

'ati   l-ēθ   šəmy-a   gàw-i?'
you.SG   NEG-COP.2SG.M   hear.PTCP-SG.M   about-me

'Hey, human, haven't you heard of me?

dax   k-iθ-ət   'ati   d-qaṭ-ət
how   IND-come-2SG.M   you.SG   SBR-cut-2SG.M

'u məndyane   d-g-əb-ət   'u là-g-əb-ət.'
and things   SBR-IND-want-2SG.M   and NEG-IND-want-2SG.M

How dare you come here and cut whatever you like, and so on?

l-ēθ   šmiy-a
NEG-COP.2SG.M   hear.PTCP-SG.M

gu   da   ṭura   dìyi=le?"
in   OBL.that.F   mountain   mine=COP.3SG.M

Haven't you heard that this mountain is mine?'

k-imər-∅,   'băle, băle,'   wən   šmiy-a
IND-say-3SG.M   indeed indeed   COP.1SG   hear.PTCP-SG.M

'u 'ana   ta   hàdax=ən   'əθy-a."
and I   for   such=COP.1SG.M   come.PTCP-SG.M

He said, 'Indeed, I have heard, and that is why I have come.'

'dàxi   ta   hadax=ət   'əθy-a?"
how   for   such=COP.2SG.M   come.PTCP-SG.M

'What do you mean that this is the reason you have come?'

(7) k-imər-∅,   'mhèmən-∅,   mer-i   b-axl-ət-ti'
    IND-say-3SG.M   believe.IMP-SG   say.PFV-1SG   FUT-eat-2SG.M-O.1SG.M

He said, 'Believe me, I thought [that if] you eat me,

ʿal ʾaqál	là-xaz-ən	yal-i	zor-e	myaθa	m-kəpna
at least	NEG-see-1SG.M	children-my	little-PL	die.INF	of-hunger

barqū́l	ʾèn-i.ˈ
before	eyes-my

at least I won't see my little children dying of hunger in front of my eyes.

ham	ʾən	ʾaxl-ət-ti	ʾati	bəš tu	mət	xāz-ən-nay.ˈ
even	if	2SG.M-O.1SG	you.SG	better	than	see-1SG.M-O.3PL

Even if you eat me, it is better than seeing them.

mayθ-ən	barqū́l	yale	zor-e	hawe-∅	bə-myaθa
die-1SG.M	before	children	little-PL	be-3PL	in-die.INF

m-kəpna	ʾu xàz-ən-nay.ˈ
of-hunger	and see-1SG.M-O.3PL

I would die in front of my little children dying of hunger, and I would see them.

naqla	ʾàti=žiˈ	b-kàypux=wən.ˈ
this time	you.SG=also	in-bondage-your.SG.M=COP.1SG.M

Now, [it's up to] you, I am at your mercy.

ʾana	gu	ḥəmayata	dìyux=iwən.ˈ
I	in	protection	your.SG.M=COP.2SG.M

I am under your protection.

g-əb-ət,ˈ	ʾana	ḥalala	tà-lux.ˈ
IND-want-2SG.M	I	prey	for-you.SG.M

If you want, I am yours.

ʾu g-əb-ət	ži,ˈ	ʾana	hun	ʾəθy-a
and IND-want-2SG.M	also	I	COP.1SG.M	come.PTCP-SG.M

[but] if you please, I've come

m-majburùθ-i'	d-máʿyəš-ən	ʾayàl	diyi.'
of-desperation-my	SBR-support-1SG.M	children	my

out of the need to feed my children.'

(8) k-imər-∅, ʿmadám t-ila hàdax,'
IND-say-3SG.M since SBR-COP.3SG.F thus

ham, hàm ṭa-li rand=ila'
even even for-me advantage=COP.3SG.F

ʾu ham ṭà-lux rand=ila.'
and even for-you.SG.M advantage=COP.3SG.F

He said, 'If that is the case, then it's good for me and good for you.'

ʿdăxi?ʾ
how

'How?'

k-imər-∅ ʾati b-awð-ət qayse ʾu b-làbl-ət,'
IND-say-3SG.M you.SG.M FUT-do-2SG.M wood and FUT-take-2SG.M

He said, 'You will cut wood and take it [to town].

ʾu ana b-yāw-ən-nux maṣraf diyux.'
and I FUT-give-1SG.M-O.2SG.M salary your.SG.M

And I will give you your living.

b-za-lux hàm ṭa-li b-aθ-ət.'
FUT-go-2SG.M even for-me FUT-come-2SG.M

You will go and come to me.

ʾaygət aθ-ət māθ-ət-ti ʾixàla,'
when come-2SG.M bring-2SG.M-O.1SG food

When you come and bring me food,

hàm	ʾana	ʾaxl-ən.'
even	I	eat-1SG.M

I too will eat.'

'ʾe,'	k-imər-∅,	'kabìra	rand=ila.'
yes	IND-say-3SG.M	great	advantage=COP.3SG.F

'Yes,' he says. 'This is a great advantage.'

(9)	kud	yom	k-izəl-∅	k-iwəð-∅	xà
	every	day	IND-go-3SG.M	IND-do-3SG.M	one

kart-ət	hənna...	ṭen-ət	qàyse,'	g-làbəl-∅.'
bundle-of	thing	load-of	wood	IND-take-3SG.M

So he goes to cut wood every day, makes a bundle of this thing, a load of wood, and carries [it].

labəl-∅	qàyse'	ʾu čʾu xa	là-labole,
take-3SG.M	wood	and no-one	NEG-take.INF

ʾàjran	gə-mzābən-∅-nay.'
expensive	IND-sell-3SG.M-O.3PL

He brings wood while no one else does, so he sells it at a high price.

k-ið-ət	ʾəstəġlal	d-šùqa.'
IND-know-2SG.M	advantage	of-market

You know, taking advantage of the market.

mhàymən-∅,'	kud-yom	hol	b-əθàya,'
believe.IMP-SG	every-day	DEIC.COP.3SG.M	in-come.INF

labole	ʾu mzabone	qàyse,'	ʾu naše	bə-xzàya,	ʾe.'
take.INF	and sell.INF	wood	and people	in-see.INF	yes

Believe me, he comes every day, transports and sells wood, people can see this, yes.

ʾu ani	xene	là-g-yar-i	za-lay.
and they	others	NEG-IND-dare-3PL	go-3PL

Others do not dare go [to the mountain].

(10) xa yoma...
    one day

One day...

ṭábʿān	d-k-i-θe-∅	d-maθe-∅	ʾixàla,
of.course	SBR-IND-come-3SG.M	SBR-bring-3SG.M	food

k-əxl-i	mùxðaðe.
IND-eat-3PL	together

Of course, when he brought food, they would eat together.

ʾawa	ʾu arya	k-əxl-i	mùxðaðe	tama.
he	and lion	IND-eat-3PL	together	there

He and the lion ate together there.

yaʿni,	hàm	ʾixal-ət	faqira	ʿala	ḥsàb-eḥ
it.means	even	food-of	poor.man	on	expense-his

k-aw-e.
IND-be-3SG.M

So the poor man's food was also at his expense.

ʾe,	ʾarya	g-yāwəl-∅-le	ʿṭa-li	ʾu ṭà-lux.'
yes	lion	IND-give-3SG.M-O.3SG.M	to-me	and to-you.SG.M

He gave him [saying] 'For you and for me.'

(11)
xa	yoma	mət	xzè-le	ʾarya,
one	day	when	see.PFV-3SG.M	lion

One day, he realized that the lion

ya'ni,	kabìra	wəd-le	faðl	ʾəll-eḥ.'
I.mean	great	do.PFV-3SG.M	favour	to-him

was doing him a great favour.

k-imər-∅,	'ba,	xòn-i,'		
IND-say-3SG.M	look	brother-my		

ham	ʾati	mšarəf-∅	gèb-an.'
also	you.SG.M	honour-3SG.M	to-us

He said, 'Brother, come over one day to ours, honour us [in this way].

ʿazm-ən-nux	xa	yoma	l-gèban,'
invite-1SG.M-O.2SG.M	one	day	to-to-ours

mənn-an	xùl-∅.'
with-us	eat.IMP-SG

I'd like to invite you to ours, eat with us.'

k-imər-∅,	'mà	y-xaləf-∅.'	b-àθ-ən.'
IND-say-3SG.M	what	IND-matter-3SG.M	FUT-come-1SG.M

He says, 'Of course, I will come.'

ba	ʾarya	mən	màni	b-zade-∅?'
look	lion	from	who	FUT-fear-3SG.M

Whom does a lion fear?

là-zad-e	mən	ču	xa.'
NEG-fear-3SG.M	from	no	one

He fears no one.

(12) | mhaymən-∅ | wə̀d-lay,' |
|---|---|
| believe.IMP-SG | do.PFV-3PL |

Believe me, they did so,

zəl-lay	mṭe-lay	l-bàyθa.
go.PFV-3PL	arrive.PFV-3PL	to-house

they went and arrived at [the man's] home.

k-imər-∅	ta	bàxt-eḥ	ʾbàxta,
IND-say-3SG.M	to	wife-his	wife

g-dary-at	ʾixala	ta	ʾàrya,
IND-put-2SG.F	food	for	lion

dre	jŭda	ʾu ṭà-li	dre	jŭda.'
put.IMP.SG.F	portion	and to-him	put.IMP.SG.F	portion

He said to his wife, 'Wife, when you serve food for the lion, serve him separately from me.'

k-imər-∅,	'lə'án	ʾegət	galize	g-nàxθ-i,	jŭda.'
IND-say-3SG.M	because	when	saliva	IND-descend-3PL	portion

galize	g-naxθ-i	gu	ʾixàla.
saliva	IND-descend-3PL	in	food

He said, 'Because when his drool runs down, it drips on the food.

ləbb-i	là-k-izəl-∅,'	yaʕni,	ʾè.
heart-my	NEG-IND-go-3SG.M	I mean	yes

I lose my appetite, yes.'

ʾay=ži	zəl-la,	θe-la	muθe-la	ʾixàla.
she=also	go.PFV-3SG.F	come.PFV-3SG.F	bring.PFV-3SG.F	food

So, she went and came back, and brought food.

dre-la	ta	ʾàrya	jŭda,	ʾu ṭà-leh	jŭda.
put.PFV-3SG.F	to	lion	portion	and to-him	portion

She served the lion separately and [the man] separately.

(13) *'u ani   pəš-lay   b-ixàla.*'
     and they begin.PFV-3PL in-eat.INF

They started eating.

xə̀l-le   'arya' 'u xləṣ-le   'u θe-le
eat.PFV-3SG.M lion   and finish.PFV-3SG.M and come.PFV-3SG.M

l-ṭùra.'
to-mountain

The lion ate his food up and came back to the mountain.

derət   yoma   zəl-le   faqìra.'
second day   go.PFV-3SG.M   poor.man

Next day, the poor man went up.

k-imər-∅,   'ha,   ha,   faqìra,'
IND-say-3SG.M   ha   ha   poor.man

kud-yom   k-əxl-ət-wa   mə̀nn-i,' *'àxxa,*'
every-day IND-eat-2SG.M-PST   with-me   here

galiz-i   là-naxθ-i-wa   gawət   ixala?'
saliva-my NEG-descend-3PL-PST   inside   food

He said, 'Hey, poor man, we had food together here every day. Did my drool never run down into food?

day   d-mṭe-li   l-gebòxun
OBL.that.F SBR-arrive.PFV-1SG   to-you.PL

kəm-ʿazm-ət-ti,'
PFV-invite-2SG.M-O.1SG

dre-lux   jŭda   ṭa-li   'u ta   gyàn-ux'   *jŭda.*
put.PFV-2SG.M   portion   to-me   and to   self-your.SG.M portion

When you invited me, you served me separately and yourself separately.

(14) 'e,   g-mestànkəf-ət   mən   galiz-i?'
    yes IND-be.revolted-2SG.M of   saliva-my

You find my [drool] revolting?

'ay,   'ày=ila   faḍl   diyi 'əll-ux?'
that.F that.F=COP.3SG.F favour   my   to-you.SG.M

Is this [how you pay back] my favour to you?

'axxa   k-əxl-ət-wa   mənn-i   ᴬᶜala   ḥsàb-iᴬ'
here   IND-eat-2SG.M-PST   with-me   on   account-my

galiz-i   là-k-iθe-∅-wa   gawət   ixala.'
saliva-my   NEG-IND-COME-3SG.M-PST   inside food

When you used to eat with me at my expense, [then] my drool was not dripping on food.

'aygət   θe-li   geb-ux,   galiz-i   nxət-le
when   come.PFV-1SG   to-your.SG.M   saliva-my   descend.PFV-3SG.M

gu   'ixala,   g-yarəm-∅   ləbb-ux   mənn-i.'
in   food   IND-elevate-3SG.M   heart-your.SG.M from-me

When I came over to yours, my drool ran down into food, you became proud.'

(15) k-imər-∅   tà-le,'   'xzi   d-amr-ən-nux,'
     IND-say-3SG.M   to-him   see.IMP.SG.M   SBR-say-1SG.M-O.2SG.M

He said to him, 'Listen to what I say.

'màθi-le   năr-ux,
bring.IMP.SG.M-O.3SG.M   axe-your.SG.M

mxi-le   gu   rèš-i.'
hit.IMP.SG.M-O.3SG.M in   head-my

Bring your axe and hit me with it on the head.'

'dằxi māx-ən-ne   b-reš-ux?'ⁿ
how   hit-1SG.M-O.3SG.M in-head-your.SG.M

'How should I hit you with it on the head?'

'ən   là-max-ət-te   b-reš-i,   dǎha b-axl-ən-nux.'
if   NEG-hit-1SG.M-O.3SG.M in-head-my now   FUT-eat-1SG.M-O.2SG.M

'If you don't hit me with it on the head, I'll devour you right now.

lazəm māx-ət-te   b-rèš-i.'
must   hit-2SG.M-O.1SG.M in-head-my

You must hit me with it on the head.'

kəm-māxe-∅-le   b-reš-eḥ.'
PFV-hit.3SG.M-O.3SG.M   in-head-his

He hit him on his head.

'u arya zəl-le   ta   gyàn-eḥ.'
and lion go.PFV-3SG.M to   self-his

The lion went away to his own [place].

'u faqira   θè-le,'
and poor.man come.PFV-3SG.M

wəd-le   qàyse' 'u θe-le   l-bàyθa.'
do.PFV-3SG.M   wood   and come.PFV-3SG.M   to-house

The poor man came, cut the wood and came back home.

(16) pəd-le   xen-a   faqìra,'
      pass.PFV-3SG.M other-SG.M poor.man

'u 'arya   l-àt-te   'alaqa   gaw-e.'
and lion   NEG-EXIST-3SG.M   relation to-him

The poor man went [to] another [place] while the lion had nothing to do with him.

ḥal	xa	yòma,'
until	one	day

ʾàrya,'	nəx-le	reš-eḥ.'	reš-eh	nə̀x-le.'
lion	heal.PFV-3SG.M	head-his	head-his	heal.PFV-3SG.M

Until, one day, the lion's head recovered. His head recovered.

ʾu θe-le,	xaze-∅	faqira
and come.PFV-3SG.M	see-3SG.M	poor.man

hole	ʾəθy-a	l-ṭura	b-waða	qàyse.'
DEIC.COP.3SG.M	come.PTCP-SG.M	to-mountain	in-do.INF	wood

He came and saw—the poor man had come to the mountain, cutting wood.

mṭè-le	faqira,'	k-imər-∅,	'hà	faqira!'
arrive.PFV-3SG.M	poor man	IND-say-3SG.M	aha	poor man

He said, 'Hello, poor man!

ʾuhu,	ʾahlan wa-sàhlan,'
oh	welcome

dằxi=wəθ?'	maqṣad:	mroḥəb-le	gàw-e.'
how=COP.2SG.M	meaning	welcome.PFV-3SG.M	to-him

Welcome, how are you?' I mean, he welcomed him.

(17)	k-imər-∅,	'faqìra,'
	IND-say-3SG.M	poor.man

də	xur-∅	gu	rèš-i,'
SBR	look.IMP-SG	in	head-my

He said, 'Oh poor man, come and look at my head.

xz-i	nìx-a	reš-i,	ʾən	là.'
look.IMP-SG.M	heal.PTCP-SG.M	head-my	or	not

See whether or not my head has recovered.'

xayer-∅	gu	rèš-eh.	k-imər-∅,	ʿmhàymən-∅ʾ
look-3sg.m	in	head-his	IND-say-3SG.M	believe.IMP-SG

hole	piš-a	bə̀š ṭu	m-qamayθa.ʾ
DEIC.COP.3SG.M	become.PTCP-SG.M	better	than-before

He looked at his head and said, 'Believe me, it's better now than it was before.

ᴬmašallaᴬ...	škìr	ʾalaha.ʾ
what.god.willed	thank.PTCP	God

Thank God!'

k-imər-∅,	ʾl-àwa	b-kayp-i	basʾ
IND-say-3SG.M	NEG-COP.3SG.F	in-desire-my	but

ʾati	kəm-jabr-ə̀t-ti	d-max-ən-wa	ʾəll-ux.'
you.SG	PFV-force-2SG.M-O.1SG	SBR-hit-1SG.M-PST	to-you.SG.M

He said, 'It wasn't what I wanted, but you forced me to hit you.'

(18)	k-imər-∅,	ʿxzi,	faqìra,	reš-i
	IND-say-3SG.M	see.IMP.SG.M	poor.man	head-my

nə̀x-le.ʾ
heal.PFV-3SG.M

He said, 'Look, poor man, my head has recovered.

bas	xabr-ux	həš	l-èle	nix-a,ʾ
but	word-your.SG.M	still	NEG-COP.3SG.M	heal.PTCP-SG.M

d-ana...	k-əmr-ət-wa
SBR-I	IND-say-2SG.M-PST

galiz-i	naxθ-i	gawət	ʾixàla.
saliva-my	descend-3PL	inside	food

But [the impact of] your words [when] you said that my drool was dripping into food has not yet healed.

băθər	mət	nəx-le	reš-i
after	when	heal.PFV-3SG.M	head-my

'u xabr-ux	l-èle	nix-a,'
and word-your.SG.M	NEG-COP.3SG.M	heal.PTCP-SG.M

ᴬḥaq 'u mustaḥàqᴬ=ile	d-axl-ən-nux.'
justified=COP.3SG.M	SBR-eat-1SG.M-O.2SG.M

Since my head has recovered and [the wound] of your word has not, it is my full right to devour you.'

qəm-le	kəm-'āxəl-∅-le	b-e	dàna.'
arise.PFV-3SG.M	PFV-eat-3SG.M-O.3SG.M	in-this.F	time

He devoured him immediately.

(19) | 'e, | qày.' |
|---|---|
| yes | so |

Yes, it is so.

šawpa,	šawp-ət	saypa	g-nàyəx-∅.'
impact	impact-of	sword	IND-heal-3SG.M

The impact of a sword heals.

šawp-ət	xabra	là-g-nayəx-∅.'
impact-of	word	NEG-IND-heal-3SG.M

[But] the impact of words does not heal.

xabra	nàxwaš,	nàxwaš=ile,	'e.'
word	evil	evil=COP.3SG.M	yes

A word can be very evil, yes.

JEWISH ARAMAIC OF DUHOK
TEXT 16: §1-11

Dorota Molin

Speaker: Sabi Avraham

Audio: https://nena.ames.cam.ac.uk/audio/184/

(1) *ʾəθ-wa   xa   beθa   d-ʿāyə̀š-∅-wa...*ˈ
    EXIST-PST one house SBR-live-3SG.M-PST

*bab-ət   beθa   d-ʿāyə̀š-∅-wa   mən sìwe.*ˈ
father-of house SBR-live-3SG.M-PST from wood.PL

There was a household who used to live on… whose father used to make his living by woodcutting.

*g-ezəl-∅-wa   go ṭùra,*ˈ   *q-qāte-∅-wa   sìwe.*ˈ
IND-go-3SG.M-PST in mountain, IND-cut-3SG.M-PST wood.PL

He used to go to the mountain and cut pieces of wood.

*g-meθè-∅-wa-lu,*ˈ   *dāré-∅-wa-lu*
IND-bring-3SG.M-PST-O.3PL, place-3SG.M-PST-O.3PL

*rəš   xmara   dìde,*ˈ
on donkey his

He would bring them, place them on his donkey.

(2) g-ewəð-∅-wā-lu   kàrta,'
    IND-make-3SG.M-PST-O.3PL   bundle

He would bind them in a bundle.

g-dāré-∅-wa-lu   kàrta' rəš xmara dìde.'
IND-place-3SG.M-PST-O.3PL bundle on   donkey his

He would put them [as] a bundle on his donkey's back.

u-g-nābə́l-∅-wa-lu   šùqa,' gə-mzābən-∅-wa-lu.'
and-IND-take-3SG.M-PST-O.3PL market, IND-sell-3SG.M-PST-O.3PL

He would take them to the market and sell them.

k-eθé-∅-wa,'   g-meθe-∅-wa   ʾĭxala
IND-come-3SG.M-PST IND-bring-3SG.M-PST food

ta yalunke   dìde.'
to children his

Then, he would come back home and bring food for his children.

u-k-eθe-∅-wa   k-əxl-i-wa   g-ʿeš-i-wa
and-IND-come-3SG.M-PST   IND-eat-3PL-PST   IND-live-3PL-PST

bət ʾànna,' mən   mzabon-ət   ṣìwe.'
in   those   from selling-of   wood.PL

When he came, they would eat and live on this, on the money from wood selling.

(3) xă   yoma zəl-le   l-ṭùra,'
    one day   go.PFV-3SG.M to-mountain

b-qaṭe-∅   ṣìwe,' xze-le   xa   gùrga.'
FUT-cut-3SG.M   wood,   see.PFV-3SG.M   one wolf

One day he went to the mountain to cut trees and he saw a wolf.

’aw	gurga	g-emər-∅	ṭa-le
that.M	wolf	IND-say-3SG.M	to-him

mằ	wət	’əθy-a?'
what	COP.PRS.2SG.M	come.PTCP-SG.M

This wolf said to him, 'Why have you come?'

g-emər-∅	’ana	g-əb-ən…'
IND-say-3SG.M	I	IND-want-1SG.M

g-ʿeš-ən	bət	qaṭ’-ən	ṣiwe.'
IND-live-1SG.M	in	cut-1SG.M	wood.PL

He said, 'I want to… I make my living by woodcutting.

gə-mzabn-ən-nu	go šuqa
IND-sell-1SG.M-O.3PL	in market

u-máʿă-yəš-ən	yalunke	dìdi.'
and-sustain-1SG	child	my

I sell it in the market and provide for my children.

bə-dè	’ana	g-ʿeš-ən.'
in-OBL.this.F	I	IND-live-1SG.M

In this way I make my living.'

(4)
g-emər-∅	’ana	b-yāw-ən-nox	kud-yom
IND-say-3SG.M	I	FUT-give-1SG.M-O.2SG.M	every-day

xă	lira	kurkamàn-a.'
one	coin	golden-SG.F

He replied 'Every day, I will give you one golden coin.

si	maṣrəf-∅	ta	yalunke	didox.'
go.IMP.SG.M	spend.IMP-SG	to	children	your.SG.M

Go, spend it on your children.'

g-emər-∅,	ᴷxerà xudèᴷ=la,'				
IND-say-3SG.M	ᴷGod's favourᴷ=COP.PRS.3SG.F				

ᴷxera xudeᴷ	bət	kərmànji	g-əmr-i.'
It is God's favour	in	Kurmanji	IND-say-3PL.

He said, 'It is God's favour, God's favour!' They said it in Kurmanji.

(5)
šqəl-le	lira	kurkamana	dide	mən	gùrga'
take.PFV-3SG.M	coin	golden	his	from	wolf

u-θe-le	l-šùqa.'
and-come.PFV-3SG.M	to-market.

He took his golden coin from the wolf and came to the market.

u-zun-ne	ta	gyane	'ixala	u-julle	ta
and-buy.PFV-3SG.M	to	himself	food	and-clothes	to

yalunke	dìde,'
children	his.

He bought food for himself and clothes for his children.

u-mabsuṭ	mər-re	ta	bàxt-e'
and-pleased	say.PFV-3SG.M	to	wife-his

walla	'ana	xze-li	xa	xùra'
indeed	I	meet.PFV-1SG	one	friend

go	ṭura'	băle	gùrgā=le.'
in	mountain	but	wolf=COP.PRS.3SG.M.

And pleased, he told his wife 'Indeed, I met a friend on the mountain, but he is a wolf.

(6)
kud-yom	g-emər-∅
every-day	IND-say-3SG.M

"Every day"—he said—

ʾana	b-yāwən-nox	xǎ	kurkamàna.'
I	FUT-give-1SG.M-O.2SG.M	one	golden

"I will give you one golden coin."

ʾùd-le	=li	ʾədyo	kurkamàna.'
make.PFV-3SG.M	=O.1SG	today	golden

He has given me a golden coin today.'

kud-yom	g-ezəl-∅	l-ṭura	u-g-ewəð-∅
every-day	IND-go-3SG.M	to-mountain	and-IND-make-3SG.M

ṣìwe'	u-k-eθe-∅	gurga	g-yāwəl-∅-le
wood	and-IND-come-3SG.M	wolf	IND-give-3SG.M-O.3SG.M

kurkamàna.'
golden

So every day, he goes to the mountain, cuts wood and the wolf comes and gives him a coin.

(7)
pəš-le	xǎ	yarxa,'	trè,'	tḷàha,'	xǎ	šàta.'
stay.PFV-3SG.M	one	month	two,	three,	one	year

One month went by, then two, three, one year.

baxt-e	g-əmr-a	waḷḷa
wife-his	IND-say-3SG.F	indeed

hatxa	xȍš	naša,'	ḅȁš=ile.'
such	good.SG.M	man	good.SG.M=COP.PRS.3SG.M

His wife said, 'What a kind man! He is good.

ʾana	g-əb-an	ʾoð-an-ne	qàðdre,'
I	IND-want-1SG.F	make-1SG.F-O.3SG.M	dishes

I want to make some dishes for him,

qaðr-an-ne	u-ʿazm-ax-le	kəs-lan	l-bèθa.'
treat-1SG.F-O.3SG.M	and-invite-1PL-O.3SG.M	by-us	to-house

I shall treat him, we shall invite him for a feast at our house.

ʾoð-ax-le	xa	ʾixala	basìm-aˈ	u-məstaʿən-∅
make-1PL-O.3SG.M	some	food	good-SG.M	and-enjoy.oneself-3SG.M

go beθa	kəs-lan	u-doq-ax	qàðre.'
in house	by-us	and-hold-1PL	banquet

We shall prepare some good food for him, he will enjoy himself at our house and we will feast together.'

(8)
g-emər-∅	ṭa-la	šùq-∅-le.'
IND-say-3SG.M	to-her	leave.IMP-SG-O.3SG.M

He says to her 'Leave him alone.

gùrgā=le.'	hèwan=ile.'
wolf=COP.PRS.3SG.M.	animal=COP.PRS.3SG.M.

He's a wolf. He's an animal.

mă	b-aθe-∅	go	naše?'	naše	b-zàdʾ-i.'
what	FUT-come-3SG.M	in	people?	people	FUT-fear-3PL

What does it mean "He will come among people?" People will be afraid.

mbàrbəʿă-∅-lu	gurga	yaʾəl-∅	go maθa.'
alarm-3SG.M-O.3PL	wolf	enter-3SG.M	in city

A wolf that enters the city will alarm them.'

g-əmr-a	là,'	là,'	mar-∅-re.	ʾàθe-∅.'
IND-say-3SG.F	no,	no,	say.IMP-SG-O.3SG.M	come-3SG.M

She said, 'No, no, tell him to come.'

(9) zəl-le   g-emər-∅   ṭà-le,ˈ
    go.PFV-3SG.M   IND-say-3SG.M   to-o.3SG.M

g-emər-∅   ʾana   l-èb-i   ʾaθ-ən.ˈ
IND-say-3SG.M   I   NEG-can-1SG   come-1SG.M

So he went and told the wolf, but he said, 'I can't come.

gùrga   =wən,   k-əxl-ən   nàše.ˈ
wolf   =COP.PRS.1SG.M IND-eat-1SG.M   man

I am a wolf. I eat people.

b-aθ-ən   go   maθa   kull-u   mbàrbəʿ-i.ˈ
FUT-come-1SG.M   in   city   all-them   alarm-3PL

If I come to town, everyone will be alarmed.'

(10) zəl-le   mər-re   ta   baxta   hàtxa
     go.PFV-3SG.M   say.PFV-3SG.M   to   wife   such

g-emər-∅   gurga.ˈ
IND-say-3SG.M   wolf

So the man went and told his wife, this is what the wolf said.

ʾaz   g-əmr-a   šud   ʾaθe-∅   b-lèle,   xə̀ška.ˈ
so   IND-say-3SG.F   let   come-3SG.M   at-night   darkness

So she said, let him come at night, when there is darkness.

bə-daw   wàxtˈ   l-əθ-wa   beherùθaˈ.
in-OBL.that.M   time.SG.M   NEG-EXIST.PST   light

At that time, there were no lights.

l-əθ-wa   ᴬʿanṭariqᴬ   ᴴmenoròtᴴ.
NEG- EXIST-PST   by.way.of   lamps

ᴬkahrabaᴬ   l-ə̀θ-wa.ˈ
ᴬelectricityᴬ   NEG-EXIST-PST

There were not, for instance, lamps. There was no electricity.

xə̀ška	wewa.¹
darkness	COP.PST.3SG.M

It was dark.

u-pāyəš-∅-wa	xə̀ška,¹	kull-a	maθa	xə̀ška
and-stay-3SG.M-PST	darkness	all-3SG.F	city	darkness

wawa.¹
COP.PST.3SG.F

When it got dark, the whole city would be dark.

(11)
g-əmr-a	dammət	payəš-∅
IND-say-3SG.F	when	stay-3SG.M

xə̀ška,¹	šud	'aθe-∅,¹
darkness	let	come-3SG.M

She said, 'Let him come after it gets dark.

beθ-an	wele	bə-dumā̀hik	dət	maθa.¹
house-our	COP.DEIC.3SG.M	in-outskirts	of	city

Our house is situated on the outskirts of town.

b-aθe-∅	kəs-lan	beθa	u-b-àzəl-∅.¹
FUT-come-3SG.M	by-us	house	and-FUT-go-3SG.M

He will come straight to our house and go back.

čŭ-xa	la	k-xāzè-∅-le.¹
no-one	NEG	IND-see-3SG.M-O.3SG.M

No one will see him.'

g-emər-∅	baxt-i	b-oð-a-lox	xa	'azime	bằš.
IND-say-3SG.M	wife-my	FUT-make-3SG.F-O.2SG.M	some	banquet	good

So he told the wolf, 'My wife will make you a great banquet.'

mər-re	ṭa-le	b-àθ-ən,'	g-emər-∅	b-àθ-ən.'
say.PFV-3SG.M	to-him	FUT-come-1SG.M	IND-say-3SG.M	FUT-come-1SG.M

He replied to him. 'I will come,' he said, 'I will come.'

g-emər-∅,	ᴴtovᴴ,	b-àθ-ən.'
IND-say-3SG.M	well,	FUT-come-1SG.M

[The wolf] said, 'Well then, I will come.'

CHRISTIAN ARAMAIC OF ENISHKE
TEXT 6: §1–13

Dorota Molin

---

(1) ʾaw   brət   màlka   wewa.ˈ
    that.M son.of   king   COP.PST.3SG.M

He was the son of a king.

brət   màlka   wewa.ˈ
son-of   king   COP.PST.3SG.M

He was the son of a king.

ʾawa   u-beθa   là-θe-le   l-ʾuxðaðe.ˈ
he   and-house   NEG-come.PFV-3SG.M to-each.other

He did not get along with his family.

šqe-le   b-dənye   xə̀š-le.ˈ
go.PFV-3SG.M   in-world   go.PFV-3SG.M

He wandered in the world, he went.

šqe-le   b-dənye   qam-xaze-∅-le   wə-re
travel.PFV-3SG.M   in-world   PFV-see-3PL-O.3SG.M   pass.PFV-3SG.M

gu   xa   ʾaθra   xèna,ˈ   xa   xayatuθa   xèna.ˈ
in   some   land   other   some   life   other

He travelled around and they saw him enter another country and [begin] a new life.

qam-dawq-i-le,	dar-i-le	gu	sə̀jən.'
PFV-seize-3PL-O.3SG.M	put-3PL-O.3SG.M	in	prison

They arrested him and put him in prison.

(2)
malka	mà	xze-le	b-xulm-e?'
king	what	see.PFV-3SG.M	in-dream-his

What did the king see in his dream?

har	malka	b-gan-e	xze-le	b-xulm-e
also	king	in-self-his	see.PFV-3SG.M	in-dream-his

The king himself saw in his dream:

'əštá	tawraθa	zằbun'	xala	əštá	ṭrìṣ-e.'
six	cows	skinny	eat.INF	six	healthy-PL

six skinny cows were devouring six healthy cows.

u-mà	xze-le	b-xulme	diyye	har	'awu	b-gan-e?'
and-what	see.PFV-3SG.M	in-dream-his	his	also	he	in-self-his

What did [Joseph] see in a dream?

'awu	b-gan-e	mà	xze-le
he	in-self-his	and-what	see.PFV-3SG.M

b-xulm-e	ᴬnafs	əl-leleᴬ?'
in-dream-his	same	DEF-night

What did he see in his dream the same night?

xze-le	b-xùlm-e,'	hole	xzada	dàxla,'
see.PFV-3SG.M	in-dream-his	COP.DEIC.3SG.M	harvest.INF	wheat

He saw in his dream that they were harvesting wheat.

'əšta	baqaθa	d-daxla	sahd-i	lbaq-e	dìyye.'
six	bundles	of-wheat	bow.down-3PL	to-his	his

Six bundles of wheat worshipped his bundles.

(3) mər-e   ʾana   yið-ən-na   mǎndi=la,
    say.PFV-3SG.M I   know-1SG.M-O.3SG.F   what=COP.3SG.F

bas   l-è-maxk-ən-na.
but   NEG-IND-tell-1SG.M-O.3SG.F

He said 'I know what it is [about], but I won't tell.'

mər-e   'mǎndi=le?'   màxke-∅-le   mǎndi=le!'
say.PFV-3SG.M   what=COP.3SG.M   tell.IMP-SG.M-O.3SG.M   what=COP.3SG.M

They said 'What is it? Tell us what it is!'

mər-e   l-è-maxk-ən-na,   l-è-hane-∅-li.
say.PFV-3SG.M   NEG-IND-tell-1SG.M-O.3SG.F   NEG-IND-please-3SG.M-O.1SG

'I won't tell, I am not comfortable telling,' he said.

ʾana   u-xunwàθ-i=wax.
I   and-brothers-my=COP.1PL

'It is about me and my brothers.

t-aθe-∅   yoma   ʾan   xunwaθ-i
FUT-come-3SG.M   day   these   brothers-my

p-sàhd-i   ʾəll-i,   bas   qam-ṭard-ì-li.''
FUT-bown.down-3PL   to-me   but   PFV-expel-3PL-O.1SG

A day will come when my brothers will kneel down before me, but they have expelled me.'

(4) mər-e   'la,   ʾad   ʾawa   b-yiðè-∅-le
    say.PFV-3SG.M   no   SBR   he   FUT-know-3SG.M-O.3SG.M

xulm-ət   dawa   màlka,   m-nabl-àx-le.''
dream-of   OBL.that.M king   FUT-take-1PL-O.3SG.M

They said 'He will be able to interpret the king's dream, let's take him [to the king].'

xəš-le	kəs-le	diyye
go.PFV-3SG.M	to-him	his

He went to him.

mər-e	mằndi=la	qəṣətta,'	faqìra?''
say.PFV-3SG.M	what=COP.3SG.F	story	poor.man

He said 'What is the story, poor fellow?

mằndi=le	qəṣətt-ət
what=COP.3SG.F	story-of

ʾəštá	tawraθa	zăbun	ʾaxl-i	ṭrìṣ-e?''
six	cows	skinny	eat-3PL	healthy-PL

What is the story of six skinny cows devouring fat ones?'

mər-e	'pt-aθe-∅-lux	ʾəštá	šənne	xa	xàḍḍa,'
say.PFV-3SG.M	FUT-come-3SG.M-to.you	six	years	some	famine

xa	garàni,'	ʾajebùθa.'
some	starvation	wonder

He said 'You will have six years of famine, a rise in prices, something astonishing.

(5)	m-daha	mhàm-i,'	mḷi-le	gunìye,
	therefore	believe.IMP-SG.M	fill.IMP.SG.M-O.3PL	sacks

ʾanna	maxazən	diyyux	xəṭṭe	u-dàbra,'
these	store.houses	your.SG.M	grains	and-wheat

b-bary-a	garani	b-xèla,'	yaʿni	xelàn-ta.'
FUT-happen-3SG.F	famine	in-strength	I mean	strong-SG.F

Therefore, believe [me], you need to gather wheat and fill your sacks, your storehouses with wheat and corn, because a severe famine will come, I mean.

ʾəštá	šənne	garani	pt-awy-a.'
six	years	famine	FUT-be-SG.F

There will be a terrible famine for six years.'

ʾawa	mjumeʿ-le	mjumeʿ-le	mjumeʿ-le
he	gather.PFV-3SG.M	gather.PFV-3SG.M	gather.PFV-3SG.M

mjumèʿ-le.'
gather.PFV-3SG.M

[The king] began to store wheat, more and more.

(6)	ʾayya	baxte	diyye	dre-la	ʾena	ʾəll-e
	this.F	wife-his	his	put.PFV-3SG.F	eye	on-him

dìyye.'
his

[Meanwhile,] his (the king's) wife began to look at him with desire.

ʾaz-a-wa	bàθr-e,'	bàθr-e,'
go-3SG.F-PST	after-him	after-him

ʾamr-a	hayyu	l-beθa	xōl-∅	u-štì.'
say-3SG.F	come.IMP.SG	to-house	eat.IMP-SG	and-drink.IMP.SG.M

She would follow him and say 'Come, eat and drink.'

hal	hàdax	qam-awð-a-le,'
until	such	PFV-do-3SG.F-O.3SG.M

mər-a	b-y-an-ne	tāj	màlka	ṭa-lux.'
say.PFV-3	FUT-give-1SG.F-O.3SG.M	crown	king	to-you.SG.M

She did this: she told him 'I'll give you the king's crown.'

(7)	mər-e	ʾana	ᴷZambil	Fròšᴷ	=iwen,'
	say.PFV-3	I	basket	seller	=COP.1SG.M

He said 'But I am a basket-seller.

y-zaqr-ən	zanbire	u-haqq-i	b-y-at-te
IND-weave-1SG.M	baskets	and-right-my	FUT-give-2SG.F-O.3SG.M

xa	lìra,ˈ	pt-àz-ən.ˈ
one	lira	FUT-go-1SG.M

I weave baskets for which I earn one lira, and then I leave.

ʾàw	wele	šuli,ˈ	ʾana	l-è-peš-ən
that.M	COP.DEIC.3SG.M	work-my	I	NEG-IND-become-1SG.M

malka	ʾana.ˈ
king	I

This is my profession. I will not become a king.

l-è-haw-ən	malka.ˈ
NEG-IND-be-1SG.M	king

I will not be a king.'

wele	šul-e	diyye	hadax.
COP.DEIC.3SG.M	work-his	his	thus

This was his job.

u-malka	qam-kəbe-∅-le	u-mən-ne	mə̀nn-e.ˈ
and-king	PFV-like-3SG.M-O.3SG.M	and-help.PFV-3SG.M	O-3SG.M

u-ʾap	ʾawa	mən-ne	mən	dàwa.ˈ
and-even	he	help.PFV-3SG.M	O-3SG.M	OBL.that.M

The king liked him and helped him, and he in turn helped him.

(8)
θe-la	xa	zawna	xunwaθa	diyye
come.PFV-3SG.F	certain	time	brothers	his

hìr-e,ˈ
distressed-PL

A time came when his brothers were in distress.

šmeʾlu	*gu*	*flan*	*dawla*	*ʾəθ*	*dabra*	*mzabòne.*ˈ
hear-PFV-3	in	a.certain	country	EXIST	wheat	sell.INF

They heard that in such-and-such a country there was wheat for sale.

xəš-le	*xa*	*b-xa*	*mə̀nn-e.*ˈ
go.PFV-3SG.M	one	with-one	of-them

They all went to him, one by one.

mà	*wed-le*	*ʾawa?*
what	do.PFV-3SG.M	he

What did he (Zambil Frosh) do?

(9)
ʾawa=le	*kyala*	*ʾàn*	*xəṭṭe*ˈ
he=COP.3SG.M	measure.INF	these	grain

u-dráyə-lla	*ṭà-lehi.*ˈ
and-place.INF-O.3SG.F	to-them

[It was] he [who] measured the grain and put it in their sacks.

šqəl-le	*xa*	*kas-ət*	*dehwa*	*ʾə́θ-wā-le*
take.PFV-3SG.M	one	cup-of	gold	EXIST-PST-3SG.M

He took out a golden cup which he had.

y-dar-i	*p-kas-ət*	*dèhwa,*ˈ
IND-put-3PL	in-cup-of	gold

They used to put [the grain] in a golden cup.

qam-ðare-∅-le	*gu*	*ṭen-et*	*xa*	*mə̀nn-e.*ˈ
PFV-put-3SG.M-O.3SG.M	in	load-of	one	of-them

And he put it in the sack of one of them.

*xə̀šle,*ˈ	*rxəq-le*	*t-maṭ-e*	*l-mðìta.*ˈ
go.PFV-3PL	go_far.PFV-3PL	SBR-arrive-3PL	to-city

They went back to their [home] city.

xəš-le har jèš baθr diyye.|
go.PFV-3SG.M even army after them

An army went pursuing them.

(10) *mər-e har ʾawa,*| *mər-e ta malka*
say.PFV-3SG.M even he say.PFV-3SG.M to king

ʾana hàtxa pt-awð-ən,|
I thus FUT-do-1SG.M

[Zambil Frosh] said, he told the king 'This is what I am going to do.

qam-ganw-i-la ʾayya ʾamana dìyyux.|
PFV-steal-3PL-O.3SG.F this.F cup your.SG.M

They have stolen your cup.'

ʾanna xunwaθa diyye=le.|
these brothers his=COP.3PL

They were his own brothers.

xəš-le baθr-e hal qurbət mòitey,|
go.PFV-3SG.M after-him until near-of city-their

They chased them outside their city.

yaʿani wàra,| *qam-dawq-ì-le,*| *meθ-ì-le.*|
I mean outside PFV-seize-3PL-O.3PL bring-3PL-O.3PL

I mean, [they were] outside when they captured them and brought them [back].

(11) *mər-e 'qày,*| *màx wið-e?*|
say.PFV-3PL how how do.PTCP-PL

They said 'But how, what have we done?

čù	məndi,	l-èx	wið-e	ʾaxni.'	'mər-e	là,'
no	thing	NEG-COP.1PL	do.PTCP-PL	we	say.PFV-3SG.M	no

Nothing, we have done [nothing].'

wutu	gniwə-lla	ṭaz-ət	dèhwa.'
COP.2PL	steal.PTCP.SG.M-O.3SG.F	cup-of	gold

You have stolen the gold cup.'

'daxxi,	ʾaxni	màṭu	b-gə́nw-ax-la?'
how	we	how	FUT-steal-1PL-O.3SG.F

'How, how could we steal it?!

yaḷḷa	yaḷḷa	mṭe-la	dabra	ʾəll-an
quickly	quickly	arrive-PFV-3SG.F	wheat	to-us

The wheat has barely arrived in our city.

u-naše	kull-a	mət-la	m-kupna	t-mamṭ-ax
and-people	all-them	die.PFV-3PL	of-hunger	SBR-bring-1PL

l-mðìta.''
to-city

Our people were dying of hunger before we would bring [it] to the city!'

mər-e	'pθux-u	gùniyat-exu.''
say.PFV-3SG.M	open.IMP-PL	sacks-your.PL

He said 'Open your sacks.'

har	ʾawa	qam-paθəx-∅-le	ʾay	gunìya.'
even	he	PFV-open-3SG.M-O.3SG.M	this.F	sack

He himself opened the sack.

mər-e	də-mbarb-i	ʾàxxa.'
say.PFV-3SG.M	SBR-empty-3PL	here

He told them to empty it here.

pḷət-la	*kas-ət*	*dehwa*	*tàma.*ˈ
come.out.PFV-3SG.F	cup-of	gold	there

The golden cup fell out.

(12) | *ʾanna* | *mà* | *wəd-le?*ˈ |
|---|---|---|
| these | what | do.PFV-3PL |

What did they do?'

qam-šaql-i-le	*ʾaw*	*xon-e.*ˈ
PFV-take-3PL-O.3SG.M	that.M	brother-their

They took [one of] their brother[s].

yaʿăni	*yðe-le*	*ʾəbb-e*	*diyye.*ˈ
I mean	know.PFV-3PL	with-him	his

I mean, they recognised him.

qam-šaql-i-le	*xunwaθa*	*diyye*	*ʾaw*	*t-ile*
PFV-take-3PL-O.3SG.M	brothers	his	that.M	SBR-COP.3SG.M

kəs	*màlka.*ˈ
with	king

[Then] they took him with them, the brother who was with the king.

(13) | *xəš-le* | *ʾabb-e* | *b-dabra* | *dìyye.*ˈ |
|---|---|---|---|
| go.PFV-3SG.M | with-them | with-wheat | their |

They went away with their grain.

kut-məndi	*t-āwèð-∅-wa,*ˈ	*l-əθ-wa*	*laʾa.*ˈ
every-thing	SBR-do-3SG.M-PST	NEG-EXIST-PST	no

There was no objection to anything he did.

ˀəštá	šənne	y-sahd-i-wa	ˀəll-e	dìyye.ˈ
six	years	IND-bow.down-3PL-PST	to-him	his

y-ʕabd-ì-wa-le.ˈ
IND-worship-3PL-PST-O.3SG.M

They would kneel before him for six years, they worshipped him.

u-hul	ˀegət	t-ile	piš-e	gor-e
and-until	when	SBR-COP.3SG.M	become.PTCP-PL	grown.up-PL

u-gwir-e	kùll-e,ˈ	ˀaw	xona	rayyəs
and-married.PTCP-PL	all-them	that.M	brother	chief

diyyehi	wèwa.ˈ
their	COP.PST.3SG.M

Until they all grew up and got married, that brother was their chief.

ˀana	ˀo	məndi	tnàyə-llax.ˈ
I	this.M	thing	tell.INF-O.2SG.F

This is what I am telling you.

JEWISH ARAMAIC OF ZAKHO
TEXT 25: §2–7, 9

Dorota Molin

Speaker: Samra Zaqen

Audio: https://nena.ames.cam.ac.uk/audio/226/

(2) ʾəs-wa   xa   ᴴbaḥùrᴴˌ,
    EXIST-PST one   young.man

ᴴmeʾód   meʾód   yăfèᴴ   we-le.ˌ
very   very   beautiful.SG.M PST.COP-3SG.M

There was [once] a young man, he was very, very handsome.

ᴴmuxšàr,ˌ   ṭòv,ˌ   yăfèᴴ.ˌ
gifted.SG.M   good.SG.M   beautiful.SG.M

[He was] talented, good, handsome.

kull-u   ʿalam   g-žăġl-iˌ
all-their   world   IND-work-3PL

u-mparnəs-i   gyàn-u,ˌ   g-oz-i   šoʾàle.ˌ
and-sustain-3PL   self.SG.F-their   IND-work-3PL   works

Everybody else worked to support themselves, doing their work.

ʾawa   g-ēr-∅,   ʾla',   là   g-be-wa.ˌ
he   IND-say-3SG.M   no   NEG   IND-want-3SG.M-PST

[But] he said no, he did not want to.

(3) bab-e   yəmm-e   mjozè-lu| mən   maḥkòye|
    father-his mother-his tire.PFV-3PL from   speak.INF

'kappàr-ox| si   žġòl-∅| d-gòr-ət|
sacrifice-your.SG.M go.IMP.SG.M work.IMP-SG   SBR-marry-2SG.M

dəd   yàtw-ət| dət ha'...,
SBR   dwell-2SG.M SBR oh

His parents exhausted themselves discussing [this with him]. 'Please, go to work so that you can marry, so that can you settle down.'

ma   p̂-awe-∅   bəd   bèsa?!|
what FUT-be-3SG.M   in   house

Why should he stay at home?

mà-l-ox?!'| la   g-žàġl-ən   g-ēr-∅.|
what-to-you.SG.M   NEG   IND-1SG.M   IND-say-3SG.M

'What is it with you?' 'I shall not work,' he said.

la   g-žàġəl-∅   ᴴᶜaṣlắnᴴ| là   g-žaġəl-∅.|
NEG   IND-work-3SG.M   lazy   NEG   IND-work-3SG.M

He does not work, the lazy [one]! He does not work.

kaṣlằn.| hè|,   ᴴᶜaṣlắnᴴ   kaṣlằn,
lazy   yes   lazy   lazy

Lazy. Yes, [he is] lazy, lazy.

hile   dmìxa   xa   te'na.|
DEIC.COP.3SG.M   sleep.PTCP-M.SG   one   fig.tree

He is sleeping under a fig tree.

(4) 'èha, ḥakoma day bàžər, ʾət-le tlaha
    this.F ruler OBL.DEF.SG.F city EXIST-3SG.M three

bnàsa. mutw-i-le kut-tla-hùn
daughters seat.PFV-O.3PL-3SG.M all-three-their

The king of that city had three daughters. He sat them down.

g-emər-∅, 'sà-wun bnàs-i,
IND-say-3SG.M go.IMP-PL daughters-my

mănibəž g-əbè-∅-li?'
who more IND-love-3SG.M-O.1SG

He said 'Come, my daughters, which [of you] loves me the most?'

(5) 'ay rab-sa g-əmr-a 'bàb-i,
    DEF.SG.F big-FS IND-say-3FS father-my

g-əb-an-nox qčin məlk-əd dùnye.
IND-love-1SG.F-O.2SG.M like king-of world

The oldest said, 'My father, I love you like the king of the world, as much as I love him.

kma g-əb-an-ne ʾe bohora-ət dùnye,
how.much IND-love-1SG.F-O.3SG.M DEF.SG.F light-of world

ʾahət g-əb-an-nox ᴴʾòtoᴴ.'
you.SG.M IND-LOVE-1SG.F-O.2SG.M same

As much as I love the light of the world, so I love *you*.'

'g-əb-àt-ti.'
IND-love-2SG.F-O.1SG.M

[The king said: 'Indeed] you love me.'

'ay xet g-ēr-∅-ra
DEF.SG.F other.INV IND-say-3SG.M-O.3SG.F

The other one—[the king] said to her,

'brat-i	kma	g-əb-àt-ti?'
daughter-my	how.much	IND-love-2SG.F-O.1SG.M

'My daughter, how much do you love me?'

g-əmr-a	'mad	mər-ra	xàs-i.
IND-say-3SG.F	like	say.PFV-3SG.F	sister-my

She said, 'Whatever my sister has said.

qčin	bohora-ət	ʾèn-i
like	light-of	eyes-my

u-^Hbriyut^H	didi	g-b-àn-nox.'
and-health	my	IND-love-1SG.F-O.2SG.M

Like the light of my eyes and my health I love you.'

g-ēr-∅,	ʾay	trè.'
IND-say-3SG.F	DEF.SG.F	two

He said... [That was] the second one.

(6)	məse-le	ʾay	zùr-ta,
	bring.PFV-3SG.M	DEF.SG.F	little-SG.F

He brought the youngest one.

'brat-i	ʾāt	kma	g-əb-àt-ti?'
daughter-my	you.SG.F	how.much	IND-love-2SG.F-O.1SG.M

My daughter, and you, how much do you love me?'

g-əmr-a	bàb-i	g-əb-àn-nox	qčin	məlxa
IND-say-3SG.F	father-my	IND-love-1SG.F-O.2SG.M	like	salt

dət	g-dare-∅	ʾəl	qəzra
SBR	IND-put-3PL	on	dish

She said, 'My father, I love you like the salt they put in cooked food,

maṭo	p̂-oy-a	basəm-ta,	ʾoto	g-əb-àn-nox.
how	FUT-be-3SG.F	tasty-SG.F	same	IND-love-1SG.F-O.2SG.M

the way it makes [the food] delicious, so I love you.'

(7)
ʾowà!	mux	məlxa	g-əb-at-ti	bàs?!
aha	like	salt	IND-love-1SG.F-O.SG.M	only

'Oh! You love me only this much?!'

g-ēr-∅,	ʾahat	la	g-nafʾ-at	tà-li.
IND-say-3SG.M	you.SG.M	NEG	IND-suffice-2SG.F	to-me

'You are not [good] enough for me.

šqol-∅	čanṭa	didax	u-s-è.
take.IMP-SG	bag	your.SG.F	and-go.IMP-SG.F

take your bag and go [away].

la	g-yaw-ən-nax	čù-məndi.
NEG	IND-give-1SG.M-O.2SG.F	any-thing

I shall not give you anything.

ʾanya	trè	bnas-i=lu,
these	two	daughters-my=COP.3PL

ʾahat	le-at	bràt-i,	wiii!ʾ
you.SG.F	NEG-COP.2SG.F	daughter-my	oh

Those two are my daughters, you are not my daughter, you!'

(9)
ʾe	šqəl-la	čanṭa	dida.
she	take.PFV-3F.SG	bag	her

She took her bag.

èka	b-ᴴʾazᴴ-a
where	FUT-go-3SG.F

Where could she go [now]

ʾəla	*daw*	^H*kerem*^H	*dət*	*bàb-a?*[|]
except	OBL.DEF-SG.M	vineyard	of	father-her

if not to her father's vineyard?

ʾət-le	^H*kerem*^H	*rùww-a,*
EXIST-3SG.M	vineyard	big-SG.M

He had a large vineyard.

g-əmr-a	*g-b-an*	*yatw-an*	*tàma*
IND-say-3SG.F	IND-want-1SG.F	sit-1SG.F	there

She said [to herself], 'I want to stay there.

b-oz-an-ni	*xa*	^H*pinà.*^{H|}
FUT-make-1SG.F-O.1SG.F	one	corner

I will make [there] a place for myself.

k-xazy-an	*hil*	*doq-an*	*gyàn-i,*[|]
IND-see-1SG.F	until	collect-1SG.F	self.SG.F-my

ma	*ʾòz-an*	*ma*	*la*	*ʾoz-àn.*[|]
what	do-1SG.F	what	NEG	do-1SG.F

I will wait there until I collect myself, [decide] what to do and what not to do.'

CHRISTIAN ARAMAIC OF ZAKHO
TEXT 10: §21–33

Dorota Molin

Speaker: Ameen Isa Shamoun

Audio: https://nena.ames.cam.ac.uk/audio/226/

(21) *fa-Toma   pləṭ-le   mən   madin-ət   Samàna.*ˈ
    and-Toma   leave.PFV-3SG.M   from   city-of   Samana

Meanwhile, Toma moved away from the town of Samana.

*xà   yoma,*ˈ *trè,*ˈ *ᴬʾəsbùʿ,* *kằða,*ˈᴬ
one   day   two   week   so

*xa   fatra   zamán=ila   mṭe-le   l-Zàxo.*ˈ
some   period   time=COP.3SG.F   arrive.PFV-3SG.M   to-Zakho

It took him a day or two, a week or so, he arrived in Zakho.

*ʾiman   mṭe-le   Zàxo…*ˈ
when   arrive.PFV-3SG.M   Zakho

When he arrived in Zakho…

*ʾamir-ət   manṭaq-ət   Bahdinằn   bə-daw   waqt,*ˈ
prince-of   region-of   Bahdinan   in-OBL.that.M   time

*ʾaw   d-iwa   b-Amèdiya,*ˈ   *b-Zàxo*   *=wa.*ˈ
that.M   SBR-COP.PST.3SG.M   in-Amediya   in-Zakho   =COP.PST.3SG.M

The prince of the region of Bahdinan, who would [later] be in Amedia, was in Zakho at that time.

(22)	šmeʾ-le	ʾə́nnuhu	te-le	xa	hòsta.ˈ
	hear.PFV-3SG.M	that	come.PFV-3SG.M	one	craftsman

He heard that a craftsman had arrived.

u-ʾawwa	hosta	ʾile	xùš	hosta.ˈ
and-that.M	craftsman	COP.3SG.M	good	craftsman

This craftsman is a good one.

hole	beny-a	hatxa	jə̀sr.ˈ
DEIC.COP.3SG.M	build.PTCP-SG.M	such	bridge

He has built such a bridge.

ᴬjəsr	ʿəmlaq	fi	flằn	manṭaqa,ˈ	u-kằða	u-kằða,ᴬ
bridge	great	in	certain	region	and-so	and-so

ʾe.ˈ
yes

A great bridge in the region called so-and-so, and so on.

fa-ʾamīr	mà	mer-e,ˈ	ʾad	Zàxo?ˈ
and-prince	what	say.PFV-3SG.M	of	Zakho

So, what did the prince of Zakho say?

(23)	mè-re,ˈ	⟨ᴬ⟩aḥsan	ši	ʾənnuᴬ	ʾawwa
	say.PFV-3SG.M	best	thing	that	he

bane-∅	xa	jəsr	ṭa-leni	gawət	mdit-ət	Zàxo.ˈ
build-3SG.M	one	bridge	to-us	inside	city-of	Zakho

He said, 'The best thing [would be] for this man to build a bridge for us in the town of Zakho.

ləʾán	l-ə́t-wā-le	ču	ràbṭ	benate-hən.ˈ
because	NEG-EXIST-PST-3SG.M	none	connection	between-them

Because there was no connection between the two sides,

ʾamr-əx	ʾənnu	ʾad	t-àra.¹
say-1PL	that	of	of-land

that is, a land (connection).

fa-ʾawwa	b-bane-∅	ṭa-leni	xa	jə̀sr.¹'
and-he	FUT-build-3SG.M	to-us	one	bridge

ʾən	ʾamr-əx	xa	gə̀šra.¹
if	say-1PL	one	bridge

So he shall build a passage for us,' let's call [it] a 'bridge'.

(24)
fa-qre-le	ʾell-ət	Tòma.¹
and-call.PFV-3SG.M	to-of	Toma

So, he summoned Toma.

ʾamer-∅	ṭà-le,¹	ʿhàyyu-∅	Toma.¹
say-3SG.M	to-him	come.IMP-SG	Toma

He said to him, 'Come, Toma.

k-əb-ən	mənn-ux	ban-ət-li	hàtxa	məndi.¹'
IND-want-1SG.M	of-you.SG.M	build-2SG.M-O.1SG	such	thing

I want you to build me such a thing.'

ʾamer-∅	ṭà-lu,¹	ʿmà	y-xaləf-∅.¹'
say-3SG.M	to-him	NEG	IND-matter-3SG.M

He said to him, 'Well then.'

fa-bdeʾ-le	Toma	bə-bnàya.¹
and-begin.PFV-3SG.M	Toma	in-build.INF

Toma began constructing the bridge.

ʾamr-i	babawàt-an,¹	ʾamr-i	ʾənnu
say-3PL	fathers-our	say-3PL	that

Our ancestors say

'Toma	bde'-le	bə-bnaya	b-jə̀sr.'
Toma	begin.PFV-3SG.M	in-build.INF	in-bridge

that he began building the bridge.

ham	là-yed-əx	xa	yoma,'	ᴬʼesbù','	šàhr,'	sǎna,'	kǎða,'ᴬ
even	NEG-know-1PL	one	day	week	month	year	so

ʼaw	hole	bə-bnaya.'"
he	DEIC.COP.3SG.M	in-build.INF

We do not know for how long he was building—a day, a week, a month, a year or so.

bə-ṭlata	bène,'	bə-ṭlata	bène,'	kəm-bāne-le
in-three	attempt	in-three	attempts	PFV-build-3SG.M-O.3SG.M

jə̀sr.'
bridge

He built the bridge in three attempts.

(25)
y-maṭe-∅	ᴬnihaya	l-ʼaxer	qànṭaraᴬ.'
IND-arrive-3SG.M	end	to-last	arch

In the end, he got to the last arch.

wəd-le	jəsr-ət	Dalál	b-xamšà	qanaṭer,'
do.PFV-3SG.M	bridge-of	Dalale	with-five	arches

mù	šawwa.'
NEG	seven

He made Dalale Bridge with five arches, not seven.

Samana	wəd-le	šǎwwa.'
Samana	do.PFV-3SG.M	seven

Samana [however] he had built with seven.

bas	ʾawwa	kəm-bānè-∅-le,'	xamšà	qanaṭər
but	that.M	PFV-build-3SG.M-O.3SG.M	five	arches

wəd-le	ṭa	jəsr.'
do.PFV-3SG.M	for	bridge

But he built this one with five arches, he made five [arches] for the bridge.

bne-le	ʾəll-ət	jəsrət	Dalál	gawət	mdit-ət
build.PFV-3SG.M	to-of	bridge-of	Dalal	inside-of	city-of

Zàxo.'
Zakho

He constructed [them for] Dalale Bridge in Zakho.

ʾamr-i	ʾənnu	ṭlata	bene	mṭe-le	Toma
say-3PL	that	three	attempts	arrive.PFV-3SG.M	Toma

nihay-ət	rabəṭ-∅-le	jə̀sr,'	y-napəl-∅	jə̀sr.'
end-SBR	connect-3SG.M-O.3SG.M	bridge	IND-fall-3SG.M	bridge

It is said that Toma reached the end to connect the bridge three times, but [every time] the bridge fell down.

(26)
fa-hole	wil-a	ʾahad-ət	ʾamir-ət	Zàxo,'
and-DEIC.COP.3SG.M	give.PTCP-SG.M	one-of	prince-of	Zakho

ʾinu...	ʾàwwa,'	ʾamir-ət	Bahdinằn,'
that	he	prince-of	Bahdinan

ʾinu	ʾ-ən	la-bane-∅	jəsr	b-qaṭə̀l-le.'"
that	if	NEG-build-3SG.M	bridge	FUT-kill-3SG.M-O.3SG.M

So, someone belonging to the prince of Bahdinan had given [a warning] that he, [that is] the prince of Zakho, would kill him if he does not build the bridge

ʾawwa	y-amer-∅	ʿàna,	ʾawwa	kəm-qaṭe-∅
he	IND-say-3SG.M	I	he	PFV-cut-3SG.M

ʾid-i	u-ʾawwa	b-qaṭe-∅	rèš-i.	ʾe,	ʿàdi.
hand-my	and-he	FUT-cut-3SG.M	head-my	yes	normal

He said 'That one severed my hand; and this one will cut my head, [to them, it's] normal.

u-ʾana	mà	ʾawd-ən-na?''
and-I	what	do-1SG.M-O.3SG.F

[But] what shall I do?'

(27)
fa-b-layle	ṭləb-le	mən	ʾalaha	u-mṣolè-le.
and-in-night	ask.PFV-3SG.M	of	God	and-pray.PFV-3SG.M

So during the night, he pleaded with God and prayed.

u-mèr-e,	ʿya	ʾalàh-i,	ʾinu	ṭalb-ən
and-sayPFV-3SG.M	Oh	Good-my	that	ask-1SG.M

mənn-ux	ʾawd-ət-li	xa	ḥằl,	ʾinu	mà
of-you.SG.M	do-2SG.M-O.1SG.M	some	solution	that	what

ʾawd-ən.
do-1SG.M

He said 'Oh, God, I ask you for some solution.

ʾana	b-xa	ʾide=wən.
I	with-one	hand=COP.1SG.M

I am with one hand.

u-b-id-ət	čaple	holi	bə-plàxa.''
and-in-hand-of	left	COP.DEIC.1SG	in-work.INF

I am working with my left hand.'

(28) mən ʿamàle,' u-har Tòma tama y-daməx-wa.'
    with workers and-even Toma there IND-sleep-3SG.M-PST

Toma [was] with the workers and even slept there.

yaʿni gəb šula dìyu,' ḥatta dāre-∅-wa bala
I mean by work his so that put-3SG.M-PST attention

l-šula dìyu,' mən ganàwe,' mən kằða,' mən
to-work his of thieves of such of

zala u-at-i ḥatta dare-∅ bala l-šula
go.INF and-come-3PL so that put-3SG.M attention to-work

diyu.'
his

That is, he was near his construction site to watch over his building [against] thieves and passers-by, to look after his building.

ᴬləʾán ʾakíd ʾə́nnuhuᴬ y-amr-i Toma gắlak
because surely that IND-say-3PL Toma very

=wa mùxləṣ b-šula diyu.'
=COP.PST.3SG.M responsible in-work his

That was also because—it was said—Toma was very loyal to his work.

fa-yom-ət ṭlàta,' mpə̀l-le.'
and-day-of three fall.PFV-3SG.M

On the third day, [the bridge] collapsed.

mà ʾawəd-∅ baʿd?'
what do-3SG.M afterwards

What shall he do now?

(29) dmə̀x-le.' mṣole-le u-dmə̀x-le.'
sleep.PFV-3SG.M pray.PFV-3SG.M and-sleep.PFV-3SG.M

So he slept. He prayed and slept.

b-layle te-le xa ròya, roya, mà?'
in-night come.PFV-3SG.M one vision vision what

He had a vision during the night.

malàxa te-le ʾamer-∅ ṭa-lu,'
angel come.PFV-3SG.M say-3SG.M to-him

An angel came and said to him:

'Tòma,' lazem ʾawwa jəsr ʾiða ʾən pàyəš-∅,'
Toma must that.M bridge if if remain-3SG.M

^Aḥày yəbqa^A,' lazem dar-ət xa rūḥ
living remains must place-2SG.M one being

gaw-u.'
inside-it

Toma, if this bridge is to stand and remain, you must put a living soul inside it.

ʾiðan rūḥ hawe-∅ barnaša ʾən hawe-∅ hàywan.'
if being be-3SG.M human or be-3SG.M animal

It may be either a human being or an animal.

^Amŭhə́m,' rūḥ ḥayya^A.' dar-ət-la gaw-u ʾaw
important living being place-2SG.M-O.3SG.F inside-it.M that.M

ḥày,' yaḷḷa jəsr diyux b-θàbət-∅.'"
being quickly bridge your.SG.M FUT-hold-3SG.M

But the important thing is that you put a living soul inside it while still living so that the bridge will stand firm.'

fa-Toma	*mṣole-le*	*u-dmə̀x-le.*'
and-Toma	pray.PFV-3SG.M	and-sleep PFV-3SG.M

So, Toma prayed and slept.

(30) | *qəm-le* | *qadàmta.*' | *mèr-e,*' | *'yà* | *'alah-i.*'' |
|---|---|---|---|---|
| arise. PFV-3SG.M | morning | say. PFV-3SG.M | oh | God-my |

He woke up in the morning. He said, 'Oh, God.'

qadamta	*dà'əman,*'	*'ə́t-wā-le*	*kalta.*'
morning	always	EXIST-PST-3SG.M	daughter.in.law

In the morning, he had a daughter-in-law.

hàmka	*qŭṣaṣ,*'	*ḥəkayat*	*y-màḥk-i-wa.*'
few	stories	tales	IND-tell-3PL-PST

xa	*y-amr-i*	*bràt-u*	*=iwa.*'
some	IND-say-3PL	daughter-his	=COP.PST.3SG.F

Some stories, that is, the versions which they used to tell, some of them say it was his daughter.

xa	*y-amr-i*	*kàltu*	*=iwa.*'
some	IND-say-3PL	daughter.in.law-his	=COP.PST.3SG.F

Some [others] say that she was his daughter-in-law.

kut-xa	*xa-məndi*	*y-amèr-∅-wa,*'	*ḥăsab*	*mà.*'
every-one	something	IND-say-3SG.M-PST	depends	what

Each one used to say something different, it depends.

'ana	*hol-i*	*šəmy-a*
I	DEIC.COP-1SG	hear.PTCP-SG.M

'inu	*y-amr-i*	*kàlt-u*	*=wa.*'
that	IND-say-3PL	daughter.in.law	=COP.PST.3MSG.F

I have heard that she was his daughter-in-law.

šəmm-aw	Dàlle,	Dàlle,	mù	Dalale.	šəmm-aw	Dàlle.
name-her	Dalle	Dalle	NEG	Dalale	name-her	Dalle

Her name was Dalle, not Dalale. Her name was Dalle.

fa-Dàlle,	kalt-ət	ʿam-an	Toma,	ʾăbū
and-Dalle	daughter.in.law-of	uncle-our	Toma	father

l-bnaya	jə̀sr,	fa,	yomiya	qadamta	y-maty-a-wa
to-build.INF	bridge	and	daily	morning	IND-bring-3SG.F-PST

fə̀ṭra,	yaʿni	fṭàrta,	ṭa	xəmyàna.
breakfast	I mean	beakfast	for	father-in-law

So, Dalle, daughter-in-law of our uncle Toma, the builder of the bridge, brought him breakfast daily in the morning, that is, breakfast, for her father-in-law.

fa-ʾət-wa-ləhən	mənn-aw...
and-EXIST-PST-3PL	with-her

ʾə́t-wā-le	b-beta	xa	kàlwa.	tə̀kram,
EXIST-PST-3SG.M	in-house	one	dog	pardon me

And they had with them... he had a dog at home, excuse me.

xa	kalwa	u-kòme	=wa.	kòme	=wa.
one	dog	and-black	=COP.PST.3SG.M	black	=COP.PST.3SG.M

A dog, and it was black. It was black.

fa-y-maty-a-wa-le	mənn-aw	u-rajʿ-à-wa.
and-IND-bring-3SG.F-PST-O.3SG.M	with-her	and-return-3SG.F-PST

She would bring it along with her and go back.

u-ham	mumkən	ʿalmud	ʾùrxa.
and-even	maybe	along	road

Maybe even the whole way.

u-kalwa y-āte-∅-wa mə̀nn-aw.'
and-dog IND-come-3SG.M-PST with-her

The dog would come with her.

hole lìp-a ʾəl,' ʾəll-ət Dalàle.'
COP.DEIC.3SG.M used.to.PTCP-SG.M to to-of Dalale

ʾəll-ət Dàlle, ʾamr-əx.'
to-of Dalle say-1PL

It had got used to Dalale, or shall we say, Dalle.

(32) fa-qadamta xzè-le...'
     and-morning see.PFV-3SG.M

So, he saw in the morning...

bə-daw wàqt,' daw wàqt,' Zaxo y-amr-i-wa
in-OBL.that.M time OBL.that.M time Zakho IND-say-3PL-PST

dàʾəman,' yaʿni, bas daw jə̀sr,' ʾə́nnuhu
always I mean only OBL.that.M bridge that

y-amr-í-wā-le jəsra ᴷmazə̀nᴷ,' ᴷpərá mazə̀nᴷ,'
IND-say-3PL-PST-O.3SG.M bridge great bridge great

jəsr ʾaw ṛàb-a.'
bridge that.M great-SG.M

At that time, at that time, Zakho was always called, I mean, the bridge was called the Great Passage, the Great Bridge, the Great Bridge.

y-amr-i l-màhi?' ləʾan,
IND-say-3PL why because

Why did they say [that]? Because,

(33) | y-àmr-i,' | ʾaykət | ʾawr-ət | daxel | ʾəpr-ət | Zàxo,'
| IND-say-3PL | when | enter-2SG.M | inside | land-of | Zakho

| y-mbayən-∅ | jəsr-ət | Dalàl.'
| IND-appears-3SG.M | bridge-of | Dalal

They say—when you enter Zakho, the Dalale Bridge is visible.

| lə'án | jəsr-ət | Dalā́l | ʿàli | =yewa,'
| because | bridge-of | Dalal | tall | =COP.PST.3SG.M

| u-ăr-ət | Zàxo | kull-a | ʿàdəl | =iwa.'
| and-land-of | Zakho | all-its.F | flat | =COP.PST.3SG.F

Because this bridge is high while the territory of Zakho is flat.

| lə'án | Zàxo | mašhúr=la | b-^Asăhəl_əs_Sə̀ndi.'
| because | Zakho | famous=COP.3SG.F | with-Plain.of.Sendi

Because Zakho is famous for the Sendi Plain.

| săhəl_əs_Sendi^A | u-Zàxo | ^Adà'əman | ʾarḍ^A | diya,'
| Plain.of.Sendi | Zakho | always | land | her

| ʾənu | ʾăra | ʿàdəl=ila.'
| that | land | flat=COP.3SG.F

Always, the Sendi Plain and Zakho [with] all of its territory—the land there is flat.

| fa-ʾaykət | pàlṭ-i,' | ʾaykət | xàz-i,'
| and-when | leave-3PL | when | see-3PL

| găr̄ək | xaz-i-le | jəsr-ət | Dalàl.'
| must | see-3PL-O.3SG.M | bridge-of | Dalal

So, from wherever [people] leave [the city] and look, they have to see the Dalale Bridge.

CHRISTIAN ARAMAIC OF HARMASHE
TEXT 33: §1–44

Paul M. Noorlander

Speaker: Salim Daniel Yomaran

Audio: https://nena.ames.cam.ac.uk/audio/229/

(1) ʾamr-i-wa   ʾəθ-wa   xàʾa,| xa   malka
    say-3PL-PST   EXIST-PST   one   a.certain   king

ʾə́θ-wa-le   ṭḷaθà   bnone.|
EXIST-PST-3SG.M   three   sons

It was said there once was a king [who] had three sons.

xa   šəm-eu   ʾAḥmád   Čălăbi=wa.| xa   Mḥămad
one   name-his   Ahmad   Chalabi=PST.COP.3SG.M   one   Muhammad

Čălăbi=w,   xa   Mərzá   Mḥằmad=wewa.| Mərzá
Chalabi=and   one   Mirza   Muhamma=PST.COP.3SG.M   Mirza

Mḥămad   ʾaw   xona   zùr-a=le.|
Muhammad   the.SG.M   brother   small-SG.M=COP.3SG.M

One was called Ahmad Chalabi; one Muhammad Chalabi, and one was Mirza Muhammad. Mirza Muhammad was the youngest brother.

ʾan   xəne   ʾan   gòr-e=nan.|
the.PL   others   the.PL   big-PL=COP.3PL

The others were the elder ones.

© 2022 Paul Noorlander, CC BY-NC 4.0   https://doi.org/10.11647/OBP.0306.11

(2) yoma=w   tre=w   tlaθa=w   'àrba,   xa   yoma
    day=and   two=and   three=and four   one   day

xa   malka   'əθ-wa-le   tlaθá   bnaθe.
a.certain   king   EXIST-PST-3SG.M three   daughters

ya'ni   bnaθe   ᴬdăraja   'ulaᴬ   xamàθe=wewa.
it.means   daughters   degree   first.SG.F beautiful.F.PL=PST.COP.3PL

A day or two, three, four [passed by]. Once a king had three daughters. You know, they were girls with beauty of the first degree.

(3) 'aw,   ma   l-àw   malka?   xpər-e   xa
    he   what   to-that.M   king   dig.PFV-3SG.M   a.certain

xàndaq;   xandaq,   ya'ni,   rwə̀x-ta.
trench   trench   it.means   wide-SG.F

He,—what about that king? He dug a trench; that is, a wide trench.

(4) mər-e: 'kut   šawər-∅-a   'àya   xandaq,
    say.PFV-3SG.M   each   jump-3SG.M-O.3SG.F this.F   trench

brat-i   gor-ta   b-yaw-ən-a   tàl-eu.'
daughter-my   big-SG.F   FUT-give-1SG-O.3SG.F to-3SG.M

He said, 'Whoever jumps [over] this trench—I shall give her to him [in marriage].'

(5) kŭl-ay   hune   b-izàla,   b-izàla=w,   b-izàala,
    all-them   DEIC.COP.3PL   in-go.INF   in-go.INF=and   in-go.INF

lène   b-iyara.
NEG.COP.3PL   in-dare.INF

Everybody was going back and forth, [but] they did not dare [to jump].

(6) *'ăxa   Mərzá   Mḥămad   tfəq-le.| qəm-le*
    here   Mirza   Muhammad   happen.PFV-3SG.M   rise.PFV-3SG.M

šqəl-e   sùst-eu| 'u   surgin-à-le.|
take.PFV-3SG.M   mare-his   and   saddle.PFV-O.3SG.F-3SG.M

Mirza Muhammad happened to be here. So he took his mare and saddled her.

'u   rku-le   l-xāṣ-t   sust-eu=w   zəl-e.|
and   mount.PFV-3SG.M-   on-back-of   mare-his=and   go.PFV-3SG.M

He mounted the back of the horse and went off.

(7) *xər-e   'əla   xandaq   xpər-ta.|*
    look.PFV-3SG.M   behold   trench   dig.PTCP-SG.F

He looked at the trench [that had been] dug.

zə-le   xðə̀-re   xa,   tre   čarxe| xðər-e,|
go.PFV-3SG.M   go.round.PFV   one   two   times   go.round.PFV

xðər-e| 'u=fiiiit   šit-à-le
go.round.PFV   and=woosh   throw.PFV-O.3SG.F-3SG.M

gan-eu   l-aw   bara   xən-a.| ḳum-šawə̀r-∅-a.|
self.SG.F-his   to-that.M   side   other.SG.M   PFV-jump-3SG.M-O.3SG.F

He went [and] walked round one, two times, walked round and round, and woosh he flung himself to the other side. He had jumped [over] it.

(8) *zə-le   qam-tar'-ət   qàṣra,| xaθa   gor-ta*
    go.PFV-3SG.M   before-door-of   castle   sister   big-SG.F

gu   šəbák   qa-maxy-a-la   xabušta   gàw-eu.|
in   window   PFV-hit-3SG.F-O.3SG.F   apple   at-him

He went to the palace gate, the eldest sister[s] [being] at the window. She hit him with an apple.

(9) | mər-i: | 'ta | xon-i | gòr-a.'|
| --- | --- | --- | --- |
| say.PFV-1SG | for | brother-my | big-SG.M |

'[This one is] for my eldest brother,' he said.

(10) | qām-šaqə-∅-la=w | matu-∅-la | baθr-ət |
| --- | --- | --- |
| PFV-take-3SG.M-O.3f.sg=and | put-3SG.M-O.3SG.F | behind-of |

xaṣ-eu=w	nàbə-∅-la	ʾaya.|	nabəl-∅-a,
back-his=and	take-3SG.M-O.3SG.F	that.F	take-3SG.M-O.3SG.F

ḵum-dare-∅-la	gu	xà	ġurfa.|
PFV-put-3SG.M-O.3SG.F	in	a.certain	room

He lifted her, put her on the horseback and took her along. After he took her, he put her in a room.

(11) | mər-e | ta | xŭlamwàθe,| |
| --- | --- | --- |
| say.PFV-3SG.M | to | servants |

ᴷhəšàrᴷ	∅-hăw-utu!	là	∅-maḥk-utu!|
alert	SBJV-be-2PL	NEG	SBJV-speak-2PL

'Be careful!' he told his servants. 'Don't say anything.

ᴬʾăbàdᴬ	la	∅-palṭ-a	m-kəm-àwxu.|
ever	NEG	SBJV-leave-3SG.F	from-mouth-your.PL

ʾixala=w	štayta=w	kul	məndi	diyaw
eating	drinking	every	thing	her

ᴬjàhəzᴬ	t-awe-∅.|
supplied	FUT-be-3SG.M

Never let a word out of your mouth. Food and drink and everything will be supplied to her.

làkun	Ø-ʾamr-utu	ʾaw	muθayθa[1]	ʾay	brata.'
NEG	SBJV-say-2PL	he	bring.PTCP.SG.F	that.F	girl

Never say he [has] brought that girl [here].'

(12) | pəš-la | brata | day | trɛy. |
|---|---|---|---|
| remain.PFV-3SG.F | girl | OBL.3SG.F | two |

The second daughter remained.

bràt-ət	trɛy,	ga	ʾərta	malka
girl-of	two	time	other.SG.F	king

hule	ʾàmər-Ø,	mər-e:
DEIC.COP.3ms	say-3SG.M	say.PFV-3SG.M

The king said once again about his second daughter, saying

(13) | 'yàba, | brat-i | ʾăya | d-trèy=la. |
|---|---|---|---|
| INJ | girl-my | this.F | of-two=COP.3SG.F |

'Folks, this is my second daughter.

kut	ʾibe	šawər-Ø-a	ʾằya	xandaq,
ever	can.3SG.M	jump-3SG.M-O.3SG.F	this.F	trench

Whoever is able to jump [over] this trench—

brat-i	ᴷpəškəšᴷ	ṭàl-eu.	yaʿni	ᴬhădiyaᴬ	ṭàl-eu.'
girl-my	gift	to-him	it.means	gift	for-him

I will give my daughter to him as a gift [in marriage].' I mean, as a present for him.

---

[1] The participle agrees here with the object in an ergative fashion, contrasting with §30 where it agrees with the agent.

(14) ga   ʾərta   Mərzá   Mḥămad   rku-le
     time other.SG.F Mirza   Muhammad mount.PFV-3SG.M

l-xaṣ-ət   susa   xwàr-a.|
on-back-of   horse white-SG.M

Once again, Mirza Muhammad rode on the back of a white horse.

ʾaw   kòm-e=wa,| ʾaw   susa   qămày-a.|
he   white-SG.M=PST.COP.3SG.M   the.SG.M horse first-SG.M

rku-le   l-xaṣ-ət   susa   xwàr-a.|
mount.PFV-3SG.M   on-back-of horse white-SG.M

It was black—the first horse. He rode on the back of a white horse.

ga   ʾərta   zəl-e=w   zəl-e=w
time other.SG.F go.PFV-3SG.M=and   go.PFV-3SG.M=and

zə-le=w,   qam-šawər-∅-a   ga   ʾərta   xandaq.|
go.PFV-3SG.M=and   PFV-jump-3SG.M-O.3SG.F time other.SG.F trench

Once more he kept going and then jumped [over] the trench again.

(15) ʾay   brata də-trɛ   qam-maxy-a-la
     the.SG.F girl   of-two   PFV-hit-3SG.F-O.3SG.F

xabušta gàw-eu.|
apple   at-him

The second daughter hit him with an apple.

(16) mər-e: ʾɛy   ta   xon-i   palgày-a.'|
     say.PFV-3SG.M   that.F   for brother-my middle-3SG.M

'This one [is] for my middle brother.'

(17) qam-šaqəl-∅-a=w   matu-∅-la   baθər
     PFV-take-3SG.M-O.3SG.F=and put-3SG.M-O.3SG.F   behind

xaṣ-eu=w   nabəl-∅-a   'ap   'aya.
back-his=and   take-3SG.M-O.3SG.F also   her

He lifted her, put her on his back and took her along as well.

k̭um-nabəl-∅-a   k̭um-matu-∅-la   gu   xà   ġurfa
PFV-take-3SG.M-O.3SG.F PFV-put-3SG.M-O.3SG.F in   a.certain room

'ərta.   ya'ni   lè   k-iðe-∅   xaθ-aw   gaw-aw.
other.SG.F it.means   NEG   IND-know-3SG.M   sister-her in-it.F

After he took her, he put her in another room. That is, she did not know her sister was there.

k̭um-matu-∅-la   gu   dè   ġurfa xərta.
PFV-put-3SG.M-O.3SG.F in   OBL.that.F room   other.SG.F

He put her in this other room.

(18) nafsə   mə̀ndi: mər-e   ta   xŭlamwàθe:
     same   thing   say.PFV-3SG.M   to   servants

'ìya   brata   ∅-masm-ùtu-la   bala.
this.F   girl   SBJV-pay-2PL-O.3SG.F   attention

The same thing: 'You take care of this girl,' he told his servants.

lakùn   'ət   ∅-palṭ-a,   'u   là   ∅-'amr-utu   ču   xa
NEG   SBR   SBJV-leave-3SG.F   and   NEG   SBJV-say-2PL   no   one

'She cannot go out and do not say tell anyone.'

(19) pə̀š-la   'ay   zur-ta.
     remain.PFV-3SG.F   the.SG.F   small-SG.F

pəš-la   'εy   zùr-ta   mər-e:
remain.PFV-3SG.F   the.SG.F   small-SG.F   say.PFV-3SG.M

The youngest remained. As the youngest remained, he said,

(20) '*ay dìyi=la.* '*àyka b-xalṣ-a!*'
    that.F mine=COP.3SG.F where fut-escape-3SG.F

'This one is mine. Where shall she escape [to]?'

(21) *'è, ga 'ərta hule malka 'àmər-∅.*
     yes time other.SG.F DEIC.COP.3SG.M king say-3SG.M

Yes, the king once again made an announcement.

mər-e: yaba, hula pəš-ta 'aya
say.PFV-3SG.M INJ DEIC.COP.3SG.M remain.PTCP-SG.F that.F

brat-i zùr-ta,
girl-my small-SG.F

He said, 'Folks, my youngest daughter is left.

kut šawər-∅-a 'ăya xàndaq
each jump.PFV-3SG.M-3SG.F this.F trench

ṭàl-eu=ila p̂-aya.
for-him=COP.3SG.F FUT-she

Whoever jumps [over] this trench—she will be for him.'

(22) *qə̀m-le rku-le l-xaṣ-ət susa smòq-a.*
     rise.PFV-3SG.M mount.PFV-3SG.M on-back-of horse red-SG.M

Then Mirza Muhammad rode on the back of a red horse.

qə̀m-le npəl-e b-àn rakawe.
rise.PFV-3SG.M fall.PFV-3SG.M at-those knights

He attacked these knights.

kut dan rakawe kum-taqəl-∅-ɛy b-xa bàra.
each OBL.the.PL knights PFV-throw-3SG.M-O.3PL at-one side

Each of the knights he threw in another direction.

(23) mər-ɛy: 'bàbu,| malàxa=le.'|
    say.PFV-3PL   father   angel=COP.3SG.M

They said, 'Dear God, he's [like] an angel.'

(24) zə-le=w   θè-le| zə-le=w
    go.PFV-3SG.M=and   go.PFV-3SG.M   go.PFV-3SG.M=and

θèle=w| šit-à-le   gan-eu   l-aw
go.PFV-3SG.M   throw.PFV-O.3SG.F-3SG.F   self.SG.F-his   to-the.M

bara   xən-a.|
side   other-SG.M

He went back and forth, back and forth. He flung himself to the other side.

(25) ham   ʾay   ḳum-maxy-a-la   xabušta   gàw-e.|
    also   she   PFV-hit-3SG.F-O.3SG.F   apple   at-him

She, too, hit him with an apple.

(26) mər-e: ʾaya   dìyi=la.'|
    say.PFV-3SG.M   that.F   mine=COP.3SG.F

'She is mine,' he said.

(27) qam-šaqəl-∅=u   matu-∅-la   baθər   xaṣ-eu=w,
    PFV-take-3SG.M=and   put-3SG.M-O.3SG.F   behind   back-his=and

He took and put her behind his back.

(28) ᴬya   ʾằlaᴬ.'|
    VOC   God

'Oh God,' [he said.]

(29) zə̀-le| [ă]ya   ḳum-nabəl-∅-a.|
    go.PFV-3SG.M   she   PFV-take-3SG.M-O.3SG.F

He went [and] took her along.

ḳum-nabə̀-∅-la,	ga	ʾərta	ḳum-dare-∅-la	b-xa
PFV-take-3SG.M-O.3SG.F	one	other.SG.F	PFV-put-3SG.M-O.3SG.F	in-one

ġurfa	xə̀rta.
room	other.SG.F

After he took her, he once again put her in another room.

(30)
mər-e	ta	xŭlamwàθe	diye:
say.PFV-3SG.M	to	servants	his

He said to his servants,

ʿdraw	bàla	lakun	ʾət	∅-ʾamr-utu	ta	čù
put.IMP.PL	attention	NEG	SBR	SBJV-say-3PL	to	NEG

naša.
person

'Be careful not to say anything to anybody.

ʾằya	brata	holi	muθy-əla.'
this.F	girl	DEIC.COP.1SG	bring.PTCP.SG.M-O.3SG.F

He said to his servants. 'I've just brought this girl [here].'

(31)
ʾap	ʾay	ḳum-ʾamə̀r-∅-ɛy:
also	she	PFV-say-3SG.M-3PL

xàlta=w	štàyta=w	ᴬkaməlᴬ	m-kùl	məndi.
food	drink	complete	from-every	thing

He told them [about] her, too, 'Her food, drink, everything [will be provided] completely.

là	∅-maḥk-utu.
NEG	SBJV-speak-2PL

Don't speak [about it].'

(32)
mər-ɛy:	"ᴬmà-y-xaləfᴬ.'
say.PFV-3PL	NEG-3SG.M-oppose

'That's all right,' they said.

(33) pəš-la xa fàtra;| bab-ay mə̀θ-le.|
    remain.PFV-3SG.F a.certain while father-their die.PFV-3SG.M

A while passed; their father died.

bab-ət Mərzá Mḥə̆́mad=u ʾAḥmád Čăl̆ăbi=w
father-of Mirza Muhammad=and Ahmad Chalabi=and

Mḥămad Čăl̆ăbi,| mǝθ-le bàb-ay.|
Muhammad Chalabi die.PFV-3SG.M father-their

The father of Mirza Muhammad, Ahmad Chalabi and Muhammad Chalabi—their father died.

malka mə̀θ-le.|
king die.PFV-3SG.M

The king died.

(34) ʾăwa xona zur-a mə̀r-e:|
    this.M brother small-SG.M say.PFV-3SG.M

The youngest brother said,

de ∅-qaym-ax ∅-jayl-ax gu qàṣra|
PTCL SBJV-rise-1PL SBJV-wander-1PL in castle

'Let's get up [and] wander in the palace

∅-xaz-ax balki məndi hàle,|
SBJV-see-1PL maybe thing situations

to see if we can find anything,

ᴷʾanbàr-anᴷ,| məndi diyan d-ilay ʾfin-e,| d-ilay
grain.repistory-PL thing our SBR-COP.3PL rotten-PL SBR-COP.3PL

xrìw-e,| xə̀tte măθalan,| b-dàw zawna.|
destroy.PTCP-PL wheat.PL for.example at-OBL.that.M time

lest our grain repositories are, for example, rotten [or] damaged at this time.'

(35) ʾè. qə̀m-le   jəl-ayd   gu   qàṣra.
     yes rise.PFV-3SG.M wander.PFV-3PL in   castle

Yes. So they wandered in the palace.

zə̀-le| pθəx-le   tarʾa day   ʾodá ʾət² xàθa
go.PFV-3SG.M open.PFV-3SG.M door   OBL.that.F room of   sister

gor-ta,| ʾay   qămày-θa.|
big-SG.F   the.F   first-SG.F

They went and opened the door of the eldest sister's room, the first one.

(36) mər-e: ʾăya   mà=yla?'|
     say.PFV-3SG.M this.F what=COP.3SG.F

'What is this?' they said.

(37) mə̀r-e:| xòn-i,| ʾaya   ṭàl-ux.|
     say-3SG.M   brother-my   she   for-you.SG.M

He said, 'My brother, she is for you.

diyux=ila   ʾaya.|
yours.SG.M=COP.SG.F   she

She is yours.'

(38) xòn-i,| ʾana lèn   zil-a.
     brother-my   I   NEG.COP.1SG.M   go.PTCP-SG.M

'My brother, I haven't been [anywhere].'

(39) mə̀-re:| ʾàn=ən   šqíl-əla.|
     say.PFV-3SG.M   I=COP.1SG.M   take.PTCP-O.3SG.F

'I [am the one who] has taken her,' he said.

---

² ʾət 'of' has a suffixal variant -ət, cf. §12, and a prefixal variant də-, cf. §41.

ṭàl-ux=ila.|	dìyux=ila	ʾaya.|
for-you.SG.M=COP.SG.F	yours.SG.M=COP.3SG.F	she

'She's for you. She's yours.'

(40) | ʾaya | k̠əm-yawəl-∅-a | ta | xòna | gor-a.| |
|---|---|---|---|---|
| she | PFV-give-3SG.M-O.3SG.F | to | brother | big-SG.M |

He gave her to the eldest brother.

(41) | pθə̀x-le | ʾoda | də-tray.| |
|---|---|---|
| open.PFV-3SG.M | room | of-two |

They opened the second room.

ʾay	brata	də-trɛy	palgày-θa.|
the.F	girl	of-two	middle-SG.F

The second, middle girl [was in there].

(42) | mər-e: | ʿxòn-i,| | ʾadiya | ʾàya=ši| |
|---|---|---|---|
| say.PFV-3SG.M | brother-my | gift | she=ADD |

dìyux=ila.ʾ|
yours.SG.M=COP.3SG.F

He said, 'My brother, now this one is yours.'

(43) | mər-e: | ʿxòn-i,| | ʾana | lèn | zil-a |
|---|---|---|---|---|
| say.PFV-3SG.M | brother-my | I | NEG.COP.1SG.M | go.PTCP.SG.M |

čə	dukθa.ʾ|
NEG	place

'My brother,' he said, 'I haven't been anywhere.'

(44) mər-e: 'bàle,| 'aya   diyux   'əll-i³
     say.PFV-3SG.M si   she   yours.SG.M by-me

šqil-a.'|
take.PFV-O.3SG.F

He said, 'Indeed, I [am the one who] took that [girl] of yours.'

---

³ The immediately preverbal agent here is expressed by means of a preposition, while the verb agrees with the object. It carries agent focus, cf. §39, and is reminiscent of focal ergative marking.

NORTHERN KURDISH OF DUHOK
TEXT 30: §1–29

Masoud Mohammadirad

Speaker: Bizhan Khoshavi Ahmad

Audio: https://kurdic.ames.cam.ac.uk/audio/242/

(1) *nāv-ē   mən   Bižān   Xošavī   ʾAhmàt.*
    name-EZ.M 1SG.OBL PN   PN   PN

My name [is] Bizhan Khoshavi Ahmad.

xalḵ-ē   bāžēr-ē   Duhoḵ-è̀.
people-EZ.M city.OBL-EZ.M PN-OBL.F

[I am] from the city of Duhok.

az=ē   čīrok-aḵ-ē,   həndak čīrok-ā   bo   hawa
1SG.DIR=FUT   tale-INDF-OBL.F   some   tale-PL.OBL for 2PL.OBL

và-gohēz-əm,
TELIC-change.PRS-1SG

I will narrate to you a tale/some tales

kū   mən   əš   dāp̄īr-ā̀   xo   go   lē
REL   1SG.OBL from grand.mom-EZ.F   REFL   ear   at.3SG.OBL

būy=na
be.PST.PTCP=COP.3PL

that I have heard from my grandmother

ū	həndàk,	həndak	dānʿàmr-ēn	davar-ē.
and	some	some	old.people-EZ.PL	region-OBL.F

and some ... some old people in the region.

(2)
čīrok-ā	ma	ā	ēk̲-ē	dē	dàst	pē
tale-EZ.F	1PL.OBL	EZ.F	one-OBL.F	FUT	hand	to

∅-k̲at-ən	čīrok-ā	Fātmā̀=ya.
SBJV-do.PRS.3SG-NA	tale-EZ.F	PN=COP.3SG

The first tale for us to start with is the tale of Fatma.

ha-bū-∅	na-bū-∅
EXIST-be.PST-3SG	NEG-be.PST-3SG

There was and there was not,

kas	šə	xodē	màs-tər	na-bū-∅
person	from	God.OBL	big-CMPR	NEG-be.PST-3SG

there was nobody greater than God,

kas	šə	banī-yā	dərawìn-tər	na-bū-∅
person	from	human-PL.OBL	liar-CMPR	NEG-be.PST-3SG

no bigger liar than man.

řož-àk̲-ē	šə	řož-ān	gund-àk̲-ē	dūradast
day-INDF-EZ.M	from	day-PL.OBL	village-INDF-EZ.M	remote

āfərat-àk̲	ha-bū-∅
woman-INDF	EXIST-be.PST-3SG

Once upon a time there was a woman in a remote village.

(3)
awḕ	āfrat-ē	šū	bə	zaḷām-ak̲-ì
DEM.DIST.OBL.F	woman-OBL.F	husband	to	man-INDF-OBL.M

k̲ər-bū
do.PST-be.PST

That woman was married to a man

kū	*bar-ī*	*wē*	*čand*	*zārok-àk̲*	*ha-bū-n.*
REL	before-OBL.M	3SG.OBL.F	some	child-INDF	EXIST-be.PST-3PL

who already had some children.

k̲əč-ak̲	*ha-bū-∅*	*bə*	*nāv-ē*	*Fāṭmà*
girl-INDF	EXIST-be.PST-3SG	by	name-EZ.M	PN

He (The man) had a girl by the name of Fatma,

k̲o	*havžìn-ā,*	*havžin-ā*	*ānk̲o*	*žənbàb-ā*
REL	partner-EZ.F	partner-EZ.F	or	step.mother-EZ.F

Fāṭmā-yē	*galak*	*haz*	*žē*	*nà-t̲-k̲ər.*
PN-OBL.F	very	liking	at.3SG.OBL	NEG-IPFV-do.PST

whom the [his] wife or her (i.e. Fatma's) stepmother did not like much.

ū	*nà-t̲-vīyā*	*bə-mīn-t=a*	*l*	*māl-ē.*
and	NEG-IPFV-want.PST	SBJV-remain.PRS-3SG=DRCT	in	home-OBL.F

She (the stepmother) did not like her (Fatma) to stay home..'

řož-ak̲-ē	*šə*	*řož-àn,*	*ət̲-bèž-t=ē,*
day-INDF-EZ.M	from	day-PL.OBL	IND-say.PRS-3SG=3SG.OBL

One day, she said to her (Fatma),

k̲əč-ā	*mən*	*har-a*	*k̲olàn-ē*	*bo*	*xo*
girl-EZ.F	1SG.OBL	go.IMP-2SG	alley-OBL.F	for	REFL

yārī-yā	*bə-k̲a.*
game-PL.OBL	SBJV-do.PRS.IMP.2SG

'My girl, go [and] play in the lane.'

(4) dam-ē   ∅-č-īt=a   k̠olān-ē
    when-OBL.F IND-go.PRS-3SG=DRCT   lane-OBL.F

yārī-yā   t̠-k̠à-t-ən|
game-PL.OBL   IND-do.PRS-3SG-NA

When she (Fatma) went to the lane to play,

kas-ak̠   šə   wānà̠   hēk-ak̠-ē   šəkēn-īt-ən|
person-INDF   from   3PL.OBL   egg-INDF-OBL.F   break.PRS-3SG-NA

ət-nāv   zavì-yā   kas-ak̠-ī   dā.|
in-middle   land-EZ.F   person-INDF-OBL.M   POST

one of them (the girls) cracked an egg on the land of a person.

dam-ē   hēk   t̠-hēt=a   šəkānd-ə̀n
when-OBL.F   egg   IND-come.PRS.3SG=DRCT   break.PST-INF

When the egg was cracked,

ət-nāv   wān   hamī   k̠əč-ān   dā| ū   har   ēk̠
in-middle   3PL.OBL   all   girl-PL.OBL POST   and   each   one

∅-k̠a-t=a   sar   yē   dì.|
IND-do.PRS-3SG=DRCT   head   EZ.M   other

each [girl] blamed the other.

ū   har   k̠əč-àk̠   t̠ə-bēž-īt-ən,| 'tà   wa   k̠ər,
and   each   girl-INDF   IND-say.PRS-3SG-NA   2SG.OBL   DEIC   do.PST

mə̀n   wa   na-k̠ər.'|
1SG.OBL   DEIC   NEG-do.PST

And each girl said [to the other], 'You did this; I didn't do this.'

(5) əl-wērē   kas-àk   t̠-hē-t=a   wērē
    in-there   person-INDF   IND-come.PRS-3SG=DRCT   there

Somebody passed by there

ət-vē-t-ən,	ət-bēž-t=ē,	ˈlāzəm=a
IND-want.PRS-3SG-NA	IND-say.PRS-3SG=3SG.OBL	necessary=COP.3SG

hīn	hamī	sìnd	bə-xò-n
2PL.DIR	all	swear	SBJV-eat.PRS-2PL

[and] said to them, 'You must all swear an oath!

kā	kḕ	av	hēk-a	šəkānd-ī=a.
EXCM	who	DEM.PROX.SG	egg-DEM	break.PST-PTCP=PERF

Let's see who has cracked the egg?

lāzəm=a	hīn	hamī	sìnd	bə-xo-n!'
necessary=COP.3SG	2PL.DIR	all	oath	SBJV-eat.PRS-2PL

You must all swear an oath!'

(6)
k̠əč-ā	ēk̠-ḕ	t̠-bēž-īt-ən,
girl-EZ.F	one-OBL.F	IND-say.PRS-3SG-NA

The first girl said,

'az	bə	sar-ē	bərā̀-yē	xo	k̠a-m-a
1SG	to	head-EZ.M	brother-EZ.M	REFL	do.PRS-1SG-NA

'I swear on my brother's head (lit. I put on my brother's head)

mən	aw	hēk-a	nà-škānd-ī=a.'
1SG.OBL	DEM.DIST.SG	egg-DEM	NEG-break.PST-PTCP=PERF

[that] I didn't break that egg.'

k̠əč-ā	du-ḕ	t̠-bēž-īt-ən,
girl-EZ.F	two-OBL.F	IND-say.PRS-3SG-NA

The second girl said,

'az	bə	sar-ē	hàr	du	bərā-yēt	xo	k̠a-m-a
1SG	to	head-EZ.M	each	two	brother-EZ.PL	REFL	do.PRS-1SG-NA

'I swear on my two brothers' heads

mən	àw	hēk-a	na-škānd-ī=a.'
1SG.OBL	DEM.DIST.SG	egg-DEM	NEG-break.PST-PTCP=PERF

[that] I didn't break that egg.'

ḳəč-ā	sē-yḕ	ṯ-bēž-īt-ən,
girl-EZ.F	two-OBL.F	IND-say.PRS-3SG-NA

The third girl said,

'az	bə	sar-ē	p̂ènǰ	bərā-yēt	xo	ḳa-m-a
1SG	to	head-EZ.M	five	brother-EZ.PL	REFL	do.PRS-1SG-NA

'I swear on my five brothers' heads

mən	aw	hēk-a	nà-škānd-ī=a.'
1SG.OBL	DEM.DIST.SG	egg-DEM	NEG-break.PST-PTCP=PERF

(that) I didn't break that egg.'

(7)
ū	har	husā	bardawā̀m	b-īt-ən.
and	EMPH	such	continual	be.PRS-3SG-NA

It continued like that.

hamī	ḳə̀č	əb	sar-ē	bərā-yē	xo	sīnd
all	girl	to	head-EZ.M	brother-EZ.M	REFL	oath

əṯ-xo-n
IND-eat.PRS-3PL

All the girls swore on their brother's head,

ko,	'mà	av	hēk-a	na-škānd-ī=a.'
COMPL	1PL.OBL	DEM.PROX.SG	egg-DEM	NEG-break.PST-PTCP=PERF

'We haven't broken the egg.'

lē	*Fātmā-ye̋*ˈ	*čūnkū*	*husà*	*hazər*	*kạr-bē*	*ča*
but	PN-OBL.F	since	such	thought	do.PST-be.PST	no

bərà	*nī-n=ən,*ˈ
brother	NEG-COP=3PL

However Fatma, as she thought that she had no brothers,

na-ẓānī	*dē*	*bə*	*čə̀*	*sīnd*	*∅-xot-ən.*ˈ
NEG-know.PST	FUT	to	what	swear	SBJV-eat.PRS-3SG-NA

did not know whom to swear on.

ū	*hamī-yā*	*kạr=a*	*sar*	*we̋*ˈ
and	all-PL.OBL	do.PST=DRCT	head	3SG.OBL.F

Everybody put the blame on her (lit. put on her head)

got=ē,	*'čūnkū*	*ta*	*sīnd*	*nà-xwār*ˈ
say.PST=3SG.OBL	since	2SG.OBL	oath	NEG-eat.PST

[and] said to her, 'Since you didn't swear,

lə-vērē	*tà*	*hēk*	*ā*	*šəkānd-ī.'*ˈ
in-here	2SG.OBL	egg	EZ.F	break.PST-PTCP

[it means that] you have broken the egg.'

(8)
ət̯-č-īt-ava	*gala*	*galak*	*dəl-ak̯-ē*
IND-go.PRS-3SG-TELIC	very	very	heart-INDF-EZ.M

ēšāyī,
distressed

She (Fatma) returned home with a broken heart

ət̯-ka-t=a	*gərī.*ˈ
IND-do.PRS-3SG=DRCT	cry.INF

[and] started to cry.

ət-bēž-īt=a	žənbā̀b-ā	xo,
IND-say.PRS-3SG=DRCT	stepmom-EZ.F	REFL

She said to her stepmother,

ət-bəž-t=ē,	'būčī	mən	čə	bərā̀	nī=n-ən?'
IND-say.PRS-3SG=3SG.OBL	why	1SG.OBL	no	brother	NEG=COP-3PL

she said to her, 'Why haven't I got any brothers?'

bo	žənbāb-ē	tə-b-īt=a	darīv-ak-ā
for	stepmom-OBL.F	IND-be.PRS-3SG=DRCT	opportunity-INDF-EZ.F

gala	galak	ā	bā̀š
very	very	EZ.F	good

It became a very good opportunity for the stepmother

kū	kəč-ḕ	žī	šə	māl-ē	bə	darē
COMPL	girl-OBL.F	ADD	from	home-OBL.F	to	out

∅-x-īt-ən.
SBJV-throw.PRS-3SG-NA

to kick her (Fatma) out of the house.

(9)
ət-bḕž-t=ē,	'wara	àz	dē
IND-say.PRS-3SG=3SG.OBL	come.IMP.2SG	1SG.DIR	FUT

jəh-ē	bərā-yē	ta	nīšā	ta	∅-dà-m.'
place-EZ.M	brother-EZ.M	2SG.OBL	showing	2SG.OBL	SBJV-give.PRS-1SG

She said to her, 'Come here, I will show you your brothers' whereabouts.'

ət-ba-t=a	sar	bān-ì,	ət-bēž-t=ē,
IND-take.PRS-3SG=DRCT	on	roof-OBL.M	IND-say.PRS-3SG=3SG.OBL

She took her on the roof of the house [and] said to her,

ꞌpə̀št	čīyā-yē	hana	pəšt	čīyā-yĩ
behind	mountain-EZ.M	DEIC.PTCL	behind	mountain-OBL.M

'Behind this mountain over there, behind the mountain [there is another mountain];

lə-pəšt	wī	čīyā-yĩ	žī,	šīnīk-ā
in-back	DEM.DIST.OBL.M	mountain-OBL.M	ADD	trace-EZ.F

čīyāy-àk̲-ī	dī	yē	hayī,
mountain-INDF-EZ.M	other	EZ.M	EXIST.PRS

Behind that other mountain there is a road to another mountain.

əškaft-àk̲=ā	ləwērē	hay
cave-INDF=EZ.F	there	EXIST

There is a cave there.

p̂è̀nǰ	bərā-yēt	ta	əl-wērè̀
five	brother-EZ.PL	2SG.OBL	in-there

Your five brothers are there.

məžīl-ī	žīyàn-ē=na	ū	řāv=ū	nēčīr-ā
busy-EZ.M	life-OBL.F=COP.3PL	and	hunt=and	hunt-PL.OBL

ṯ-kà-n.
IND-do.PRS-3PL

They are busy living and hunting.'

(10)
Fātmā,	gala	galak	əṯ-mīn-t=a	hayərì.
PN	very	very	IND-remain.PRS-3SG=DRCT	astonished

[On hearing this] Fatma was very astonished.

əṭ-bēž-īt-ən,	garak=a	az	bə-čə̀-m
IND-say.PRS-3SG-NA	necessary=COP.3SG	1SG.DIR	SBJV-go.PRS-1SG

bərā-yēt	xo	paydā	∅-ḳà-m
brother-EZ.PL	REFL	visible	SBJV-do.PRS-1SG

She said, 'I shall go [and] find my brothers

ū	gal	wā̀nā	dā	bə-žī-m.
and	with	3PL.OBL	POST	SBJV-live.PRS-1SG

and live with them.'

čūnkū	ṭə-zằn-īt-ən	žənbāb-ḕ	gala	galak
since	IND-know.PRS-3SG-NA	stepmom-OBL.F	very	very

hāl-ē	wānā	nāxoš	ḳər-ī=ya
condition-EZ.M	3PL.OBL	unpleasant	do.PST-PTCP=PERF

She knew that the stepmother had upset them a lot,

ū	ṭə-vē-t-ən	bə-zəvəř-īt-avà	dav
and	IND-want.PRS-3SG-NA	SBJV-turn.PRS-3SG-TELIC	side

bərā-yēt	xo.
brother-EZ.PL	REFL

and that it was necessary for her to go to [live with] her brothers.

(11)
ḳəčək	dam-ē	∅-č-īt-ə̀n,	gala	galak
girl	when-OBL.F	IND-go.PRS-3SG-NA	very	very

ṭə-wastīy-ḕt-ən.
IND-exhaust.PRS-3SG-NA

On the way [to the mountain], the little girl (i.e., Fatma) became very tired.

gala	galak	māndì	ṭ-b-īt-ən
very	very	tired	IND-be.PRS-3SG-NA

She became very exhausted

hatā̀|	čīyā-yak̲-ḕ	ṯa-bahūrīn-īt-an=ū|
until	mountain-INDF-OBL.M	IND-pass.PRS-3SG-NA=and

by the time she passed the first mountain

čīyā-yē	du-ē	ṯa-bahūrīn-īt-an=ū|
mountain-EZ.M	two-OBL.F	IND-pass.PRS-3SG-NA=and

and the second mountain

aṯ-gah-īt=a	čīyā-yē	sḕ.|
IND-arrive.PRS-3SG=DRCT	mountain-EZ.M	three

and [finally] arrived at the third mountain.

(12)	dam-ē	aṯ-gah-īt=a	čīyā-yē	sḕ,|
	when-OBL.F	IND-arrive.PRS-3SG=DRCT	mountain-EZ.M	three

On arriving at the third mountain,

aškaft-ak̲-ā	gala	galak	ā	balà̄nd	∅-bīn-īt-an.|
cave-INDF-EZ.F	very	very	EZ.F	high	IND-see.PRS-3SG-NA

she saw a very big (lit. high) cave.

ū	ṯ-hē-t=a	hazar-ā	wē
and	IND-come.PRS-3SG=DRCT	thought-EZ.F	3SG.OBL.F

It crossed her mind (lit. It came to her memory)

kū	ṯa-vē-t-an	barā-yēt	wē	la
COMPL	IND-should.PRS-3SG-NA	brother-EZ.PL	3SG.OBL.F	in
vè̄	aškaft-ē	va	∅-b-an|	
DEM.PROX.OBL.F	cave-OBL.F	POST	SBJV-be.PRS-3PL	

that her brothers should be in that cave

har	wakī	žanbāb-ḕ	gotī.|
just	like	stepmom-OBL.F	say.PST.PTCP

—just as the stepmother had said.

(13) dam-ē　　ṭ-č-ìt=ē|
     when-OBL.F　IND-go.PRS-3SG=3SG.OBL

'When she (Fatma) went inside

ū　　sah　　ṭə-kà-t=ē|
and　look　IND-do.PRS-3SG=3SG.OBL

and looked around,

əṭ-bīn-īt-ə̀n,|　čə̀　ṭ-bīn-īt-ən?|
IND-see.PRS-3SG-NA　what　IND-see.PRS-3SG-NA

she saw that ... what did she see?

p̂ènǰ　　taxt-ēt　　dərēžkəri,|
five　　bed-EZ.PL　lain.on.the.ground

Five beds lying [on the ground],

p̂ènǰ　āmān-ēt　　xārən-ē,|
five　utensil-EZ.PL　eat.INF-OBL.F

five sets of eating utensils,

p̂ènǰ　ǰəl,|　p̂ènǰ　kavčək.|
five　garment　five　spoon

five sets of clothes, five spoons.

har　　təšt　　ət　　wē　　　　　　əškaft-ē　va　　p̂ènǰ-ē
each　thing　in　DEM.DIST.3SG.OBL.F　cave-OBL.F　POST　five-OBL.F

p̂ènǰ　boy=a.|
five　be.PST.PTCP.3SG=PERF

Each thing in that cave was in five [sets] (lit. five in five).

(14) dam-ē　　wān　　p̂ēnǰ-ā　ṭ-bīn-īt-ə̀n|
     when-OBL.F　3PL.OBL　five-PL　IND-see.PRS-3SG-NA

When she saw all those [things] in five sets,

ēksar ṭə-ẓān-īt-ən
totally IND-know.PRS-3SG-NA

she was sure

avà   jəh-ē   bərāy-ē   wē=ya.
DEM.PROX.3SG.DIR place-EZ.M brother-EZ.M 3SG.OBL.F=COP.3SG

that it was the place of her brothers.

bar-ē   xo   dà-t=ē   wēri   galak=ā
front-EZ.M REFL give.PRS-3SG=3SG.OBL there.OBL very=EZ.F

bēsarūbàr=a.
messy=COP.3SG

She looked around [the cave and saw that] it was very messy.

ahā̀, bərā-yak̲-ì   ṭ-bīn-īt-ən   sar ēk̲ šə
PRST brother-INDF-OBL.M IND-see.PRS-3SG-NA on   one from

wān   taxt-ā   yē   nəvəstì=ya.
DEM.PL.OBL bed-PL.OBL EZ.M sleep.PST.PTCP=COP.3SG

Lo, she saw a brother sleeping on one of the beds.

(15) *Fātmā dā-kū   wi   bərā-yì̄   go   lē*
       PN   so-that 3SG.OBL.M brother-OBL.M ear at.3SG.OBL

na-b-īt-ən,
NEG.SBJV-be.PRS-3SG-NA

In order for her brother not to hear,

baṭanì-ak̲-ā   mazən ṭ-ʿīn-īt-ən
canvas-INDF-EZ.F big   IND-bring.PRS-3SG-NA

Fatma brought a big lining canvas

dān-t=a   sar bərā-yē   xo   yē   bəčīk
PVB.put.PRS-3SG=DRCT on   brother-EZ.M refl EZ.M small

[and] put it on her young brother

kū	bərā-yak̲-ī	bəčĭk=a.
REL	brother-INDF-EZ.M	small=COP.3SG

—the one who was the young[est] brother.

dā-n-t=a	sar	wī	bərā-yī̀.
PVB-put.PRS-3SG=DRCT	on	DEM.DIST.3SG.OBL.M	brother-OBL.M

She put it (the canvas) on that brother.

ū	Fātmā	ř̌ā-t̲-b-īt-ən	dast=əb	kār-ī
and	PN	PVB-IND-be.PRS-3SG-NA	hand=to	work.OBL.M

t̲-k̲a-t-ə̀n.
IND-do.PRS-3SG-NA

And Fatma rose [and] started to work (lit. put hands to work).'

(16)	Fātmā̀	ř̌ā-t̲-b-īt-ən	dast=əb	kār-ī
	PN	PVB-IND-be.PRS-3SG-NA	hand=to	work.OBL.M

t̲-k̲a-t-ən.
IND-do.PRS-3SG-NA

Fatma rose (and) started to work.

ēh	taxt-ā	hamī-yā̀	pāqəž	ət̲-k̲a-t-ən.
INTJ	bed-PL.OBL	all-PL.OBL	clean	IND-do.PRS-3SG-NA

She cleaned all the beds.

ǰəlk-ā̀	t̲-šo-t-ən.
garment-PL.OBL	IND-wash.PRS-3SG-NA

She washed the clothes.

āmān-ā̀	hamī-yā	pāqəž	tə-k̲a-t-ən.
utensil-PL.OBL	all-PL.OBL	clean	IND-do.PRS-3SG-NA

She cleaned all the dishes.

əškaft-ē	hamī	yē	ət̪-māl̥-īt-ə̀n.ˈ
cave-OBL.F	all	EZ.M	IND-sweep.PRS-3SG-NA

She swept all [inside] the cave.

ū	l-ēk	də-da	bəsarūbàr	ət̪-k̲a-t-ən,ˈ
and	at-one	IND-give.PRS.3SG	orderly	IND-do.PRS-3SG-NA

She had put everything in order,

hatā	bərā-yēt	wē	t̪-hē-n-avà.ˈ
until	brother-EZ.PL	3SG.OBL.F	IND-come.PRS-3PL-TELIC

before her brothers returned.

(17)
pəšt-ī	Fātmā	kār=o	bār-ēt	xo
after-OBL.M	PN	job=and	RDP-EZ.PL	REFL

t̪-k̲à-t-ən,ˈ
IND-do.PRS-3SG-NA

After Fatma finished her [cleaning] tasks,

xārən-àk̲-ā	gala	galak	ā	xoš	žī	čē
meal-INDF-EZ.F	very	very	EZ.F	delicious	ADD	LVC

t̪-k̲a-t	bo	bərā-yēt	xoˈ
IND-do.PRS.3SG	for	brother-EZ.PL	REFL

she cooked a very good meal for her brothers

kā	čə̀	lə-vērē	ha=ya
EXCM	what	in-here	EXIST=COP.3SG

out of what there was in the cave

čə̀	nēčīr	k̲ərī=ya,	ətgal	həndak̲	nān-ī̀ˈ
what	hunt	do.PST-PTCP=COP.3SG	with	some	bread-OBL.M

and what they had hunted—together with bread

bo	wānā̀	ḥāzər	ət-ka-t-ən.
for	3PL.OBL	ready	IND-do.PRS-3SG-NA

—she prepared [a meal] for them.

(18)
ət-bēž-ī,	'dam-ē	bərā̀-yēt	mən,	har	čār
IND-say.PRS-3SG	when-OBL.F	brother-EZ.PL	1SG.OBL	each	four

bərā-yēt	mən-ē	dī	ṯ-hē-n-avà,	dā
brother-EZ.PL	1SG.OBL-EZ.M	other	IND-come.PRS-3PL-TELIC	HORT

vērē	ā	bəsarūbàr	∅-b-īt-ən.'
here	EZ.F	tidy	SBJV-be.PRS-3SG-NA

She said, 'Let it be orderly and clean here by the time my brothers, my other four brothers are back.'

Fātmā	yaksar	č-īt=a	ət-bən	taxt-ak-ī̀-va
PN	totally	go.PRS-3SG=DRCT	in-under	bed-INDF-OBL.M-POST

ān	bən	sērk-àk-ē	'arzāq-ī-va
or	under	basket-INDF-EZ.M	food-OBL.M-POST

'Fatma immediately went under a bed/or under a large cooking basket.

xo	va-ṯ-šēr-ìt-ən
REFL	TELIC-IND-hide.PRS-3SG-NA

She hid herself

ū	čāvařē	ṯ-b-īt-ən	hatā	bərā̀-yēt	wē
and	eyes.on.road	IND-be.PRS-3SG-NA	until	brother-EZ.PL	REFL

ṯ-hē-n.
IND-come.PRS-3PL

and waited (lit. eyes on road) [there] until her brothers returned.'

(19)
dam-ē	bərā-yēt	wē	ət-hè-n,
when-OBL.F	brother-EZ.PL	3SG.OBL.F	IND-come.PRS-3PL

When her brothers arrived,

bərā-yē	mažə̀n	ǰo	t̩-kav-īt-ən.
brother-EZ.M	big	LVC	IND-fall.PRS-3SG-NA

the eldest brother bludgeoned his way [through his brothers]

ət̩-bēž-t=ē,	'ā	ava	čan	təšt-ak-ī
IND-say.PRS-3SG=3SG.OBL	EXCM	DEM.PROX.3SG	how	thing-INDF-EZ.M

sàyr=a	čē	bo-y-∅!
bizzare=COP.3SG	good	be.PST-PTCP-3SG

[and] said to them, 'Oh, what has been happening here is indeed surprising!

bərā-yē	ma	yē	bəčīk	husā	na	yē	zīràk̩
brother-EZ.M	1PL.OBL	EZ.M	little	such	NEG	EZ.M	striving

bo-∅
COP.PST-3SG

Our youngest brother did not used to be so conscientious.

av	āmằn-a	xa	šīšt-ən=ū
DEM.PROX.3SG	utensil-DEM	REFL	wash.PST-3PL=and

He has washed the dishes all by himself.

av	jəlk-à	šīšt-ən=ū
DEM.PROX.3SG	garment-DEM	wash.PST-3PL=and

He has washed the clothes.

av	taxt-a	bə-sar-ū-bàr	k̩ər.
DEM.PROX.3SG	bed-DEM	orderly	do.PST

He has put the beds in order.'

řāwra	b-ən	dasxoší-yè	lē	da-n,
LVC	be.PRS-3PL	thanking-OBL.F	at.3SG.OBL	give.PRS-3PL

They (the brothers) started to thank him (the youngest brother),

ʿsaḥàt-ā	ta	xoš;
health-EZ.F	2SG.OBL	nice

'Bravo! (lit. may your health be nice!)

ta	kār-aḵ-ē	jằn=ē	ḵərī.'
2SG.OBL	job-INDF-EZ.M	beautiful=EZ.M	do.PTCP

You have done a wonderful job.'

(20)	bərā	dam-ē	əš	xaw	ř̌ā-ṭ-b-īt-avà
	brother	when-OBL.F	from	sleep	PVB-IND-be.PRS-3SG-TELIC

When the [youngest] brother woke up

əṭ-bīn-īt	wērē	yā	pāqə̀ž=a.
IND-see.PRS-3SG	there	EZ.F	clean=COP.3SG

and saw that the house was clean,

əṭ-bēž-īt-ən,	ʿhamā	bo	mən	lē-hàt-∅!
IND-say.PRS-3SG-NA	INTJ	for	1SG.OBL	PVB-come.PST-3SG

he said, 'It simply occurred to me (lit. it simply came to me).

bə	ḥəsāb,	al-ʾasās	mə̀n	ī	aw
by	counting	on-basis	1SG.OBL	EZ	DEM.DIST.SG

šol-a=ya	ḵərī.'
work-DEM=EZ.F	do.PST.PTCP

Indeed, it was me who has done these tasks!"

ət-bēž-t=ē,		ʿwaḷā	bərā	az	gala	galak	ī
IND-say.PRS-3SG=3SG.OBL		by.God	brother	1SG.DIR	very	very	EZ

māndī̀	bū=m	kū	mən	av	vērē	hamī̀
tired	COP.PST=1SG	COMPL	1SG.OBL	DEM.PROX.SG	here	all

pāqəž	ḳər.'
clean	do.PST

He said [to the eldest brother], 'By God, brother, after cleaning everything in the house I got very tired!'

(21)
ət-bēž-n=ē	bərā	saḥàt-ā	ta	xoš.
IND-say.PRS-3PL=3SG.OBL	brother	health-EZ.F	2SG.OBL	nice

They (the brothers) said to him, 'Bravo, brother.'

ṣəbāhī̀	dor-ā	bərā-yē	ma	yē	mazən=a.
tomorrow	turn-EZ.F	brother-EZ.M	1PL.OBL	EZ.M	big=COP.3SG

Tomorrow is our eldest brother's turn.'

ʿafù	dūr-ā	bərā-yē	ma	yē	dìv	dā=ya!
pardon	turn-EZ.F	brother-EZ.M	1PL.OBL	EZ.M	after	POST=COP.3SG

aw=ḕ	šə	wī̀	mazən-tər.
DEM.DIST.SG=EZ.M	from	3SG.OBL	big-CMPR

Pardon, 'It's our penultimate brother's turn [, the one who was born before the youngest one]; the one [who is] older than him (the youngest one).'

(22)
ət-b-īt=a	řož-ā	p̂āš-tə̀r.
IND-become.PRS-3SG=DRCT	day-EZ.F	after-CMPR

The next day, (Lit. It became the next day.)

bərā-yēn	dī	dar	ṭ-kav-ən=a	nēčīr-ḕ.
brother-EZ.PL	other	outside	IND-fall.PRS-3PL=DRCT	hunt-OBL.F

the other brothers went hunting.

bərā	žī	tə-bēž-īt-ə̀n,	'ē	bāwar	ka	vḕrē
brother	ADD	IND-say.PRS-3SG-NA	INTJ	belief	do.IMP.2SG	here

galak	ā	pāqə̀ž=a.				
very	EZ.F	clean=COP.3SG				

The brother said, 'Believe it [or not], it is very clean here;

na	ā	pīs=a.
NEG	EZ.F	dirty=COP.3SG

it's not untidy.

kā	dā	az	bəxo	bə-nv-ə̀m;
INTJ	HORT	1SG.DIR	simply	SBJV-sleep-1SG

az	gala	galak	yē	wastīà̱y=ma.
1SG	very	very	EZ.M	tired=1SG.COP

I shall simply sleep. I'm very tired.'

bərā	∅-č-īt	ət̰-nəv-īt-avà.	
brother	IND-go.PRS-3SG	IND-sleep.PRS-3SG-TELIC	

The brother went [and] slept again.

(23)

dam-ē	bərā	t̰-nəv-īt-avà,
when-OBL.F	brother	IND-sleep.PRS-3SG-TELIC

After the brother fell asleep,

kạčək	bar-ē	xo	∅-da-t=ē	hēštā
girl	front-EZ.M	REFL	IND-give.PRS-3SG=3SG.OBL	still

bərā	yē	nəvəstī=a.
brother	EZ.M	sleep.PST.PTCP=COP.3SG

the girl (i.e., Fatma) noticed that he was still sleeping.

zīkā	ət̰-hē-t=a	dar-è̱.
soon	IND-come.PRS-3SG=DRCT	outside-OBL.F

She came out quickly.

wàn	jəl=ū	barg-ā|	wān...	aw	təšt-ēn
3PL.OBL	garment=and	cover-PL.OBL	3PL.OBL	DEM.PROX.SG	thing-EZ.PL

wē	dəhī	na-pāqəžkərì=n|	hamī-yā
DEM.DIST.OBL.F	yesterday	not-cleaned=COP.3PL	all-PL.OBL

ət-ba-t=a	žə	dar-va-y	aškaft-è.|
IND-take.PRS-3SG=DRCT	in	outside-POST-EZ	cave-OBL.F

She took the dirty clothes and dirty stuff from the previous day out of the cave.

ū	bəsarūbar	ət-ka-t-ən=ū	čè	t-ka-t-ən|
and	orderly	IND-do.PRS-3SG-NA=and	good	IND-do.PRS-3SG-NA

She arranged them all and cleaned them.

(24)	ū	ḥawẓ-ak-ā	gul-à	žī	əl-bar	dar
	and	garden-INDF-EZ.F	flower-PL.OBL	ADD	in-front	door

aškaft-ē	čē	t-ka-t-ən|
cave-OBL.F	good	IND-do.PRS-3SG-NA

In addition, she made a small garden of flowers in front of the cave

ū	gul-ā	tē-dā	t-čīn-ìt-ən=ū.|
and	flower-PL.OBL	in.3SG.OBL.POST	IND-plant.PRS-3SG-NA=and

and planted some flowers in it.

řax-ē	dī	žī	wəsā	pəčak-ē	pāqəž
side-EZ.M	other	ADD	such	a.little-OBL.F	clean

ət-ka-t-ən
IND-do.PRS-3SG-NA

Also, she cleaned the other side [the area around the cave]

bəsarūbàr	ət-ka-t-ən.|
orderly	IND-do.PRS-3SG-NA

[and] put the things [around the cave] in order.

(25) b-īt=a   ēvār   kū   dē
    become.PRS-3SG=DRCT evening COMPL FUT

bərā-yēt   wē   ∅-hē-n-avà,
brother-EZ.PL   3SG.OBL.F   SBJV-come.PRS-3PL-TELIC

[When] it became evening, [and time] for her brothers to come back,

Fātmā   ǰār-ak-ā   dī   ət-č-īt=a   bən
PN   time-INDF-EZ.F   again   IND-go.PRS-3SG=DRCT   under

sērk-ē   'arsāq-ī́   va
basket-EZ.M   nutrition-OBL.M   POST

Fatma again went under the cooking basket

ū   pātà-y   t-īn-t=a   xār-ē
and   canvas-OBL.M   IND-come.PRS-3SG=DRCT   down-OBL.F

and brought down the cotton canvas,

dā   bərā-yēt   wē   wề   na-bīn-in.
COMPL   brother-EZ.PL   3SG.OBL.F   3SG.OBL.F   NEG-see.PRS-3PL

so that her brothers wouldn't see her.

(26) bərā   t-hē-n-avà   sah   ət-ka-n-ē
     brother   IND-come.PRS-3PL-TELIC   looking   IND-do.PRS-3PL=3SG.OBL

The brothers returned home [and] looked around

tə-bēž-ēt-ən   bərā-yē   mazə̀n   čūnkū   šə   wānā
IND-say.PRS-3SG-NA   brother-EZ.M   big   since   from   3PL.OBL

maz-tər=ū   bə-āqəl-tə̀r   bo   got=ī,
big-CMPR=and   with-wise-CMPR   COP.PST.3SG   say.PST=3SG

'[and] said—The eldest brother, given that he was older and more clever than the rest, said,

ʿava	təšt-ak̲-ē	na	yē,	na	yē
DEM.PROX.SG	thing-INDF-EZ.M	NEG	EZ.M	NEG	EZ.M

ṭabēʿì	řūy	ət̲-da-t-ən.
normal	happening	IND-give.PRS-3SG-NA

'This is not something natural that has been happening here!

čūnkū	bərā-yēt	mən	hamī	gāv-ā	husā	nà
because	brother-EZ.PL	1SG.OBL	all	time-PL.OBL	such	NEG

zīrak	būˑn!
thriving	COP.PST=3PL

Since my brothers were not that conscientious before,

husā	vār-ā	pāqəž	nà-t̲-k̲ər!
such	place-PL.OBL	clean	NEG-IPFV-do.PST

they wouldn't clean the house like this.

husā	vērē	bəsarūbar	nà-t̲-k̲ər!
such	here.OBL.F	orderly	NEG-IPFV-do.PST

They wouldn't arrange the things in the house in such a way.'

ava	čì=ya	čē	būy-∅?
DEM.PROX.SG	what=COP.3SG	good	be.PST.PTCP-3SG

'What has happened here?

àz	nə-ẓān-əm.
1SG.DIR	NEG-know.PRS-1SG

I don't know!'

baz	ē	∅-ẓān-īn	pəšt-ī	am	čīrok-ā	xo
but	FUT	SBJV-know.PRS-1PL	after-OBL.M	1PL.DIR	tale-EZ.F	REFL

kaməl	∅-ḳà-yn.
complete	SBJV-do.PRS-1PL

However, we [the listeners] are going to figure it out after we finish our tale.

(27) ət-bēž-īt=ē, 'bərā̀, bərā!'
  IND-say.PRS-3SG=3SG.OBL brother brother

He (the eldest brother) said, 'Brother, brother!'

šə	xaw-ē	šīyār	ət-ḳà-t-ən.
from	sleep-EZ.M	awake	IND-do.PRS-3SG-NA

He woke him up.'

ət-bēž-t=ē,	'ta	čə̀	ḳərī=ya?'
IND-say.PRS-3SG=3SG.OBL	2SG.OBL	what	do.PST.PTPC=PERF

[and] said, 'What did you do?'

bərā	bar-ē	xo	t-dà-t=ē	aw
brother	front-EZ.M	REFL	IND-give.PRS-3SG=3SG.OBL	DEM.DIST.SG

bərā-yē	wī	∅-təřs-īt-ən	awalīkā.
brother-EZ.M	3SG.OBL.M	IND-fear.PRS-3SG-NA	in.the.beginning

He (the sleeping brother) looked at him. He was scared at first.

də-vē-t	∅-bēž-t=ē,	'bə-bor-a
IND-want.PRS-3SG	SBJV-say.PRS-3SG=3SG.OBL	SBJV-pass.PRS-IMP.2SG

mən	šol	nà-ḳər;
1SG.OBL	work	NEG-do.PST

He wanted to say, 'Excuse me! I didn't do my job.

ān	mən	wār-ā	pāqəž	nà-k̲ər;
or	1SG.OBL	place-PL.OBL	clean	NEG-do.PST

I didn't clean our house;

ān	mən	xwārən	čē	nà-k̲ər.
or	1SG.OBL	food	good	NEG-do.PST

I didn't cook food.'

(28)
baġ	∅-da-t=a	wār-à̲,
looking	IND-give.PRS-3SG=DRCT	place-PL.OBL

He (the sleeping brother) looked around

wār-ā	bəsarūbàr=a.
place-PL.OBL	orderly=COP.3SG

[and saw that] that everything was in order.

t̲ə-bēž-t=ē,	'bərā,	mən	šol-ē	xo	hamì̲
IND-say.PRS-3SG=3SG.OBL	brother	1SG.OBL	work-EZ.M	REFL	all

yē	k̲əri
EZ.M	do.PTCP

He said, 'Brother, I did my job entirely

az	bə-xo	nəvə̀st-əm.
1SG.DIR	in-REFL	sleep.PST-1SG

[and then] I simply slept.'

bərā	t̲-bēž-t=ē,	'āhā	galak	bā̀š=a.
brother	IND-say.PRS-3SG=3SG.OBL	INTJ	very	good=COP.3SG

The [elder] brother said, 'Ah! It's very nice.

dast-ē	ta	dē	xoš	∅-b-ə̀n.'
hand-EZ.M	2SG.OBL	FUT	nice	SBJV-be.PRS-3PL

Thank you (lit. May your hands be nice!)!'

(29) xārən-ằ   xo   ṯ-xo-n.
     food-EZ.F REFL   IND-eat.PRS-3PL

They ate their meal.

jəlk-ēt   xo   ṯ-guhoř-ən   dē   ∅-nəv-ən.
garment-EZ.PL   REFL   IND-change.PRS-3PL FUT   SBJV-sleep.PRS-3PL

They changed their clothes to [get ready for] sleep.

dam-ē   řož   əṯ-hal-ē-t-ən,
when-OBL.F   day   IND-PVB-come.PRS-3SG-NA

When dawn broke (lit. the sun rose)

ṯə-vē-t-ən   bə-čə-n=a   řāv=ū   nēčīr-ằ.
IND-want.PRS-3SG-NA   SBJV-go.PRS-3PL=DRCT   hunt=and   hunt-PL.OBL

they intended to go hunting.

bər-ī   řož   bə̀-hal-ē-t-ən
before-OBL.M   sun   SBJV-PVB-come.PRS-3SG-NA

əṯ-čə-n=a   řāv=ū   nēčīr-ằ.
IND-go.PRS-3PL=DRCT   hunt=and   hunt-PL.OBL

Before the dawn broke, they would go hunting.

NORTHERN KURDISH OF DURE
Text 20: §1-13

Masoud Mohammadirad

Speaker: Herish Rashid Tawfiq Beg
Audio: https://kurdic.ames.cam.ac.uk/audio/249/

(1) *nāv-ē   mə   Hèrəš=a.*|
    name-EZ.M   1SG.OBL   PN=COP

My name is Herish.

az   ḳuř-ē   Řašīd   Bag-ē   Barwārì=ma=ū| *az*
1SG.DIR   son-EZ.M   PN   PN-EZ.M   PN=COP.1SG=and   1SG.DIR

Barwārì=ma,|
PN=COP.1SG

I am the son of Rashid Bag Barwari, and I am from Barwari.

navī-yē   Tawfiq   Bag-ē   ḳuř-ē
grandson-EZ.M   PN   PN-EZ.M   son-EZ.M

hajī   Řašīd   Bàg-ē   Barwārī.|
PN   PN   PN-EZ.M   PN

[I am] the grandson of Tawfiq Bag Barwari, [who is] the son of Haji Rashid Bag Barwari.

az=ē	bo	wa	čīròk-ā	ḥasp-ē	māḷbàt-ē
1SG.DIR=FUT	for	2PL.OBL	tale-EZ.F	horse-EZ.M	family-OBL.F

b-ēž-əm
SBJV-say.PRS-1SG

I am going to tell you the story of 'the family horse',

wakī	bāb=ū	bāpīr-ā	bo	mə
like	father=and	grand.father-PL.OBL	for	1SG.OBL

và-gařyā-yī.
TELIC-turn.PST-PTCP

the way I have been told it by the elders.

(2)
ṭ-bēž-ən	ha-bū-∅	na-bū-∅,
IND-say.PRS-3PL	EXIST-COP.PST-3SG	NEG-COP.PST-3SG

It is said that there was and there was not,

kas	šə	xodē	màẓ-tər	na-bū-∅,
person	from	god.OBL.M	big-CMPR	NEG-COP.PST-3SG

[but] there was nobody greater than God,

kas	šə	banī-yā	žī	dərawìn-tər	na-bū-∅
person	from	human-PL.OBL	ADD	liar-CMPR	NEG-COP.PST-3SG

and no bigger liar than man.

zamān-ak-ī	wē	davar-è	xalḵ-è	čə
period-INDF-OBL.M	DEM.DIST.OBL.F	region-OBL.F	people-OBL.F	what

ṭ-ḵər?
IPFV-do.PST

What did the people in this region do once?

har	bənamàḷ-ak-ē	hàsp-ak-ē	makən-ē,	jəhēl-è
each	family-INDF-OBL.F	horse-INDF-EZ.M	solid-EZ.M	young-EZ.M

Each family had a young, reliable horse

galà gala gala gala lāv ha-bū-∅|
very very very very strong EXIST-be.PST-3SG

that was very, very strong.

(3) *ṱ̂ə-bēž-ən àv ḥaṣp-ē hanē*| *har*
IND-say.PRS-3PL DEM.PROX horse-EZ.M DEICT.PTCL each

ṱ̂ə-nāv-ē bənamāḷ-ē əṱ̂-hāt-∅=a nīyā̀s.|
in-middle-EZ.M family-OBL.F IPFV-come.PST-3SG=DRCT knowing

It is said that this [particular] horse (i.e. the horse of a certain family) was known in every family.

yaʿnī xalk-ē av ḥaṣp-a bənamā̀ḷ-ē
that.is people-OBL.F DEM.PROX horse-DEM family-OBL.F

ṱ̂-nīyāsī|
IPFV-know.PST

That is, people knew this horse as the 'family horse'.

kas lə vī ḥaṣp-ī sīyār
person at DEM.PROX.3SG.OBL.M horse-OBL.M rider

nà-ṱ̂-bū-∅.|
NEG-IPFV-become.PST-3SG

Nobody would mount this horse.

sāḷ-ē jār-ak-ē av ḥaṣp-a darè ṱ̂-xəst|
year-OBL.F time-INDF-OBL.F DEM.PROX horse-DEM out IPFV-throw.PST

nīšā xalk-ē əṱ̂-dā̀|
showing people-OBL.M IPFV-give.PST

Once a year, they (i.e. the family) would bring [the horse] out for people to see it.'

ū	xalk̂-ē	madhà	pē	tə-k̂ər-ən.
and	people-OBL.M	praising	to.3SG.OBL	IPFV-do.PST-3PL

And people would praise it (i.e. the horse)

ū	xalk̂-ē	ḥasp-ē	xo	bə	wā
and	people-OBL.M	horse-EZ.M	REFL	to	DEM.PL.OBL

ḥasp-ā	tə-šəbəhànd-ən.
horse-PL.OBL	IPFV-compare.PST.3PL

and compare their horses to those [family] horses.

(4)
ḥasp-ē	bənamāl̟-ē	yē	čāwà	bū-∅?
horse-EZ.M	family-OBL.F	EZ.M	how	COP.PST-3SG

[But] what was the family horse like?

bàb-ē	ḥasp-ī	yē	bənamāl̟-ē	bū-∅,	Pəxīnè.
father-EZ.M	horse-OBL.M	EZ.M	family-OBL.F	COP.PST-3SG	PN

Its father, Pekhine, also belonged to this family.

k̂uř-ē	wī	ḥasp-ī	žī	bə	wē
son-EZ.M	DEM.DIST.OBL.M	horse-OBL.M	ADD	with	DEM.DIST.OBL.F

bənamāl̟-ē	t̟-mā-∅.
Family-OBL.F	IPFV-stay.PST-3SG

Its colt also stayed with the same family.

kas-ē	lə	vī	ḥasp-ī	žəbar
person-EZ.M	at	DEM.PROX.OBL.M	horse-OBL.M	because.of

qīmàt-ā	wī	lē	sīyār	na-bū-∅
value-EZ.F	3SG.OBL.M	at.3SG.OBL	rider	NEG-COP.PST-3SG

Because of its value, nobody would mount the [family] horse.

tənē	dàrē	tə-xəst	bo	jānī̀
only	out	IPFV-throw.PST	for	grandeur

It was only brought out of the stable for people to see its grandeur,

ū	va-šārt-ava	tə	gov-ḕ	dā.
and	TELIC-hide.PST-TELIC	in	stable-OBL.F	POST

and then hidden again in the stable.

(5)
t̰-bē-n	sāḷ-ak-ḕ	ḥasp-ē	bənamāḷ-ak-ḕ
IND-say.PRS-3PL	year-INDF-OBL.F	horse-EZ.M	family-INDF-OBL.F

ko	gala	gala	galak	yē	barnīyằz	bū
COMPL	very	very	very	EZ.M	known	COP.PST.3SG

It is said that the horse of [a] family became so famous

ū	xalk-ē	hamī,	ʿyaʿnī	nāv=ū	dang-ēt
and	people-OBL.M	all	well	name=and	voice-EZ.PL

vī	ḥasp-ī	čə̀	bū-n?'
DEM.PROX.OBL.M	horse-OBL.M	what	COP.PST-3PL

that everybody [said], 'Well, what is [so] special about this horse?'

ēk	hāt-∅=a	dəzī̀-ēt	ḥasp-ī.
one	come.PST-3SG=DRCT	roberry-EZ.PL	horse-OBL.M

A [certain] person came to steal the horse.

xo	āvēt=a	tə	gov-ḕ-va
REFL	throw.PST=DRCT	in	stable-OBL.F-POST

He went into the stable

ū	xo	āvēt=a	sar	pəšt-ā	ḥasp-ē	wằ.
and	REFL	throw.PST=DRCT	on	back-EZ.F	horse-EZ.M	3PL.OBL

and mounted the family horse.

vā	ḥasp-ē	wā	řavằnd.
DEM.PROX.3SG	horse-EZ.M	3PL.OBL	abduct.PST

He stole the horse.

(6) zaḷâm žî| xodān-ē ḥasp-ī pē
    man add owner-EZ.M horse-OBL.M at.3SG.OBL

hasằ-∅.|
understand.PST-3SG

The man, the owner of the horse found out [about the robbery].

dīt ēk̲-ī ḥasp-ē wā bə̀r.|
see.PST one-OBL.M horse-EZ.M 3PL.OBL take.PST

He saw that a person had taken their horse.

got=a k̲ùř-ēt xo,|
say.PST=DRCT son-EZ.PL REFL

He said to his sons,

'həlừ-n vē řā-bə-gah-ən|
get.up.IMP-2PL DEM.PROX.OBL.F PVB-SBJV-arrive.PRS-2PL

'Get up, go and reach the thief,

hatk-ā ma čừ-∅|
honour-OBL.F 1PL.OBL go.PST-3SG

for we are disgraced.

ēk-ì̄ ḥasp-ē ma bər,| yē bənamằḷ-ē.'|
one-OBL.M horse-EZ.M 1PL.OBL take.PST EZ.M family-OBL.F

Someone has taken our horse—the family horse—

av-ē bāb-ē ḥasp-ì̄| əv bāb-ē
DEM.PROX-EZ.M father-EZ.M horse-OBL.M DEM.PROX.3SG father-EZ.M

bənamāḷ-ḕ.|
family-OBL.F

[Both] the horse's father [and] the father of the family [said so].

(7) ya‛nī   žə   bāb=ū   kāl-ā-va   ḥasp=ū
    that.is from   father=and   elder-PL.OBL-POST   horse=and

bənamāḷ   pēkvà   bū-n   nažāt   bo   nažāt-ī̀.
family   together   be.PST-3PL generation   by   generation-OBL.M

From the days of old (lit. from fathers and grandfathers), from one generation to the other, the horse and the family had lived together.

gotī̀   àv   zaḷām-ē   xodān-ē   ḥasp-ī
say.PTCP   DEM.PROX.3SG   man-EZ.M   pwner-EZ.M   horse-OBL.M

čū-∅
go.PST-3SG

It is said that the owner of the family horse went

lə   ḥasp-ē   xwa   sīyằr   bū-∅.
at   horse-EZ.M   REFL   rider   COP.PST-3SG

and mounted his [other] horse.

ū   kuř-ēt   wī   žī   dā   dìv.
and   son-EZ.PL   3SG.OBL   ADD   give.PST   after

And his sons followed him.

kat-n=a   dīv   ḥasp-ī̀   kat-n=a   dìv
fall.PRS-3PL=DRCT   after   horse-OBL.M   fall.PRS-3PL=DRCT   after

They went after the [family] horse, they went after it.

ū   ḥasp   řā-gər-ən   čārgāvằ.
and   horse   PVB-grab.PRS-3PL   galloping

They galloped on their horses off [to the thief].'

(8) ḵùř-ēt   wī   žī   ēk   bə-dīv-va
    son-EZ.PL   3SG.OBL.M   ADD   one   in-after-POST

The sons [went] behind their father,

ū	bāb=ē	bə-dīv	dəzīḵar-i̭-va.
and	father=EZ.M	in-after	thief-OBL.M-POST

and the father went after the thief.

dəzīḵar=ē	lə	ḥasp-ē	bənamāḷ-ē	sīyàr=a.
thief=EZ.M	at	horse-EZ.M	family-OBL.F	rider=COP.3SG

The thief was riding the family horse.

bāb	žī	lə	ḥasp-ē	xo	sīyàr=a.
father	ADD	at	horse-EZ.M	REFL	rider=COP.3SG

The father was on his [other] horse.

har	du	ḵuř	žī	av	dā	wař-ēt
each	two	son	ADD	DEM.PROX.3SG	give.PST	thus-EZ.PL

wằ-y	dī
3PL.OBL-EZ.M	other

Similarly, his two sons followed each other.

ḵā	kī	žə	bāgìr	ha=ya	lē	lē
EXCL	who	at	windy	PTC=COP.3SG	but	at.3SG.OBL

sīyằr	būy=n.
rider	COP.PST.PTCP=COP.3PL

Even though it was [extremely] windy, they were riding their horses.

(9)
tə-bēž-ən	bāb	gahəšt=a	dəzīḵar-i̭.
IND-say.PRS-3PL	father	arrive.PST.3SG=DRCT	thief-OBL.M

It is said that the father reached the thief.

dast-ē	xwa	hāvèt,	dā	gah-ət	pātk-ằ	wī
hand-EZ.M	REFL	throw.PST	AUX	reach.PRS-3SG	scarf-EZ.F	3SG.OBL.M

He stretched out his hand to grab the thief's scarf

nà-gahašt=ē|	dast-ē	xwa	zəvəřānd-avà.|
NEG-arrive.PST.3SG=3SG.OBL	hand-EZ.M	REFL	turn.PST-TELIC

[but since] his hands did not reach it [the thief's scarf], he withdrew them.

ū	havsār-ē	ḥasp-ī	bə	ləxāv-va	kēšà|
and	halter-EZ.M	horse-OBL.M	with	bridle-POST	pull.PST

He (the father) pulled the reins of his horse

ū	ḥasəp	řā-wəstànd.|
and	horse	PVB-stop.PST

and made it stop.

dəzīkar	žī	žē	falətì-∅.|
thief	ADD	from.3SG.OBL	run.away.PST-3SG

The thief rode away (lit. the thief scaped from him).

(10)	hatā	k̲uř-ēt	wī	gahīšt-ən=ē|
	until	son-EZ.PL	3SG.OBL.M	arrive.PST-3PL=3SG.OBL

When his sons caught up with him,

got=ē,	'bāb-o!	ta	čə̀	māḷ-ā	ma
say.PST=3SG.OBL	father-VOC	2SG.OBL	why	home-EZ.F	1PL.OBL

xərā	k̲ər?|
ruined	do.PST

they said, 'Dad, why did you ruin our home?

wē	gāv-ē	dastē	ta
DEM.PROX.3SG.OBL.F	time-OBL.F	hand-EZ.M	2SG.OBL

tə-gàhəšt=ē!|
IPFV-arrive.PST=3SG.OBL

A while ago you could have reached the thief!

ta	bȕčī̆	na-gərt?'ˈ
2SG.OBL	why	NEG-grab.PST

'Why didn't you grab him?'

got=ē,	'rün-ə̀n,ˈ
say.PST=3SG.OBL	PVB.sit.PRS.IMP-2PL

The father said, 'Calm down! (lit. Sit down!)

mə	ʿaql	xarəj	k̠ə̀r.'ˈ
1SG.OBL	wisdom	consumption	do.PST

I acted wisely.'

(11)	go	'waxt-ē	az	gahəštī=m
	say.PST	time-OBL.F	1SG.DIR	arrive.PST.PTCP=COP.1SG

ḥasp-ē	bənamāḷ-ȅ,ˈ
horse-EZ.M	Family-OBL.F

He (the father) said, 'When I approached the family horse—

av=ē	hənda	sāḷ=a	am	əb	bāb=ū
DEM.PROX.3SG=EZ.M	so.many	year=COP.3SG	1PL.DIR	with	father=and

bāpȉr-va	madh-ā	pē	t̠ə-ka-ynˈ
grandfather-POST	praise-PL.OBL	to.3SG.OBL	IND-do.PRS-1PL

the one which we have been praising for so long

ū	t̠ə-ba-yn	nāv	xalk̠-ȅˈ
and	IND-take.PRS-1PL	into	people-OBL.M

and which we take around for people to see

tu	∅-ẓān-ī	čə	hāt-∅	sar-ē	mə̀n?ˈ
2SG.DIR	IND-know.PRS-2SG	what	come.PST-3SG	head-EZ.M	1SG.OBL

—do you know what I thought of?'

(12) gotī,   'waxtē   mə   dītī̀   mə   dastē   xwa
     say.PST.PTCP when   1SG see.PTCP 1SG.OBL   hand-EZ.M   REFL

dā   hàvē-m| pātək-ā   dəz-ī   dā   gēr-əm|
AUX   throw.PRS-1SG   scarf-EZ.PL   thief-OBL.M AUX   grab.PRS-1SG

He (the father) said, 'When I saw that I could stretch out my arms and grab the scarf of the thief.

dā   xalək   hamì   zān-īt-ən|
AUX   people   all   know.PRS-3PL-NA

[I thought that] people would figure out

dəzīḳar-aḳ   hāt-∅   ḥasp-ē   mà   dəzī|
thief-INDF   come.PST-3SG   horse-EZ.M   1PL.OBL   steal.PST

that a thief had come to steal our horse

yē   bənamāḷ-è| av=ē   sar-ē   həndasāḷ=a
EZ.M   family-OBL.F   DEM.PROX.SG=EZ.M   on-EZ.M   so.many.year=COP.3SG

nàv=ū   dang-ēt   wī   čūy=n.|
name=and   voice-EZ.PL   3SG.OBL.M   go.PST.PTCP=3PL

—the family horse— the one which has been famous and well-known for so many years.'

(13) dā   bēž-ən   ēk-ī   ḥasp-ē   wa   dəzì.|
      AUX   say.PRS-3PL   one-OBL.M   horse-EZ.M   3PL.OBL   steal

[The father continued] '[Later] people would say, "Someone stole your [family] horse.

ū   hīn   bə   ḥasp-ēt   xwà| yèt   sīyārī-ē| bə
and   2PL.DIR   with   horse-EZ.PL   REFL   EZ.PL   riding-OBL.F   to

ḥasp-ē   bənamāḷ-ē   řā   gahəšt-ə̀n.|
horse-EZ.M   family-OBL.F   POST   arrive.PST-3PL

And you could reach the family horse with your riding horses.

bəlā	ḥàṣəp	bo	wī	∅-b-īt
HOR	horse	for	3SG.OBL.M	SBJV-be.PRS-3SG

[So instead,] let the [family] horse be the thief's,

bas	bəlā	madh-ēt	ḥaṣp-ī	bə-mīn-ì.
just	HOR	praise-EZ.PL	horse-OBL.M	SBJV-stay.PRS-3SG

but let the praise of the [family] horse remain with us!'

NORTHERN KURDISH OF KHIZAVA
Text 7: §1-19

Masoud Mohammadirad

Speaker: Ahmed Abubakir Suleiman
Audio: https://kurdic.ames.cam.ac.uk/audio/247/

(1) nāv-ē   mə̀n   ʾAhmad   ʾAbūbakər   Səlēmǎ̀n.
    name-EZ.M 1SG.OBL PN   PN   PN

My name [is] Ahmad Abubakir Sleman.

az   xalk-ē   gund-ē   Xīzavà̀=ma,   ʾašīr-ā   Gulīà̀
1SG.DIR   people-EZ.M   village-EZ.M PN=COP.1SG   tribe-EZ.F PN.PL.OBL

I come from the village of Khizava, (from) Guli tribe.

ū   az   žə   dāyəḵbū-yē   həzār=ū
and   1SG.DIR from   mother.born-EZ.F   thousand=and

nahsad=ū   šēst=ū   hàšt-ē=ma.
nine.hundred=and   sixty=and   eight-OBL.F=COP.1SG

I was born in 1968.

ʾamā   dərəstāhī-yā   mən   dā   tārīx=əm   xàlaṭ=ən,
but   reality-EZ.F   1SG.OBL   POST   date.DIR.PL=1SG   wrong=COP.3PL

But in reality ... my date [of birth] is wrong.

šēst=ū   dù=ma.
sixty=and   two=COP.1SG

I was born in 1962.

(2) zanbīlfəròš du   goř-ēt   zanbīlfəroš yēṭ
    basket.seller two tomb-EZ.PL basket.seller EZ.PL

hay=n   əl   davar-ā   kurd-ā̀   dā,
EXIST=COP.3PL in   region-EZ.F Kurd-PL.OBL   POST

The basket seller—there are two tombs of [associated with] the basket seller in Kurdish regions:

ēk   lə   Kurdəstān-ā Bākòr,
one   in   PN-EZ.F   north

one in northern Kurdistan,

ēk   lə   Kurdəstān-ā Bāšòr.
one   in   PN-EZ.F   south

one in southern Kurdistan.

yē   Bākòr, yē   lə   Vārqin-ē   lə   qazā
EZ.M   north   EZ.M   in   PN-OBL.F   in   county.EZ.F

Səlīvā lə   vīlāyat-ā   Dīyằrbakər.
PN   in   province-EZ.F   PN

The one in the northern Kurdistan is located in Farqin in the Siliva county, Diyarbakir province.

(3) ʾamā yē   av-ē   haček̇o   lə   Kurdəstān-ā
    but   EZ.M DEM.PROX-EZ.M   that.is in   PN-EZ.F

Bāšòr
south

But, as for the one in southern Kurdistan,

ava   ṭə-kat   sar jằʿdā   nāvbayn-ā
DEM.PROX.SG   IND-fall.PRS.3SG on   road.EZ.F in.between-EZ.F

Bātīfē   ū   Zāxo dā.
PN.OBL.F   and PN   POST

the tomb is located on the road between Batifa and Zakho.

əl-sàr	ǰaˤdē=ya[|]	bə-řax	gund-ē	Sīrkotkī-yȅ-da
on-top	road.OBL.F=COP.3SG	to-side	village-EZ.M	PN-OBL.F- POST

It is on the road next to the Sirkotki village.

taqrīban	rošāvā-yē	nə̀hīyā	Bātīfā	p̂ēnǰ
approximately	west-EZ.M	region.EZ.F	PN	five

kīlomīṭr-ā.[|]
kilometer-PL.OBL

It [is located] approximately less than five kilometres west of the Batifa region.

(4)	àv	zanbīlfəroš-a	wak	həkāyat-ā	wī
	DEM.PROX	basket.seller-DEM.SG	as	story-EZ.F	3SG.OBL.M

hāt-ī-∅	gotən-ē[|]
come.PST-PTCP-3SG	say.INF-OBL.F

As for the basket seller—the way his adventure has been told

yḕt	xalk-ē	ma=ū	bāv=ū	bāp̂ir-ēt
EZ.PL	people-EZ.M	1PL.OBL=and	father=and	grandfather-EZ.PL

ma	ēk	bo	ēk	yē	gòt-ī[|]
1PL.OBL	one	to	one	EZ.M	say.PST-PTCP

[and] from what our ancestors have passed on to each other:

lə-sar	vē	kalhā	šȁbānī-yē	ṭ-īn-ən,[|]
from-top	DEM.PROX.OBL.F	castle-EZ.F	PN-OBL.F	IND.bring.PRS-3PL

av	kalh-ā	šābȁnī-yē.[|]
DEM.PROX	castle-EZ.F	PN-OBL.F

his story comes from the citadel of Shabani, this citadel of Shabani.

(5) ava   yē   ḳo   lə-daf   ma   nằv-ē
    DEM.PROX.SG.DIR EZ.M REL at-side 1PL.OBL name- EZ.M

wı̆| mīr   Məhsən   ḳuř-ē   mīr   Avdulazīz-ē
3SG.OBL   prince PN   son-EZ.M   prince PN-EZ.M

mīr-ē   Müsəl=a,| yē   vē   kalh-ằ   Müsəl.|
prince-EZ.M   PN=COP.3SG   EZ.M   DEM.PROX.3SG.OBL.F   castle-EZ.F PN

He (the basket seller) was called Mir Muhsin in our region. [He is] the son of Mir Avdulaziz, the prince of Mosul, [at] this citadel of Mosul.

mīr   Məhsən   ḳuř-ē   mīr   Avdulazīz-ē   mīr-ē
prince   PN   son-EZ.M   prince PN-EZ.M   prince-EZ.M

Müsəl=a.|
PN=COP.3SG

Mir Muhsin (the basket seller) was the son of Avdulaziz, the prince of Mosul.

tabʿan   wak   ava   wak   həkằyat-ā   wı̆
evidently   as   DEM.PROX.SG   as   story-EZ.F   3SG.OBL.M

ət-bēž-ən|
IND-say.PRS-3PL

Evidently, his story was like this:

zanbīlfəroš   ḳuř-ē   mīr-ı̆   bī-∅.|
basket.seller   son-EZ.M   prince-OBL.M   be.PST-3SG

the basket seller was the prince's son.

(6) ʾənsān-aḵ-ī   lāw-aḵ-ī   ǰahēl   yē   barkatı̀
    human-INDF-EZ.M   boy-INDF-EZ.M   young   EZ.M   handsome

bī-∅|
be.PST-3SG

He was a handsome young man.

gařhā-∅	*nāv*	*jahēl-ā*	*dā=ū*
wander.PST-3SG	among	youth-PL.OBL	POST=and

He would wander around with other youths.

pāra	*lə-bar*	*dast=ī*	*zàhəf*	*bī-n=ū.ǀ*
money	in-front	hand=3SG	a.lot	be.PST-3PL=and

He had a lot of money at his disposal.

ət̯-bēž-ən	*waxt-ak̯-ī*	*kas-ak*	*šə*	*māl-ā*
IND-say.PRS-3PL	time-INDF-OBL.M	person-INDF	from	house-EZ.F

mīr-ī	*mə̀r-∅.ǀ*
prince-OBL.M	die.PST-3SG

It is said that a member of the prince's family once passed away.

(7) *waxt-ē*	*mər-i-∅*		*tabʿan*	*xalk-ē*
when-OBL.F	die.PST-PTCP-3SG		evidently	people-EZ.M

davar-ē	*lē*	*kòm*	*bī-n=ūǀ*
region-OBL.F	at.3SG.OBL	group	be.PST-3PL=and

When he died, the people of the region obviously gathered around him,

bərən-ā=(a)v	*zīyārat-è=ūǀ*
take.INF-EZ.F=DRCT	tomb.visiting-OBL.F=and

took [him] to the cemetery,

aw	*gořˇ*	*k̯olà̯=ūǀ*
DEM.DIST	tomb	dig.PST=and

dug a grave,

k̯ər	*tḛ̄*	*da=ūǀ*	*va-šằrt=ū.ǀ*
do.PST	in.3SG.OBL	POST=and	TELIC-hide.PST=and

put [him] in it, and buried [him].

awī	*žī*	*got=ē,*
3SG.OBL.M	ADD	say.PST=3SG.OBL

He (Muhsin) said,

'mā	*dē*	*ava*	*hamā*	*lə-vè-dē*	*b-ē!?'*
EXCM	FUT	DEM.PROX.SG	EMPH	in-DEM.PROX.3SG.OBL.F-POST	be.PRS-3SG

'Is he going to rest in this grave forever?

got=ē,	*'ava*	*dē*	*lə-vē*
say.PST=3SG.OBL	DEM.PROX.SG	FUT	in- DEM.PROX.3SG.OBL.F

∅-b-ē	*hatà*	*qīyāmat-ē.'*
SBJV-be.PRS-3SG	until	resurrection-OBL.F

They (the people at the funeral) said, 'Yes, he will stay here until the resurrection.

(8)
'qīyāmat	*ḵangī̀=ya?'*	*gotī=ū.*
resurrection	when=COP.3SG	say.PST.PTCP=and

When is the resurrection?', [he said].

'čo	*qīyāmat-ē-va*	*řā*	*čo*	*šə*	*hē*
no	resurrection-OBL.F-POST	POST	none	of	yet

dīyānat-ē	*nə̀-zān-a,*	*čo*	*dīyānat-à̄.'*
religion-OBL.F	NEG-know.PRS-3SG	no	religion-PL.OBL

[They said to him], 'No religion knows for sure about [when] the resurrection [happens], no religion!'

ṭərs-ề	*xwa*	*lə*	*dəl-ī*	*dā.*
fear-EZ.M	REFL	at	heart-OBL.M	give.PST

Fear took hold of him (Muhsin).

gotī,	'ava	dē	t̯-nāv	vē
say.PST.PTCP	DEM.PROX.SG	FUT	in-middle	DEM.PROX.OBL.F

ằx-ē	řā-b-ət̯?'
soil-OBL.F	PRV-be.PRS-3SG

He said, 'Is he going to get out from under the soil [at the resurrection]?'

got=ē	'à.ˈ	bə	šàv-ē=ū	bə	rož-ē
say.PST=3SG.OBL	yes	at	night-OBL.F=and	at	day-OBL.F

Yes, day and night,' they said.

go	məstamər	lə-vē-dē	b-ē
say.PST.3SG	continually	in-DEM.PROX.OBL.F-POST	be.PRS-3SG

'He will stay here day and night continually.

ava	xəlằs.'ˈ
DEM.PROX.SG	over

It is finished [for the dead].'

(9)
řā-bī	wak	awadī-ak̯-ē	bə	sàr-ī
PVB-be.PST.3SG	like	thing-INDF-OBL.F	to	head-OBL.M

kat-∅ˈ
fall.PST-3SG

[Upon seeing this scene] something came to his mind

malā-yàk̯	hāt-∅	bo	āxàft	rož-ak
mullah-INDF	come.PST-3SG	for	speak.PST	day-INDF

du	sē	čār.ˈ
two	three	four

A mullah came to talk to him for one, two, three, four days.

har	*řo*	*dā*	*bēž-ē,*
each	day	AUX	say.PRS-3SG

Every day, he would say,

'malē	*war-a*	*bo*	*mə̀n*	*bə-āxav-a.'*
mullah.OBL	come.IMP-2SG	for	1SG.OBL	SBJV-speak.PRS-IMP.2SG

'Mullah! Come [and] talk to me [about religion].'

hatā	*bahs-ē*	*dīyằnat-ē*	*bo*	*ī*	*kər.*
even	talk-EZ.M	religion-OBL.F	for	3SG.OBL.M	do.PST

Mullah talked to him about the religion.

(10)
'dīyānat	*husằ=na=ū*
religion	such=COP.3PL=and

[The mullah said] 'Religion is like this.

dīyānat-ā,	*masīhī̀*	*yā*	*hay,*
religion-EZ.F	Christian	EZ.F	EXIST.3SG

There is the Christian religion.

dīyānat-ā	*əslāmatī̀*	*yā*	*hay.*
religion-EZ.F	Islamic	EZ.F	EXIST.3SG

There is the Islamic religion.

har	*dīyānat-ak̠=ā*	*ha-b-ə̀t'*	*tab'an*	*'ərf=ū*
EMPH	religion-INDF=EZ.F	EXIST-SBJV.be.PRS-3SG	naturally	custom=and

'ādāt=ū	*'awādī-yēṭ*	*manhaǰ-ē*	*dīyānat-ē.*
tradition.PL=and	INTJ-EZ.PL	way-EZ.M	religion-OBL.F

Each religion has a set of liturgies and customs.'

aw	*lə-sar*	*əslāmatī-yè*	*bī-∅*
DEM.DIST	on-top	Islam-OBL.M	be.PST-3SG

He (Muhsin) had Islamic faith.

əslāmatī   nīšā   dằ.|
Islam   showing   give.PST

[The Mullah] showed him the principles of Islam.'

(11) mằ-∅| bə   čand   hayv-ak̲-ằ   mā-∅|
      rest.PST-3SG by some month-INDF-EZ.F   rest.PST-3SG

Things remained [like this] for a couple of months.

gotī   'p̱ā   az   k̲ò   bə-k̲ə-m,|
say.PST.PTCP   EXCM   1SG.DIR   what   SBJV-do.PRS-1SG

He (Muhsin) said, 'What shall I do

az=ē   žə   vē   ʾawādì   xalās|
1SG.DIR=EZ.M   from   DEM.PROX.OBL.F   thing   relieved

to be relieved of this thing,

žə   wī   qabl-ì̲| ṭang=ū   ṭārī-yā
from   DEM.DIST.OBL.M   grave-OBL.M   tight=and   darkness-EZ.F

vī   qabl-ī   xalằs   ∅-b-əm.'|
DEM.PROX.OBL.M   grave-OBL.M   relieved   SBJV-be.PRS-1SG

[to be relieved] of this dark narrow grave?'

(12) got=ē,   'tə-vē-t   ṭù| ēh   ṭu
      say.PST=3SG.OBL   IND-should.PRS-3SG   2SG.DIR   INTJ   2SG.DIR

nəvềž-ēt   xwa   bə-k̲ē!|
prayer-EZ.PL   REFL   SBJV-do.PRS.2SG

'He (the Mullah) said, 'You, eh, you should recite your prayers!

ṭu   taʿat=ū   ʾəbādàt-ēt   xwa   bə-k̲ē!|
2SG.DIR   obedience=and   praying-EZ.PL   REFL   SBJV-do.PRS.2SG

You should perform your worship!

tu	hārīkằr	∅-bē	ləgal	xalk-ak̯-ē=ū
2SG.DIR	helper	SBJV-be.PRS.2SG	with	people-INDF-OBL.M=and

You should help people.

tu	yē	bə-řàhm	∅-bē=ū,
2SG.DIR	EZ.M	with-mercy	SBJV-be.PRS.2SG=and

You should be merciful.

tu	zolm=o	zordārī	lə	xalk-ak̯-ē	nà-k̯ē.
2SG.DIR	injustice=and	tyranny	to	people-INDF-OBL.M	PROH-do.PRS.2SG

and should not do any injustice nor cruelty to people.

hagàr	tu	zolm-ē	bə-k̯ē
if	2SG.DIR	injustice-OBL.F	SBJV-do.PRS.2SG

If you're unjust [to people],

tāʿat=ū	ʾībādat-ē	ta	qabül	nà-b-ət.
obedience=and	praying-EZ.M	2SG.OBL	acceptance	NEG-be.PRS.3SG

your obedience and prayer will not be accepted [by God].'

(13)
'bā́š=a	p̂ānē	bàv-ē	mən-ē	tə-k̯ēt
well=COP.3SG	EXCM	father-EZ.M	1SG.OBL=EZ.M	IND-do.PRS.3SG

[Muhsin said], 'Isn't it so that my father does [injustice]!

az=ē	wē	xwàrən-ē	də-xo-m.'
1SG.DIR=EZ.M	DEM.DIST.3SG.OBL.F	food-OBL.F	IND-eat.PRS.1SG

I'm living off him.'

got=ē,	'walạ	ā	bàv-ē	ta	zolm-ề
say.PST=3SG.OBL	by.God	INTJ	father-EZ.M	2SG.OBL	injustice-OBL.F

bə-k̯ə-t
SBJV-do.PRS.3SG

He (the Mullah) said, 'By God if your father does injustice [and you live off him],

taʿat=ū	ʾibādat-ē	ṭa	qabül	nà̀-b-ət.'
obedience=and	praying-EZ.M	2SG.OBL	acceptance	NEG-be.PRS-3SG

your prayers will not be accepted.'

ʿp̄ā	az	kò	bə-k̂ə-m
EXCM	1SG.DIR	what	SBJV-do.PRS-1SG

[Muhsin said], 'What shall I do

az=ē	žə	vē	zolm=ū	zordārī-yē
1SG.DIR=EZ.M	from	DEM.PROX.OBL.F	injustice=and	tyranny-EZ.M

bāv-ē	xwa?'
father-EZ.M	REFL

[to be relieved] of the injustice caused by my father?'

(14)	həndī	go	bāv-ē	xwà.
	so.much	say.PST	father-EZ.M	REFL

He talked so much to his father.

bāv-ē	wī	řāzī	nà-bī-∅	vī
father-EZ.M	3SG.OBL.M	content	NEG-be.PST-3SG	DEM.PROX.OBL.M

ṭəšt-ī	bə-hēl-ēt.
thing-OBL.M	SBJV-let.PRS-3SG

[But] his father did not agree to abandon this thing.

got,	ʿagar	ṭu	kad-ak̂-è̄	bə	dast-ē
say.PST	if	2SG.DIR	tailor-INDF-OBL.F	with	hand-EZ.M

xwa	bə-k̂ē
REFL	SBJV-do.PRS.2SG

The Mullah (lit. he) said, 'If you do a job with your own hands,

ū	ṭu	xwa	xwadằn	bə-k̂ē=ū
and	2SG.DIR	REFL	owner	SBJV-do.PRS.2SG= and

take care of yourself

'ayằr-ā	xwa	xwadān	∅-ḵē
standard-EZ.F	REFL	owner	SBJV-do.PRS.2SG

and manage to live by your own means

dē	həngē	taʿat=ū	ʾibādat-ē	ta	qabùl
FUT	then	obedience=and	praying-EZ.M	2SG.OBL	acceptance

də-b-əṭ.'
IND-be.PRS.3SG

then your prayers will be accepted.'

(15)	řā-bī-∅	dàr-kat-∅,	dar-kat-∅	žə	màl
	PVB-be.PST-3SG	PVB-fall.PST-3SG	PVB-fall.PST-3SG	from	home

dar-kat-∅
PVB-fall.PST-3SG

He rose [and] left [the house].

bə-žə	žənk-àḵ	ha-bī=ū	du	bəčēk.
in-of	woman-INDF	EXIST.be.PST=and	two	baby.DIM

He had a wife and two babies.

got	žənk-ā	xwà,
say.PST	wife.DIM-EZ.F	REFL

He said to his wife,

ʿaz=ē	∅-čə-m	bo	mà	šūl	∅-ḵə-m.'
1SG.DIR=FUT	SBJV-go.PRS-1SG	for	1PL.OBL	work	SBJV-do.PRS-1SG

'I will go and make a living (lit. work) for us.'

(16) ŗā-bī-∅ hằt-∅ dast̠ ap̂ zanbīl-ā-w
    PVB-be.PST-3SG come.PST-3SG hand to basket-PL.OBL-POST

c̠ē-k̠ərən-ề k̠ər.
good-do.INF-OBL.F do.PST

He rose, came [and] started making baskets.

zanbīl-ēt kurdawārī-yē bo fēqi̠ bə k̠ār
basket-EZ.PL Kurdish.region-OBL.F for fruit to work

t̠-īn-a xalk-ē ma.
IND-bring.PRS-3SG people-EZ.M 1PL.OBL

Our people use the Kurdish baskets for fruit.

əš šəfk̠ằt hāt-∅ c̠ē-k̠ərən-ē.
from stick come.PST-3SG good-make.INF-OBL.F

They are made of sticks.

lə hāt-∅ ba rūbār-ằ=ū
in come.PST-3SG to river-PL.OBL=and

He came to the river

zanbĩl c̠ē-k̠ər-ən.
basket well-do.PST-3PL

and made baskets.

ma gòt wī sardam-ĩ žīyān ət̠
1PL.OBL say.PST DEM.DIST.OBL.M period-OBL.M life in

kalh-ā dā bī-∅
citadel-PL.OBL POST COP.PST-3SG

We said that back then people would live in citadels.

ū	hāt-∅=ū	hāt-∅=ū	mantaqa	hatā
and	come.PST-3SG=and	come.PST-3SG=and	region	until

hātī-∅	kalh-ā	šàbānī-yē.'
come.PST.PTCP-3SG	citadel-EZ.F	PN-OBL.F

He (i.e. Muhsin) kept coming until he arrived at the gate of the Shabani citadel.

(17)
hāt.'	waxt-ē	lə	darok̯-ē
come.PST.3SG	when-OBL.F	at	small.gate-EZ.M

dargah-ā	hawằ	katī-∅=ū'
gate-PL.OBL	air	fall.PST.PTCP-3SG=and

He arrived. When the [lock of the] gate of the citadel flew open,

zēṛavān-ā	go,	'tē	k̯ò	∅-čē?'
guard-PL.OBL	say.PST	2SG.OBL.FUT	where	SBJV-go.PRS.2SG

the guards asked, 'Where are you going?'

got=ē	tab'an	zanbĭlk-ē	məl=ī-và
say.PST=3SG.OBL	naturally	basket.DIM-OBL.F	shoulder=3SG-POST

bī-∅'
COP.PST-3SG

He (the basket seller) said—well he had baskets on his shoulders—,

go,	'az=ē	∅-čə-m	zanbīl-ằ
say.PST(3SG)	1SG.DIR=FUT	SBJV-go.PRS-1SG	basket-PL.OBL

∅-fəroš-əm.'
SBJV-sell.PRS-1SG

'I'm going to sell baskets.'

əl	k̯olằn-ēt	bāžēr-ē	hāt-∅=o	čo-∅.'
from	alley-EZ.PL	city.OBL-OBL.F	come.PST-3SG=and	go.PST-3SG

He strolled from street to street in the city.

(18) ət-bēž-ən awādī hačko kəč-ā mīr-î̄
    IND-say.PRS-3PL INTJ as.for daughter-EZ.F prince-OBL.M

It is said that the prince's daughter

ət qasr-ē ət panǰarē dā
from palace-OBL.F from window.OBL.F POST

aw kuř-à lāw-ē barkatī dī=ū
DEM.DIST.DIR boy-DEM youth-EZ.M handsome see.PST=and

zanbīl-ā ∅-fəroš-ət.
basket-PL.OBL IND-sell.PRS-3SG

saw the handsome man, that is the basket seller, who was selling baskets, through the windows of the palace.

kuř-ē mīr-ī=a=w
son-EZ.M prince-OBL.M=COP.3SG=and

He was the prince's son.

lāw-ak-ī barkatī̀=ya.
youth-INDF-EZ.M handsome=COP.3SG

He was a handsome young man.

(19) ǰəhēdā vīyān-ā kuřk-ī kat-∅
    immediately love-EZ.F boy.DIM-OBL.M fall.PST-3SG

dəl-ē kəčk-è.
heart-EZ.M girl.DIM-OBL.F

Immediately, she (the prince's daughter) was filled with love for the boy.

got ǰārī-yā xwà,
say.PST maid-EZ.F REFL

She said to her maidservant,

ʕhař-a	∅-bēž-a	wī	zanbīlfəroš-ī̀
go-IMP.2SG	SBJV-say.PRS-2SG	DEM.DIST.OBL	basket.seller-OBL.M

bəlā	b-ət	vē-dḕ.ʾ|	
HOR	SBJV-come.PRS.3SG	DEM.PROX.3SG.OBL.F-POST

'Go and ask the basket seller to come here.'

čū-∅	got=ē,
go.PST-3SG	say.PST=3SG.OBL

She (the maidservant) went and said to him (the basket seller),

ʕwar-a!	àm=ē	zanbīl-ā	žə	ṭa
come.IMP-2SG	1PL=FUT	basket-PL.OBL	from	2SG.OBL

∅-kəř-īn.ʾ|
SBJV-buy.PRS-1PL

'Come here. We would like to buy baskets from you.'

NORTHERN KURDISH OF ZAKHO
Text 11: §1-24

Masoud Mohammadirad

Speaker: Saeid Rezvan

Audio: https://kurdic.ames.cam.ac.uk/audio/245/

(1)	az	nāv-ē	mən	Saʿīd	Hajī	Sadìq˩	Zāxoyī
	1SG.DIR	name-EZ.M	1SG.OBL	PN	PN	PN	PN

I—my name [is] Saʿid Haji Sadiq Zakhoyi

žə	bənamāl-ak-ē	Zāxo	yā꞊t	kavə̀n˩	nāv-ē
from	family-INDF-EZ.F	PN	EZ.F꞊EZ.PL	old	name-EZ.M

bənamāl-ā	Řazvān-ằ˩
family-EZ.F	PN-PL.OBL

[I am from] an old family in Zakho, called the Razvans' family.

t-ē-m	bar-nīyāsīn	Saʿīd	Řazvānì.˩
IND-come.PRS-1SG	front-know.PST.INF	PN	PN

I am known as Saʿid Razvani.

(2)	az	dē	nūka	sar	afsānā	pər-ā	Dalằl
	1SG	FUT	now	on	tale.EZ.F	bridge-EZ.F	PN

∅-āxav-əm.˩
SBJV-speak.PRS-1SG

Now, I will talk about the myth of 'the bridge of Dalal'

mən	pēnj	šàš	partūk	sar	Zāxo	čē
1SG.OBL	five	six	book	on	PN	good

kər-ī=na|
do.PST-PTCP=COP.3PL

I have written (lit. produced) five, six books on Zakho,

žə	kalapòr=o|	afsānà=w|	mažū̀=w|	pēzānī̀-yē
from	heritage=and	myth=and	history=and	knowing-EZ.M

Zāxo|	bə	zəmān-ē	Kurdī̀=o	ʿArabì.|
PN	in	language-EZ.M	Kurdish=and	Arabic

in Kurdish and in Arabic, on its heritage, myths, history, and general information.

(3)
afsānā	pər-ā	Dalàl|	būčī	nāv-ē	wē
tale.EZ.F	bridge-EZ.F	PN	why	name-EZ.M	3SG.OBL.M

kər-ī=na	pər-ā	Dalàl?|
do.PST-PTCP=COP.3PL	bridge-EZ.F	PN

The myth of the bridge of Dalal —why is it (i.e., the bridge) called the bridge of Dalal?

ākənjī̀-yēt	Zāxo	yēt	kavən|	yēt	Zāxo	āvà
habitant-EZ.PL	PN	EZ.PL	old	EZ.PL	PN	prosperous

kər-ī=n|	Juhì	bī-n.|
do.PST-PTCP=COP.3PL	Jew	COP.PST-3PL

The old inhabitants of Zakho, the ones who built Zakho were Jewish.

av	afsānà|	yā	Jəhī-yằn=a.|
DEM.PROX.3SG.DIR	myth	EZ.F	Jew-PL.OBL=COP.3SG

This myth belongs to the Jews.

(4) ū   ma   əš   Jəhī-yằ   go   lē
    and   1PL.OBL from   Jew-PL.OBL   ear   at.it

bī=ya.|
be.PST.PTCP=PERF

We have heard it [the myth] from the Jews.

ū   ma   əž   day   bằb-ēt   xo| əb
and   1PL   from   mother father-EZ.PL   REFL   in

vī   šəkl-î̀   go   lē   bī=ya|
DEM.PROX.3SG.OBL.M   manner-OBL.M   ear   at.it be.PST.PTCP=PERF

We have heard it from our parents

awē   às   bo   wa   t-bḗž-əm.|
3SG.OBL.F   1SG.DIR   for   2PL.OBL   IND-say.PRS-1SG

in the manner I am going to tell you about.

(5) ət-bēž-ən   pər-àk   dī   wusā   əl   Jəzīr-ā
    IND-say.PRS-3PL   bridge-INDF   other   such   in   PN-EZ.F

Botā   hāt-bī-∅   āvākərən-ē|
PN   come.PST-COP.PST-3SG   build.PST.INF-OBL.F

nāv-ē   wē   pər-ā   Bāfət.|
name-EZ.M   3SG.OBL.F   bridge-EZ.F   PN

It is said that another bridge like this (i.e. the bridge of Dalal) had been built in Cizre Bohtan, called the bridge of Bafit.

(6) waxt-ḕ   pər   bə   dumāhî̀   inā-yī|
    when-EZ.M   bridge   to   end   bring-PST-PTCP

When the construction of the bridge was finished,

mīr-ē   yē   Jəzīr-ā   Botằ| gāzī   hostā-yî̀   kər.|
prince-EZ.M   EZ.M   PN-EZ.F   PN   calling   master-OBL.M   do.PST

the emir of Cizre Bohtan summoned the builder (the master)

got=ē,	'dē	ta	xalàt	∅-kə-m.'
say.PST=3SG.OBL	FUT	2SG.OBL	gift	SBJV-do.PRS-1SG

[and] said, 'I will give you a gift.' (lit. I will gift you)

(7)
dast-ē	wī	yē	řāst-ē	žè	va-kər
hand-EZ.M	3SG.OBL.M	EZ.M	right-OBL.F	from.it	TELIC-do.PST

[The emir] cut off his right hand

got=ē,	'tā	tu	čə̀	pər-ē	dī	əl	čə
say.PST=3SG.OBL	so.that	2SG.DIR	no	bridge-EZ.M	other	in	no

jəh-ē	dī	āvā	nà-kī!'
place-EZ.M	other	prosperous	NEG.SBJV-do.PRS.2SG

[and] said to him, 'Lest you make another bridge [like] this anywhere else!

az	šānāzī-yè	bə	vē	pər-ē ..'
1SG.DIR	pride-OBL.F	to	DEM.PROX.3SG.OBL.F	bridge-OBL.F

I [take] pride in this bridge.'

(8)
dam-ằ	hāt-ī-∅	Zāxo	řavī-∅
time-EZ.F	come.PST-PTCP-3SG	PN	flee.PST-3SG

hāt-∅	Zāxò	bə	xo
come.PST-3SG	PN	by	REFL

When the builder (lit. he) came to Zakho—he fled and simply came to Zakho—

mìr-ē	Zāxo	dāxoz	žē	kər
prince-EZ.M	PN	request	from.3SG.OBL	do.PST

the emir of Zakho demanded that

pər-ak-ē	lə-sar	ġābīr-ì	čē	∅-kə-t
bridge-INDF-OBL.F	on-top	river-OBL.M	good	SBJV-do.PRS-3SG

əl	řožhalā̀t-ē	bāžēr-i.
in	east-EZ.M	city-OBL.M

he build a bridge on the Khabur river in the east of the city.

(9)
aw	bə-ʿàks-ē=t	mīr-ē	Jəzīr-ē	got,
3SG.DIR	in-reverse-OBL.F=EZ.PL	prince-EZ.M	PN-OBL.F	say.PST

'bəlā	az	dē	āvà	∅-kə-m.'
alright	1SG.DIR	FUT	prosperous	SBJV-do.PRS-1SG

Contrary to [what] the emir of Cizre [had told him], he (i.e., the builder) said, 'Alright, I will build [one].'

aw	čū-∅	bə	xo	hustā	lə	xo	kòm	kər.
3SG.DIR	go.PST-3SG	by	REFL	master	at	REFL	collection	do.PST

He went and gathered some builders around him.

aw	banā̀	bī-∅
3SG.DIR	mason	COP.PST-3SG

He himself was a mason,

yaʿnī	[əp	hang-ē]	andāzyār	nà-bī-∅
that.is	as	much-EZ.M	architect	NEG-COP.PST-3SG

that is, he was not an architect.

bas	àw	yē	āvā	kər-ī.
but	3SG.DIR	EZ.M	prosperous	do.PST-PTCP

However, he had built that the bridge.

(10)
lè	gařā-∅
at.it	search.PST-3SG

He looked around.

əl	darkār-ē	bākòr-ē	Zāxū	bə	taqrīban
in	surrounding-EZ.M	north-EZ.M	PN	by	approximately

pāzda	bīst	kīlomətr-ằ		bar
fifteen	twenty	kilometers-PL.OBL		rock

žə	wē-rē		īnằ-n.	
from	DEM.DIST.3SG.OBL.F-POST		bring.PST-3PL	

He brought the stones [necessary for the construction of the bridge] from [a distance of] around 15–20 kilometres north of Zakho.

du	bar	ži	bə	řē-vē	ət-katì̱=n
two	stone	add	at	road-POST	TAM-fall.PST.PTCP=COP.3PL

Two of the stones were dropped on the road [to Zakho];

hatā	nūkà	ži	lə	Dārozān-ē	mawjud=ən.
until	now	ADD	in	PN-OBL.F	existent=COP.3PL

they can still be seen (lit. are existent) in Darozan.

(11)	ū	dàs	āvēt=a	pər-ē	ā
	and	hand	throw.PST=DRCT	bridge-OBL.F	EZ.F

čēkərə̀n-ā	pər-ē.
build.PST.INF-EZ.F	bridge-OBL.F

He started building the bridge (lit. He threw hands at the bridge, at building the bridge)

dam-ā	t-gahašt-∅=a	kəvān-ā	nīv-è	dā
time-EZ.F	IPFV-arrive.PST-3SG=DRCT	arch-EZ.F	half-OBL.F	AUX

tamằm	∅-kə-t.
finished	SBJV-do.PRS-3SG

Whenever he completed constructing the arch in the middle of the bridge,

řož-ā	dī	dā	∅-ề-t
day-EZ.F	other	AUX	SBJV-come.PRS-3SG

aw	kəvằn	wē	həl-wəšā-yi̋-∅.
DEM.DIST.3SG.DIR	arch	FUT	PVB-pour.PST-PTCP-3SG

the next day, he would come to the bridge [and] the arch had collapsed.

(12)
awì	pərsyār-ā	əb	'Arabī	t-bḗž-n=ē
3SG.OBL.M	question-EZ.F	in	Arabic	IND-say.PRS-3PL=3SG.OBL

"arrằf"
fortune.teller

The builder (lit. he) asked [a fortune-teller, who is] called *'arāf* in Arabic.

bə	kurdī	am	ət-bḗž-n=ē	'xēvzằnk'
in	Kurdish	1PL.DIR	IND-say.PRS-1PL=3SG.OBL	fortune.teller

In Kurdish, we call them *xēvzānk*,

yān	aw-ē	təšt-ī	bə	xo	b-zằn-ət
or	3SG.DIR-EZ.M	thing-OBL.M	by	REFL	SBJV-know.PRS-3SG

meaning 'someone who knows about things by themselves.'

got=ē,	'az	pər-ē	husā	āvằ
say.PST=3SG.OBL	1SG.DIR	bridge-OBL.F	such	prosperous

t-kə-m
IND-do.PRS-1SG

He said, 'I am building such a bridge,

ət-həl-waš-ə̀t!
IND-PVB-pour.PRS-3SG

[but] it keeps collapsing.'

(13) got=ē,   'ṣəbà| kī   xodān   gīyằn|
     say.PST=3SG.OBL tomorrow.morning who   owner   soul

awəl b-ē   sar pər-ē|
first SBJV-come.PRS.3SG on   bridge-OBL.F

[The fortune-teller] said, 'Tomorrow morning, any living soul (lit. the owner of soul) that comes onto the bridge—

dù   got-got=ēt   hay=n|
two said-said=EZ.PL EXIST=COP.3PL

there are two sayings [regarding the fortune-teller's advice].

èk   žə   wān   ət-bēž-ət,| 'sàr   žē   ka=w|
one of   3PL.OBL IND-say.PRS.3SG head   from.it do.IMP.2SG=and

the first is [the fortune-teller] said, 'Bhead the living soul

xwin-ā   wī   pē   řā   dà.'|
blood-EZ.F 3SG.OBL to.it POST give.IMP.2SG

and rub its blood on the bridge.'

yā   du-ḕ   pətər| ya'nī   ət-hāt-∅=a   gotən-ḕ|
EZ.F two-OBL.F   more   that.is IPFV-come.PST-3SG=DRCT   say.INF-OBL.F

The second saying is narrated more frequently.

tə-bēž-ət   sāxēnì haykal-ē   pər-ē   bə-ka-t|
IND-say.PRS.3SG alive   body-EZ.M bridge-OBL.F SBJV-do.PRS.3SG

[According to this the fortune-teller] said that he (i.e. the builder) should put [the living soul] alive into the bridge.

'haykal dà| ū   farš-ā̀   da-yn-a
body   give.IMP.2SG   and carpet-PL.OBL PVB-put.PRS-IMP.2SG

sar=ū| ū   bə-gr-à!'|
on=and   and SBJV-seal.PRS-IMP.2SG

[The fortune-teller said,] 'Cover it with a carpet, and seal it (i.e. the bridge).

(14) řož-ā   dī   səpḕ   dḗ   Dalāl-ē   bo   yē
     day-EZ.F other   morning   POST PN-OBL.F for   EZ.M

xā̀rən   īnāt.
food   bring.PST

The next day, in the morning, Dalal brought him (the builder) food.

Dalāl   bı̆k-ā   wī   bī-∅.
PN   daughter.in.law-EZ.F   3SG.OBL.M   COP.PST-3SG

Dalal was his daughter-in-law.

ṣa-ē   Dalāl-ē   əl   pēšĭ-yḕ   bī-∅.
dog-EZ.M PN-OBL.F   in   front-OBL.F   COP.PST-3SG

Dalal's dog was in front of her.

(15) kayf-ā   hustā-yī   galàk   hāt-∅.
     pleasure-EZ.F master-OBL.M very   come.PST-3SG

The builder was very pleased.

dəm-ā   gahašt-ī-∅   nèzīk   pər-ḕ
time-EZ.F arrive.PST-PTCP-3SG   near   bridge-OBL.F

When they came closer to the bridge,

ṣa-yī   məšk-àk   dīt   bàr   dā=yḕ
dog-OBL.M mouse-INDF   see.PST   front   give.PST=3SG.OBL

the dog saw a mouse [and] headed towards it.

Dalàl   ət-sar   pər-ē   kat-∅
PN   on-top   bridge-OBL.F   fall.PST-3SG

Dalal walked onto the bridge (lit. Dalal fell on the bridge).

ava   dē   b-ət=a   qurbānī̀.
DEM.PROX.3SG.DIR FUT   be.PRS-3SG=DRCT   sacrifice

[meaning that] she was going to be the sacrifice [for the bridge].

(16) **màm-ē   wē   got=ē**
     uncle-EZ.M 3SG.OBL.F say.PST=3SG.OBL

Her uncle (i.e., her father's brother) said to her—

waxt-ē   čūyī-∅   màm-ē   wē   gərī-∅
time-EZ.M   go.PST.PTCP-3SG uncle-EZ.M 3SG.OBL.F cry.PST.3SG

when she came, her uncle cried,

řāndək   əž   čāv-ē   wī   hāt-n=a   xār-ē.
teardrop   from eye-EZ.M 3SG.OBL.M come.PST-3PL=DRCT   down-OBL.F

tears streamed down his face (lit. teardrops came down from his eyes).

gòt=a   màm-ē   xo,
say.PST=DRCT   uncle-EZ.M REFL

She said to her uncle,

'mām,   tu   bočī̀   t-gərī?
uncle   2SG.DIR   why   IND-cry.PRS.2SG

'Uncle, why are you crying?'

(17) **got=ē,   'ḥāl=ū   masal=ēt   'arrāf-ī**
     say.PST=3SG.OBL state=and   problem=EZ.PL   fortune.teller-OBL.M

yēt   xēxzānk-ī   avà=na
EZ.PL   fortune.teller-OBL.M   DEM.PROX.3SG.DIR=COP.3PL

He said, 'The fortune-teller's saying is like this (lit. the state and problem of the fortune-teller is such).

ət-vē-t   az   tà   bə-kə-m   haykal-ē
IND-be.necessary.PRS-3SG   1SG.DIR   2SG.OBL   SBJV-do.PRS-1SG body-EZ.M

pər-ē   dā.'
bridge-OBL.F   POST

I must put you into the construction of the bridge.'

(18) ē got=ē, ˈbəlằ!
     INTJ say.PST=3SG.OBL alright

She said, 'Alright!

akar	av	pər-a	sar	mằ	čē
if	DEM.PROX.3SG.DIR	bridge-DEM	on	1SG.OBL	good

bə-b-ət
SBJV-be.PRS-3SG

If this bridge is going to be built on me,

az=ē	xo	∅-kə-m	qurbānī̀-yā
1SG.DIR=FUT	REFL	SBJV-do.PRS-1SG	sacrifice-EZ.F

vī	bā̀žēr-ī.
DEM.PROX.3SG.OBL.M	city-OBL.M

[then] I will make myself a sacrifice on behalf of the city.

ya'nī	čūnko	az	žən-ə̀k=əm
that.is	because	1SG.DIR	woman-DIM=COP.1SG

Just because I am a woman,

hīn	mə	bə	čāv-ak-ī	nērīnì	əl
2PL.DIR	1SG.OBL	in	eye-INDF-EZ.M	negative	at

mə	ət-fəkər-ən?
1SG.OBL	IND-think.PRS-2PL

do you have a false belief in me (lit. You think of me through a negative eye)?

(19) řā-bī jəh-ē wē čề kər=o
     PVB-COP.PST.3G place-EZ.M 3SG.OBL.F good do.PST=and

[The builder] made her a place [in the bridge],

dərēž	*kər=o*	*fàrš*	*da-ynā-n*	*sar.*
long	do.PST=and	carpet	PVB-put.PST-3PL	on

laid her down and put a carpet on her [and successfully built the bridge].

(20)
havžìn-ē	*wē*	*zaḷằm-ē*	*wē*	*nà*	*l*
spouse-EZ.M	3SG.OBL.F	husband-EZ.M	3SG.OBL.F	NEG	at

māl	*bī-∅.*
home	COP.PST-3SG

Her (i.e., Dalal's) spouse, her husband, was not home.

pəšt-ī	*řož-ak-ē*	*zəvəř̃ì-∅-va*
after-EZ	day-INDF.OBL.F	turn.PST-3SG-TELIC

He returned [home] a day later

pərsyār	*kər,*	*'kằ*	*havžìn-ā*	*mən?*
question	do.PST	where.is	spouse-EZ.F	1SG.OBL

[and] asked, 'Where is my spouse?'

(21)
bằb-ē	*wī*	*got=ē,*	*hāl=ū*
father-EZ.M	3SG.OBL.M	say.PST=3SG.OBL	state=and

masala	*avà=ya*
problem	DEM.PROX.3SG=COP.3SG

His (Dalal's husband's) father (i.e., the builder) said, 'The story is as follows:

ma	*yē*	*kər-ī*	*ət*	*pər-è*	*dā.*
1PL.OBL	EZ.M	do.PST-PTCP	in	bridge-OBL.F	POST

we have put her into the bridge [for the bridge to hold together].'

(22)
'čāwà	*wa*	*wa*	*kər?*	*čāwà?*
how	2PL.OBL	such	do.PST	how

[Dalal's husband said] 'How could you do this? How?!'

das	*hāvēt=a*	*māhūl-ī*
hand	throw.PST=DRCT	stone.hammer-OBL.M

He grabbed the stone hammer.

got,	*'dē*	*∅-č-əm*	*∅-īn-m=a*	*dàr.'*
say.PST	FUT	SBJV-go.PRS-1SG	SBJV-bring.PRS-1SG=DRCT	out

[and] said, 'I will go and take her out.'

(23)	*čò-∅*|	*həndī*	*māhol-ā*	*da-ynằd=ē.*|
	go.PST-3SG	much	stone.hammer-PL.OBL	PVB-put.PST=3SG.OBL

[Dalal's husband] went and hammered the bridge so much.

awē	*kər=a*	*gāzī*|	*got=ē,*	*'bàs=a!*|
3SG.OBL.F	do.PST=DRCT	call	say.PST=3SG.OBL	enough=COP.3SG

Dalal (lit. she) started to call him [and] said to him, 'That's enough!

tu	*wusā*	*mə*	*pətə̀r*	*də-ēšī-n-ī!*|
2SG.DIR	such	1SG.OBL	more	IND-hurt.PRS-CAUS-2SG

You are hurting me more by doing so!

àv	*pər-a*	*dē*	*∅-mīn-t=a*	*sar*
DEM.PROX.3SG.DIR	bridge-DEM	FUT	SBJV-remain.PRS-3SG=DRCT	on

məl-ēt	*mən*|
shoulder-EZ.PL	1SG.OBL

This bridge will stand on my shoulders

həndī	*mən*	*šīyā-yī̀.'*|
much	1SG.OBL	can.PST-PTCP

as long as I am able [to hold it].'

(24) ya'nī   ava   kurtī̀-yā   afsānā
     DISC   DEM.PROX.3SG   summary-EZ.F   myth.EZ.F

pər-ā   Dalāl.ǀ
bridge-EZ.F   PN

This [was] a summary of the myth of the bridge of Dalal's myth.

bas   wak   mə̀   got-ī   taǀ
but   as   1SG.OBL   say.PST-PTCP   2SG.OBL

However, as I had told you,

ava   əž   Jəhī-yà̄   hāt-ī-∅=ya
DEM.PROX.3SG   from   Jew-PL.OBL   come.PST-PTCP-3SG=DRCT

sətāndən.ǀ
take.PST.INF

the myth has been transmitted (lit. taken) from the Jews.

CENTRAL KURDISH OF SHAQLAWA
TEXT 19: §9–22

Masoud Mohammadirad

Speaker: Hawsar Najat Bapir
Audio: https://kurdic.ames.cam.ac.uk/audio/236/

(9) *haqāyat-aka   la   nāw-ī   mař=ū   bəzə̀n| yā   xod*
    tale-DEF   by   name-EZ.M   ewe=and   goat   or   REFL

mař=ū   dābəřằn-ī   mař-ak.|
ewe=and   separation-EZ.M   ewe-INDF

The tale is called 'ewe and goat', or 'the separation of a ewe'.

a-r-ē   ha-bū-∅   na-bū-∅|
IND-say.PRS-3SG   EXIST-be.PST-3SG   NEG-be.PST-3SG

It is said that there was [and] there was not

kas   la   xwā-y   gawrà-tər   na-bū-∅.|
person   from   god-OBL.M   big-CMPR   NEG-be.PST-3SG

[but] there was no one greater than God.

l-aw   dunyā-ya   p̂ān=ū   barìn-a-y| šūwān-àk
in-DEM   world-DEM   vast=and   vast-DEM-OBL.M   shepherd-INDF

ha-bū-∅.|
EXIST-be.PST-3SG

In this vast world, there was a shepherd.

mēgalàkʸ=ī	*galak*	*la*	*mař=ū*	*bəzən=ī*	
female.herd=3SG	many	of	ewe=and	goat=3SG	

tē-dā	*ha-bū-∅.*
in-POST	EXIST-be.PST-3SG

He had a sheep flock which contained many ewes and goats.

řož-ak	*la*	*řož-ān*	*la*	*ēwārà-(a)kʸ-ī*	*pāyīz-ān*
day-INDF	of	day-PL	in	evening-INDF-EZ.M	autumn-PL

dərang-ān-àkʸ-ī	*šaw-ē*	*mař*	*lagar*	*barx-ī*	*xo*
late-PL-INDF-EZ.M	night-OBL.F	ewe	with	lamb-EZ.M	REFL

dā-a-bəř-ềt.
PVB-IND-cut-3SG

Once, on a late autumn evening, a ewe and her lamb lost (lit. were separated from) the flock.

(10)	*a-gā-t=a*	*dzē-yakʸ-ī*	*tařàš=ī*
	IND-reach.PRS-3SG=DRCT	place-INDF-OBL.M	rock=3SG

lē=ya=w	*mērg=a.*
at=COP.3SG=and	meadow=COP.3SG

She (the ewe) reached a place which was [full of] rocks and was a meadow.

wāta	*mērg-àkʸ-ī*	*dzīyā*	*aw*	*šət-ān-a=ya.*
that.is	meadow-INDF-EZ.M	separate	DEM	thing-PL-DEM=COP.3SG

That is, it was a separate meadow and so forth.

šaw-ē	*lo*	*xo=y*	*a-mēn-ēt-awà.*
night-OBL.F	for	REFL=3SG	IND-stay.PRS-3SG-TELIC

She stayed there for the night.

a-kā-t=a	dzḕ-y	xo=y.
IND-do.PRS-3SG=DRCT	place-EZ.M	REFL=3SG

She made the place her habitat.

hatā	zəstān=ū	hāwìn=iš	dḗ	aw	mař-a
until	winter=and	summer=ADD	IND.come.PRS.3SG	DEM	ewe-DEM

har	l-aw	dzē-y	a-mĭn-ēt-ò.
EMPH	in-DEM	place-OBL.M	IND-remain.PRS.3SG-TELIC

She stayed there the [coming] winter until the [next] summer.

(11)
yaʿnī	kurīt-àkʸ-ī	lo	xo	durust	a-kā=w
that.is	shed-INDF-OBL.M	for	REFL	right	IND-do.PRS.3SG=and

That is, she made a shed in it for herself

lē=y	a-žē.
in=3SG	IND-live.PRS.3SG

and lived there.

řož-ak	la	řož-ằn	la-nāw	sarmā=w	sora=w
day-INDF	from	day-PL	in-middle	cold=and	RDP=and

bastalakʸ-ī,	gurg-akʸ-ī	bərsī	fērbằz	lo=y
frost-OBL.M	wolf-INDF-EZ.M	hungry	cunning	at=3SG

d-ēt=a	pḗš.
IND-come.PRS.3SG=DRCT	front

Once, in the middle of cold weather and frost, a cunning hungry wolf came to her.

a-r-ē,	ʿkʸḕ	řē=y	ba	to	dāy=a
IND-say.PRS.3SG	who	road=3SG	to	2SG	give.PST.PTCP=PERF

la-nāw	murkʸ-ī	mən	dā-nəš-ī?
in-middle	property-EZ.M	1SG	PVB-sit.PRS-2SG

He said, 'Who has let you live on my property!?'

mař=īš	*wâq=ī*	*wəř*	*a-mīn-ē.*
ewe=ADD	mood=3SG	perplexed	IND-remain.PRS-3SG

The ewe was astonished (lit. her mind remained dazed) [and said],

'ē	*bāš=a*	*gurg-ò!*	*ba-xo*	*gurg*	*har*
INTJ	nice=COP.3SG	wolf-VOC	in-REFL	wolf	each

řož-a=w	*la*	*dzēy-ak^y-ì̄=ya.*
day-DEM=and	in	place-INDF-OBL.M=COP.3SG

'Well, wolf! A wolf is normally in a different place each day.

bařawà=ya=w	*harčē*	*řož-a=w*	*la*
wanderer=COP.3SG=and	every	day-DEM=and	in

mantəq(a)-ak^y-ì̄=ya.
region-INDF-OBL.M=COP.3SG

It is a wanderer and is in a different region each day.

ma'qū̀l=a?	*'ārd=ī*	*ha-bī*	*amən*
logical=COP.3SG	earth=3SG	EXIST-be.PRS.SBJV.3SG	1SG

nà-zānī-bī=m!
NEG-know.PTCP-be.SBJV=1SG

Is it conceivable that a wolf had land and that I had not known about?'

(12)
aw=īš	*a-r-ē*	*'pēš-tər*
3SG.DIST=ADD	IND-say.PRS-3SG	before-CMPR

nà-hātī=ya.
NEG-come.PST.PTCP=COP.3SG

She said [to herself], 'He had not come earlier [to this place].

bas	*ka*	*mən*	*l-ērà=ma*
but	since	1SG	in-here=COP.1SG

However, now that I am here,

da=y-hawē	*bə=m-xwà*	*tabʿan.*
IND=3SG-want.PRS	SBJV=1SG-eat.PRS.3SG	naturally

he wants to eat us.

handza	[*dān=yān*	*pē*	*xwāz-īn.*]
then	seed=3PL	to	want.PST?-1PL

That's why he is creating a trap for us.'

a-r-ē,	*ˈšət-ī*	*wā*	*nì=ya!*
IND-say.PRS.3SG	thing-EZ.M	DEIC	NEG=COP.3SG

She said [to the wolf], 'It is not so!

aw	*murk-à*	*murk^y-ē*	*xwā=ya.*
DEM	property-DEM	property-EZ.F	god=3SG

This property belongs to God.

nà	*murk^y-ē*	*tu-w=a=w*	*nà*	*murk^y-ē*
neither	property-EZ.F	2SG-EP=COP.3SG=and	nor	property-EZ.F

mən=īš=a.
1SG=ADD=COP.3SG

This is neither your property nor my property!'

(13)	*ˈkū*	*ato*	*a-kē-y*	*ē*	*xo?*
	how	2SG	IND-do.PRS-2SG	PRON.EZ	REFL

[The wolf said], 'How is it that you claim it is yours?'

a-rē,	*ˈmən*	*šāhēd=ū*	*ʾəsbàt=əm*	*ha=na,*
IND-say.PRS.3SG	1SG	witness=and	proof=1SG	EXIST=COP.3PL

He said, 'I have a witness

ka	*àw*	*murk-a*	*murk^y-ē*	*mən=a=w*
COMPL	DEM	property-DEM	property-EZ.F	1SG=COP.3SG=and

[who can prove that] this property is mine

la	bāb=ū	bāpīr-àn	lo=m	māwīy-t-oawa.'
from	father=and	grandfather-PL	to=1SG	remain.PST.PTCP-3SG-TELIC

and has been passed on to me from my elders (lit. fathers and grandfathers).'

mař=īš	a-r-ē,	'bə-řo	b-īn-à!'
ewe=ADD	IND-say.PRS-3SG	SBJV-go.2SG.IMP	SBJV-bring.PRS-2SG.IMP

The ewe said, 'Go and bring him!'

a-r-ēt	'řàz	∅-bē=ū	la	řēga-y
IND-say.PRS-3SG	correct	SBJV-be.PRS.2SG=and	in	road-EZ.M

šēr-ì	ba!'
lion-OBL.M	be.PRS.IMP.2SG

[As] the saying goes (lit. it says), 'Say the truth and be courageous! (lit. be in the path of the lion).'

(14)	mař-aka=š	ràst=a.	gùrg	fērbāz=a.
	ewe-DEF=3SG	right=COP.3SG	wolf	cunning=COP.3SG

[Now] the ewe is right [but] the wolf is being cunning.

da=y-hawē	məndār-akà=y	lē	bə-xwā.
IND=3SG-want.PRS	child-DEF=3SG	from	SBJV-eat.PRS.3SG

He wants to eat her (the ewe's) lamb.

a-r-ē,	'səbaynē-kà	sa'āt	dwāzdà-y
IND-say.PRS-3SG	tomorrow.OBL.F-DEF	hour	twelve-EZ.M

nīwařwān-ē	yā xod	wàxt-ī	ēwārē	amə̀n
noon-PL-OBL.F	or else	time-EZ.M	evening.OBL.F	1SG

šāhēd=ū	ʾəsbāt-ī	xo=m	da-yn-əm.
witness=and	proof-EZ.M	REFL=1SG	IND-bring.PRS-1SG

He (the wolf) said, 'Tomorrow at noon or in the evening I will bring my witness [here].

d-ē-m	a-salmīn-əm	ka	awa	mùrkʸ-ē
IND-come.PRS-1SG	IND-prove.PRS-1SG	COMPL	DEM	property-EZ.F

mən=a.ˀ|
1SG=COP.3SG

I will come and prove that this is my property!'

(15)
a-r-ē	řož	hāt-∅=ū	řož	řòy-∅.|
IND-say.PRS-3SG	sun	come.PST-3SG=and	sun	go.PST-3SG

It is said [that] the dawn broke (lit. the sun came and the sun went).

mař	hàr	pərsyār=ī	a-kərd	'da-bī|	šāhēd-ī
ewe	EMPH	question=3SG	IND-do.PST	IND-AUX	witness-EZ

gurgʸ-ī	kʸè	bī?ˀ|
wolf-OBL.M	who	COP.PRS.3SG

The ewe kept asking [herself], 'Who is going to be the wolf's witness?'

səbaʿynè	lo=y	wa	dīyār	kat-∅|	gùrg=ū
tomorrow.OBL.F	for=3SG	to	visibility	fall.PST.3SG	wolf=and

řēwī	pēkawa	bū-n.|
fox	together	be.PST-3PL

One morning the wolf and fox became visible to her [from afar].

wət=ī,	ʿba	xwā-y	hār=əm	šàř=a.|
say.PST=3SG	by	god-OBL.M	situation=1SG	bad=COP.3SG

She (the ewe) said, 'By God, I'm in a bad situation!

amən	kù	bār=yān	bə-ba-m?ˀ|
1SG	how	load=3PL	SBJV-take.PRS-1SG

How am I supposed to get rid of them? (lit. how can I load them?)'

čū-∅	hānā=y	bərd=a	bar	sagʸ-ì.
go.PST-3SG	refuge=3SG	take.PST=DRCT	front	dog-OBL.M

She went to ask the dog for help.

(16)
kəsok-àkʸ=ī	lē	bū-∅,	kəsok-akʸ-ī	zor	zor
dog-INDF=3SG	at	COP.PST-3SG	dog-INDF-EZ.M	very	very

ba-wàj=ū	ba-wafà.
with-face=and	with-loyalty

There was a dog in it [in the meadow], a respectful, faithful dog.

dīfàʿ=īš=ī	la	mař-aka-y	a-kərd.
defence=ADD=3SG	at	ewe-DEF-OBL.M	IPFV-do.PST

He would defend the ewe.

got=ī,	'hār=ū	masla=m	awà=ya=w	ba
say.PST=3SG	situation=and	problem=1SG	DEM=COP.3SG=and	to

hānà=m	ga!'
aid=1SG	arrive.PRS.2SG.IMP

She said [to the dog], 'The situation is like this, [please] come to my aid.'

got=ī	'xam=ət	nà-bī!
say.PST=3SG	sorrow=2SG	NEG-be.PRS.SBJV.2SG

He (the dog) said, 'No worries!

la-nāw	ama	yak	šət	zor	bàw=a.
in-middle	1PL	one	thing	very	common=COP.3SG

Something in customary among us [the members of the dog family],

aw=īš	wədzàġ=a,	wədzàġ-ī	bāb=ū	bāpīr-àn,
3SG=ADD	clan=COP.3SG	clan-EZ.M	father=and	grandfather-PL

[and] that is the clan, that is, the clan passed from elders.

bā̀š=a?'
nice=COP.3SG

All right?

(17) *pē=yī   bə-rḕ!*
     to=3SG SBJV-tell.PRS.2SG

[The dog continued] 'Tell him [the wolf to come]!

amən	*a-č-əm*	*la-pəšt*	*aw*	*dār-à-y*	*xò*
1SG	IND-go.PRS-1SG	in-back	DEM	tree-DEM-OBL.M	REFL

a-šār-m-awa.
IND-hide.PRS-1SG-TELIC

I will go and hide behind that tree.

har	*kāt-ak*	*řēwī*	*hằt-∅*	*sùnd=ī*	*xwārd*	*ba*
each	time-INDF	fox	come.PST-3SG	swear=3SG	eat.PST	to

wədzāġ=ī	*yān*	*ba*	*har*	*šət-àkʸ=ī,*
clan=3SG	or	to	EMPH	thing-INDF-3SG

Whenever he [the fox] comes over and takes an oath on his clan or on anything else,

awā	*mən*	*řēk*	*lat=ū*	*pàt=ī*	*a-ka-m.*
DEIC	1SG	directly	piece=and	RDP=3SG	IND-do.PRS-1SG

I will tear him to pieces right away.

nè-wēr-ən	*sond-ī*	*ba-dro*	*bə-xo-n.'*
NEG-dare.PRS-3PL	swear-OBL.M	with-lie	SBJV-eat.PRS-3PL

They will not dare to make a fake oath.'

a-r-ē	*hamān*	*xuta=yān*	*dzē-ba-dzḕ*	*kərd.*
IND-say.PRS-3SG	same	saying=3PL	place-by-place	do.PST

It is said that they (i.e. the ewe and the dog) made the same plan.

ṣa-y	xo	šārd-awa	la-pəž	dā̀r-ī.
dog-OBL.M	REFL	hide.PST-TELIC	in-back	tree-OBL.M

The dog hid behind the tree.

ū	gurg=ū	řēwī=š	hāt-ən	lo	šahādadān-è.
and	wolf=and	fox=ADD	come.PST-3PL	to	witness.INF-OBL.F

And the wolf and fox came to bear witness.

(18)	got=ī	got=ī,	'awà=š	šāhēd-ī	mən.'
	say.PST=3SG	say.PST=3SG	DEM=ADD	witness-EZ.M	1SG

[The wolf] said, 'Here is my witness!'

řēwī	ba	jəwāb	hāt-∅	zor	ba	murtahī̀,
fox	to	response	come.PST-3SG	much	with	comfort

The fox started to speak (lit. came to answer) comfortably.

got=ī,	'amə̀n	šāhēdī	a-da-m	ka	aw
say.PST=3SG	1SG	witnessing	IND-give.PRS-1SG	COMPL	DEM

murk-à	mùrk^y-ē	gurg-ī̀=a.
property-DEM	property-EZ.M	wolf-OBL.M=COP.3SG

[and] said, 'I testify that this land is the wolf's

atò	hāt-ī́	la-sar=ət	dā-kotā̀=ya,	ba-bē
2SG	come.PST-2SG	on-top=2SG	PVB-hit.PST.PTCP=COP.3SG	with-no

hàq=ū	ba-bē	mằf.'
right=and	with-no	right

and that you have come [into this land and] taken it over without any [legitimate] rights.'

(19)	mař-aka=š	got=ī	'àxər	nà-bī!
	ewe-DEF=ADD	say.PST=3SG	well	NEG-be.PRS.3SG

The ewe said, 'It does not work like this!

la	ʿādằt=ū	ʿurf-ē	ma	sūnd	xwārdə̀n
in	habit=and	custom-EZ	1PL	swear	eat.INF

aw-ja	salmāndə̀n.'
DEM-time	prove.INF

In our customs, one first takes an oath, then one proceeds to presenting proof.'

got=ī	'bāš	ama	sūnd	ba	čə̀	bə-xo-yn?'
say.PST=3SG	all.right	1PL	swear	to	what	SBJV-eat.PRS-1PL

He (the fox) said, 'All right! What should we take an oath on?'

got=ī	ʿa-bī	sūnd	ba	wədzằġ-ī	bāb=ū
say.PST=3SG	IND-be.PRS.3SG	swear	to	clan-EZ.M	father=and

bāpīr-ān=əm	bə-xo-y!',	mař-akà	got=ī.
grandfather-PL.OBL=1SG	SBJV-eat.PRS-2SG	ewe-DEF	say.PST=3SG

'You should take an oath on the clan of my ancestors!', the ewe said.

(20)
řēwī=š	got=ī,	'zor	ʾaʿtīyādì=ya.
fox=ADD	say.PST=3SG	very	normal=COP.3SG

The fox said, 'It is totally fine.

wədzằġ=ət	la	kēndarḕ=ya	tā	sūnd=ī	pē
clan=2SG	in	where.OBL.F=COP.3SG	so.that	swear=3SG	to

bə-xo-yn?'
SBJV-eat.PRS-1PL

Where is your clan for us to take an oath on?'

got=ī,	'wədzằġ-ē	mən	la-pəšt	àw	dār-a=ya.'
say.PST=3SG	clan-EZ.M	1SG	in-back	DEM	tree-DEM=COP.3SG

She said, 'My clan is behind that tree!'

ka	řēwī	dīt-ī	sag-àkʸ-ī	gawra	la-pəž
when	fox	saw.PST=3SG	dog-INDF-EZ.M	big	in-back

dār-akà=ya.	har	zərāw=ī	čù-∅		
tree-DEF=COP.3SG	EMPH	gall.bladder=3SG	go.PST-3SG		

On seeing a big dog behind the tree, the fox was frightened (lit. his gallbladder went).

got=ī	'na	ba	xwà-y	bak	pīrozī	wədzàġ=ət
say.PST=3SG	no	by	God-OBL.M	by	greatness.EZ.M	clan=2SG

ato	wədzāġ=ət	gala	galak	mubàràk=a.		
2SG	clan=2SG	very	very	sacred=COP.3SG		

He said, 'By God, [and] by your clan's sanctity, your clan is very holy.

nə̀-tān-əm	sūnd=ī	pē	bə-xo-m.'			
NEG-can.PRS-1SG	swear=3SG	to	SBJV-eat.PRS-1SG			

I cannot take an oath on it.'

řīwì	řoy-∅.
fox	go.PST-3SG

The fox went away.

(21)
got=ī	gurg	got=ī	'nà-bīt!
say.PST=3SG	wolf	say.PST=3SG	NEG-be.PRS.3SG

The wolf said, 'It does not count!

řīwī	tərsà=ya.
fox	scared=COP.3SG

The fox became scared.

aga-nā	qat	qàt	pəšt	la	mən	nā-kā=w
if-not	never	never	back	at	1SG	NEG-do.PRS.3SG=and

Otherwise, he would never turn his back on me.

šā́hēd	àw=a	ka	awa	murkʸ-ī	mə̀n=a.ʼ
witness	3SG=COP.3SG	COMPL	DEM	property-EZ.M	1SG=COP.3SG

He is the witness that this property is mine.'

got=ī	ka	gurg	lē=y	nəzīk	bū-∅-w-awa
say.PST=3SG	when	wolf	to=3SG	near	become.PST-3SG-EP-TELIC

sūnd	bə-xwà!
swear	SBJV-eat.PRS.3SG

When it was the time for the wolf to take the oath,

got=ī	ʽmən	sūnd	nak	ba	wədzāġ-ē	tò
say.PST=3SG	1SG	swear	no.only	to	clan-EZ.F	2SG

ba	hamū	šət-ḕkʸ-ī	a-xo-m.ʼ
to	all	thing-INDF-OBL.M	IND-eat.PRS-1SG

he said, 'I will take an oath not only on your clan but also on anything else!'

(22)
ka	dīt=ī	ṣàgʸ=ī	lē=ya
when	see.PST=3SG	dog=3SG	in=COP.3SG

When he (the wolf) saw that a dog was there [behind the tree],

ṣa	pəř=ī	dā=ya=w	quřk=ī	gə̀rt.
dog	movement=3SG	give.PST=COP.3SG=and	throat=3SG	grab.PST

the dog jumped on the wolf and seized [him by] his neck.

got=ī,	ʽāmà̀n,	amə̀n	hìč	nī=ma.
say.PST=3SG	EXCL	EXCL	nothing	NEG=COP.1SG

He (the wolf) said, 'Please, please! I'm nothing!

aw	murk-a	murkʸ-ī	tò=a.ʼ
DEM	property-DEM	property-EZ.M	2SG=COP.3SG

This property is yours!'

jā	a-r-è	l-aw	hāḷat-a-y	dā	ūdzāġ
then	IND-say.PRS-3SG	in-DEM	tale-DEM-OBL.M	POST	clan

awanda	pīròz	bū=a	la-nāw	komaḷgā-y	kurdì
that.much	sacred	be.PST=PERF	in-middle	society-EZ.M	Kurdish

It is said that the clan was so holy in the Kurdish society

ya'nī	sùnd=ī	pē	xor-ā=ya.
that.is	swear=3SG	to	eat.PRS-PASS.PST=COP.3SG

that one would take an oath on it.

har	lò=ya=š	a-bīn-īn	haqāyat	kurdī-yakàn
EMPH	why=COP.3SG=ADD	IND-see.PRS-1PL	tale	kurdish-DEF.PL

b-aw	amānj-a-y	a-bà-n.
to-DEM	purpose-DEM-OBL.M	IND-take.PRS-3PL

That is why we see that it's referred to in Kurdish tales.

amn=īš	hāt-m-àw
1SG=ADD	come.PST-1SG-TELIC

I came back [from the events of the story]

hìč=əm	pē	na-bəř-ā-∅
nothing=1SG	to	NEG-cut.PRS-PASS.PST-3SG

and nothing was given to me [by the characters in the story].

xalās=ū	řòy-∅.
over=and	go.PST-3SG

It is finished (lit. it is finished and gone).

INDEX

additive particle, 86, 102, 104, 107, 142, 155
affricate, 2, 8
alliteration, 111, 119; *See also* rhyme
Alqosh, 29
anaphora, 129, 134–136; *See also* demonstrative, pronoun, personal
anecdote, 37, 42, 52, 65, 72, 75, 84
animal, 36, 38–39, 42, 61–63, 65–67, 70, 124, 137
Arabic, xiv, 7, 16, 27, 29–31, 90, 93, 95–96, 98, 100–101, 107–108, 114–115, 117, 125, 131–132, 138, 146, 149, 152, 154, 303, 308
Aramaic, *See* Neo-Aramaic
areal, 86, 154
Armenian, 76, 78, 80–81, 92, 95, 98, 147, 154
article, definite, 6, 11, 29
aspiration, 13, 30
Azeri, 92–93, 95, 98, 154
ballad, 27, 29, 43, 54–55, 93
Barwar, 3, 6, 16, 27, 45, 109, 274

Behdinī, *See* Kurdish, Northern
clitic, 6, 9, 11, 13, 14, 18, 29
closing formula, 86, 87, 90–94, 98, 154
deictic, 87, 133–134, 138–139
demonstrative, 31, 107, 109, 114, 133–135
discourse marker, 31, 34, 86, 99, 100, 107, 115, 154
ditransitive, 3
dramatic visualisation, 153
Duhok, 2–11, 18–27, 30, 43, 54–68, 72, 74–81, 176, 196, 248
89–94, 100–110, 112–113, 115–127, 129, 131–132, 136–153
Dure, 2, 3, 6, 7, 25, 26, 27, 30, 54–55, 59, 64, 82, 83, 93, 119, 122, 141
Enishke, 2, 3, 25, 28, 37, 46–48, 51–54, 82, 129, 205
epic, 76, 93, 151
epiphora, 129
episode, 31–32, 77, 99, 107, 128
Erbil, 6, 134
event cohesion, 130

evidentiality, 116, 144, 147, 155
ezafe, 8, 11, 32–33, 63–64, 114
fable, 42, 66
filler, 27, 111, 113– 114, 116–117, 154
folklore, Christian, 51, 57, 62, 67
folklore, European, 61, 68, 78
folklore, Jewish, 53, 55, 62, 64, 68–69
folklore, Kurdish, 37, 42, 45–47, 49, 50–52, 55, 58, 67, 74, 83
folktale, 23, 27, 32, 38, 42, 45, 66–68, 74–75, 98, 146, 153
foregrounding, 112, 130
future, 8, 11, 15, 52, 58, 138
Harmashe, 2, 3, 26, 28, 76, 79, 87, 91, 110, 122–123, 141, 148, 150
ideophones, 119, 120; *See also* onomatopoeia, sound symbolism
idiom, 85, 86, 111–112, 124, 149, 154
impersonal, 30, 32, 89
indefiniteness, 133, 143
inderdental, 3, 4, 27, 28
indicative, 3–4, 9–10, 11, 15, 49, 86, 89, 94, 106, 110, 117, 121–122, 126, 128, 130, 133, 137, 139, 144, 146
intonation, 19, 20, 115
Italian, 98
Jerusalem, 27, 30
Khizava, 6–7, 9, 11, 25, 31, 46–48, 52, 74, 99, 113–114, 118, 131, 135, 148, 286
Kurdish, Central, 6–8, 10–11, 23, 26, 30–32, 64–68, 71, 74, 79, 82, 84, 87–88, 91, 94–95, 102–104, 106–107, 111, 116–117, 120–122, 125, 130, 132–135, 147, 148
Kurdish, Northern, 5–10, 20, 23, 25–26, 30–32, 46–48, 52, 54, 55–56, 60–61, 62, 64, 66–68, 74–77, 79–80, 82–83, 89–91, 93, 94, 99106, 108–127, 129, 131–132, 134–135, 137, 139–142, 146, 148–150, 153
Kurmanji, *See* Kurdish, Northern
legend, 36, 42, 47, 49, 54–56, 60, 76, 82
lengthening, 119, 123

loanword, 7, 29–31, 131–132
L-suffix, 4–5, 10–11, 27–28, 101, 143
moral lesson, 38, 61, 86, 94
Mukri, 6
multilingual, 85, 131
narrative imperative, 146, 155
narrative present, 145–146, 155
negation, 15, 28, 29, 88, 126, 149
Neo-Aramaic, 1–3, 8, 12–17, 19, 21, 23, 25–27, 29–30, 32–33, 44–48, 55, 57, 59, 61– 62, 65, 67–78, 81, 83, 85–87, 89, 92–94, 97, 100–102, 108, 111, 114–115, 119, 126, 128–135, 137–139, 143, 145, 149–153
object, indirect, 9–11, 139
oblique (case), 9, 11, 31–33, 118
opening formula, 86–90, 95–98, 107, 154
onomatopoeia, 119, 120, 124, 155; *See also* ideophones, sound symbolism
oral literature, xiii, 1, 36–37, 81, 85–86, 92, 119, 128, 154
participle, 33, 238

particle, existential, 3
perfective, past, 10, 15, 26, 28, 101, 146
Persian, 49, 95–96, 107, 109, 124, 147
pharyngealization, 7, 13, 30
possessor, 4–5, 10–11, 29
preposition, 15, 28, 247
preverb, 3–4, 10–11, 14–15, 26–28, 100–101, 143, 247
pronoun, personal, 6, 8, 33, 142; *See also* demonstrative
proverb, 24, 64, 86, 94, 111, 117
questions, 28, 119, 125–127
reduplication, 119, 124–125, 155
repetition, 34, 86, 109, 119, 122–124, 128–131, 140, 148, 150–152, 154–155
rhyme, 90, 98, 111, 118; *See also* alliteration
Sanskrit, 96
Serbo-Croatian, 98
Shaqlawa, 2–3, 6–11, 17, 23–32, 37, 46–47, 50–52, 64–68, 71–72, 74–75, 82–84, 87–92, 94–95, 99–100, 102–107, 111, 113, 115–125, 130, 133, 134–135, 137–

139, 143–144, 147–148, 165
social status, 6, 38, 43, 68, 70–74
Sorani, *See* Kurdish, Central
sound symbolism, 86, 120, 128, 154–155; *See also* onomatopoeia, ideophone
stress, 20
subjunctive, 9, 15, 28
syllable, 17–19, 28, 124
tail-head linkage, 86, 109, 128, 130, 140, 155; *See also* repetition
telicity, 32
thematisation, 128
Ṭuroyo (Neo-Aramaic), 1, 78–79, 100–101, 125
verbal syntax, 87, 144, 155
vowel, 3, 8, 13–17, 19, 28, 123
word order, 87, 128, 140–143
Zakho, 2–6, 10–11, 25, 29–31, 45, 47, 54–58, 60, 68, 70, 72–73, 93, 121, 124, 126–127, 132, 140, 159, 163–164, 216, 222–223, 226, 232–233, 287, 302–303, 305, 307

Cambridge Semitic Languages and Cultures

General Editor Geoffrey Khan

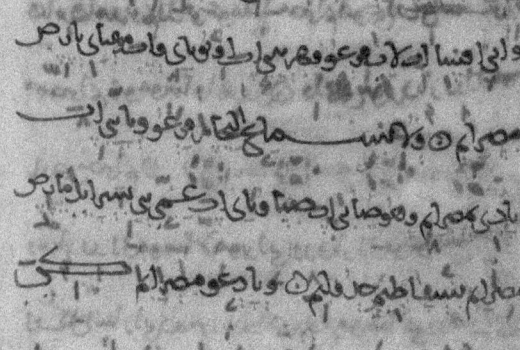
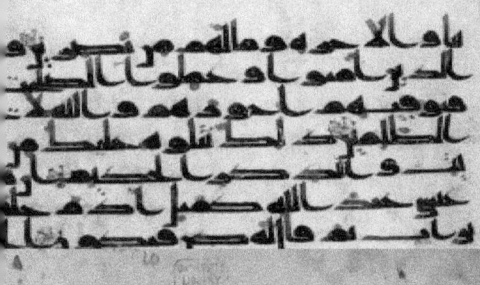

Cambridge Semitic Languages and Cultures

About the series

This series is published by Open Book Publishers in collaboration with the Faculty of Asian and Middle Eastern Studies of the University of Cambridge. The aim of the series is to publish in open-access form monographs in the field of Semitic languages and the cultures associated with speakers of Semitic languages. It is hoped that this will help disseminate research in this field to academic researchers around the world and also open up this research to the communities whose languages and cultures the volumes concern. This series includes philological and linguistic studies of Semitic languages, editions of Semitic texts, and studies of Semitic cultures. Titles in the series will cover all periods, traditions and methodological approaches to the field. The editorial board comprises Geoffrey Khan, Aaron Hornkohl, and Esther-Miriam Wagner.

This is the first Open Access book series in the field; it combines the high peer-review and editorial standards with the fair Open Access model offered by OBP. Open Access (that is, making texts free to read and reuse) helps spread research results and other educational materials to everyone everywhere, not just to those who can afford it or have access to well-endowed university libraries.

Copyrights stay where they belong, with the authors. Authors are encouraged to secure funding to offset the publication costs and thereby sustain the publishing model, but if no institutional funding is available, authors are not charged for publication. Any grant secured covers the actual costs of publishing and is not taken as profit. In short: we support publishing that respects the authors and serves the public interest.

UNIVERSITY OF
CAMBRIDGE
Faculty of Asian and Middle
Eastern Studies

You can find more information about this serie at:
http://www.openbookpublishers.com/section/107/1

Other titles in the series

The Neo-Aramaic Oral Heritage of the Jews of Zakho
Oz Aloni

https://doi.org/10.11647/OBP.0272

Points of Contact
The Shared Intellectual History of Vocalisation in Syriac, Arabic, and Hebrew

Nick Posegay

https://https://doi.org/10.11647/OBP.0271

A Handbook and Reader of Ottoman Arabic
Esther-Miriam Wagner (ed.)

https://doi.org/10.11647/OBP.0208

Diversity and Rabbinization
Jewish Texts and Societies between 400 and 1000 CE

Gavin McDowell, Ron Naiweld, Daniel Stökl Ben Ezra (eds)

https://doi.org/10.11647/OBP.0219

New Perspectives in Biblical and Rabbinic Hebrew
Aaron D. Hornkohl and Geoffrey Khan (eds)

https://doi.org/10.11647/OBP.0250

The Marvels Found in the Great Cities and in the Seas and on the Islands
A Representative of 'Aǧā'ib Literature in Syriac

Sergey Minov

https://doi.org/10.11647/OBP.0237

Studies in the Grammar and Lexicon of Neo-Aramaic
Geoffrey Khan and Paul M. Noorlander (eds)

https://doi.org/10.11647/OBP.0209

Jewish-Muslim Intellectual History Entangled
Textual Materials from the Firkovitch Collection, Saint Petersburg
Camilla Adang, Bruno Chiesa, Omar Hamdan, Wilferd Madelung, Sabine
Schmidtke and Jan Thiele (eds)

https://doi.org/10.11647/OBP.0214

Studies in Semitic Vocalisation and Reading Traditions
Aaron Hornkohl and Geoffrey Khan (eds)

https://doi.org/10.11647/OBP.0207

Studies in Rabbinic Hebrew
Shai Heijmans (ed.)

https://doi.org/10.11647/OBP.0164

The Tiberian Pronunciation Tradition of Biblical Hebrew
Volume 1

Geoffrey Khan

https://doi.org/10.11647/OBP.0163

The Tiberian Pronunciation Tradition of Biblical Hebrew
Volume 2

Geoffrey Khan

https://doi.org/10.11647/OBP.0194

www.ingramcontent.com/pod-product-compliance
Lightning Source LLC
Chambersburg PA
CBHW051535230426
43669CB00015B/2606